CISTERCIAN FATHERS SERIES: N

The New Monastery

Texts and Studies
on the Earliest Cistercians

CISTERCIAN FATHERS SERIES: NUMBER SIXTY

The New Monastery

Texts and Studies
on the Earliest Cistercians

Edited by E. Rozanne Elder

Cistercian Publications
Kalamazoo, Michigan — Spencer, Massachusetts
1998

Available from
Cistercian Publications
Distribution Centre
Saint Joseph's Abbey
167 North Spencer Road
Spencer, MA 01562–1233

Editorial Offices
Institute of Cistercian Studies
Western Michigan University
Kalamazoo, MI 49008

The work of Cistercian Publications
is made possible in part by support from Western Michigan University
to The Institute of Cistercian Studies

Erratum
The New Monastery
page 88, line 20 should read
...corde et corpore usque ad mortem...

Printed in the United States of America

In commemoration of

The Nine-hundredth Anniversary

of the founding of Citeaux

21 March 1098

Table of Contents

Exordium Cistercii

The Beginnings of the New Monastery

Cîteaux is Given to
the New Monastery

Be it known to all Christian believers present and future that Reynard, viscount of Beaune, his wife, Hodierna by name, and their sons Hugh, Hubert, Raynard, and Hagan and their sister Raimunda, for the remission of their sins and those of their forebears, have bestowed upon Robert and the brothers, who with him are desirous of observing the Rule of Saint Benedict more strictly and faithfully than they have hitherto done, their estate called Cîteaux from time immemorial along with everything necessary to them and to their successor servants of God, for the purpose of building a monastery and monastery buildings, of working the land, and all necessary uses.

This same Reynard and his wife, from whose patrimony this same allod has legally been inherited, and their aforenamed sons make this legitimate gift for the use of these brothers principally and especially in honor of the most blessed Mother of God and ever-virgin Mary in whose honor the place, which is now called the New Monastery, is dedicated, located in the territory of the aforesaid allod of Cîteaux. And to the aforesaid brothers he turns over for the worship of God the church at the site which he has owned until now, and because the abbot and the other brothers consider it hardly appropriate to accept it from his hand, because he is a layman, he relinquishes and utterly renounces any further ownership of any kind.

As for the rest of this land which at the time it had pleased Reynard to retain: Odo, Duke of Burgundy, arranged that for its concession and for its free release and transfer to the undertakings of these same monks he would receive for that land each year twenty pounds at the castle at Beaune. Furthermore in the same exchange the duke granted him and his sons permission to plant vineyards of any size in the territory of Beaune and to cultivate them as their own

11

demesne. The same Reynard, however, retained two serfs on this allod, Theoderic and Martin, and a certain female servant named Osanna, and as much land as they needed to farm for their own keep. They are, however, to cultivate only as much land as the same duke and the oft-mentioned Reynard and his wife, if they chose to be present, and the lord abbot is to divide and assign it to them in parts removed from the monks' fields.

Following the dedication of the church of the New Monastery, [16 November 1106], the duke Reynard, with his wife, renewed this gift, in plain view of the many persons who had attended, granting it into the hand of Dom Walter, bishop of Chalon, for the use of the above—mentioned brothers for as long as they reposed quietly in the service of their Creator under the protection of their pastor, free from lay control and all worldly strife. The same duke granted the brothers the full use as well of the forests adjacent to the aforesaid cenobium as well as of all his lands surrounding it. At this above transfer and gift was present Hugh, the duke's son, who also agreed to it; and his brother Henry agreed to the same later on. The undersigned witnesses attended: Hugh of Mont Saint John, Walter of Salives, Segwin of Beaune and his son Hugh, Hugh of Grancey, Milo of Frôlois, Robert, the provost of Argilly, John of Pommard and Landric his son, Hugh the Gamekeeper. Peter, son of Tetbert, granted this and Hugh of Monesteith is a witness.

Which act was affirmed after two years, in the time of Dom Alberic the abbot, who took the place of abbot Robert who had departed. . . .

Pater ipsius monasterii

Robert of Molesme

Robert of Molesme

Robert, the man of God, . . . took the brothers [living around his hermitage] to a certain forest called Molesme. There, working with their own hands, they cut branches from the trees and with them built huts in which they could take their rest. Similarly they also completed a chapel in which they regularly offered up to the Lord the Saving Victim and the sacrifice of a contrite spirit. Because they had no bread with which to nourish their bodies after a day's work, they ate only vegetables.

As it happened, the bishop of Troyes[1] was making his way through the forest where the men of God were serving the Lord in severe poverty and humbleness and he reached the place at suppertime with a large retinue of companions. The men of God gave them a warm welcome, although they were somewhat embarrassed at not having the wherewithal to give them a meal. The bishop, astounded and not a little edified at their poverty and humbleness, bade the brothers farewell and went away.

As time went on and the brothers had not even the slightest means of support, they had recourse to blessed Robert to ask him what to do. He, of course, never *relied on gold or put his trust in riches.*[2] He taught them *to place their hope in the Lord God*[3] for he knew that *God would never allow the soul of the just to suffer hunger*[4] for long. Although they had not the means, he sent them to Troyes to procure food, literally obeying the prophet's advice: 'You who have no silver, come. Hurry, buy and eat'.[5] No sooner had they entered the city of Troyes in their bare feet, however, than report of them reached

1. Philip or Milo II de Pont, 1083–1121
2. Job 31:24
3. Ps 73:28
4. Prov 10:3
5. Is 55:1

the bishop. Having had them brought to him, he welcomed them warmly and demonstrated the love he had for God by the humane treatment he accorded His servants. Then he fitted them out with new clothes and sent them back to their brothers with a four-horse cart laden with clothes and victuals. This blessing encouraged the brothers no end and they learned patience in adversity. Though, in fact, from that day forward there was no dearth of people bestowing food or clothing on them.

After they had persevered a very long time in God's service, many others came to them, fleeing the world and having set aside worldly baggage to bend their necks to *the Lord's easy yoke.*[6] Still others sent them the necessities of life from distant places so that *they might receive the reward of the just*[7] for having given to those already just. But because an oversupply of goods often begets a want of moral fibre, once they began to abound in temporal goods they started to slip in spiritual, to the point that *their wickedness seemed to grow as though from fatness.*[8]

ROBERT LEAVES MOLESME

Blessed Robert, however, did not *set his heart on growing rich,*[9] but strove to advance ever more and more towards God and *to live soberly, righteously, and godly*[10] according to the institutes of Saint Benedict. When the sons of Belial[11] noticed this, they rose up horribly against the man of God, provoking him to bitterness and by their evil deeds torturing the soul of this just man. Reader, do not be surprised that wickedness should make a place for itself in this holy company, for pride too is native to heaven and when it invades minds which live in heaven, it is returning, as it were, to its birthplace and hiding *in sackcloth and ashes*[12] even though its more usual garments are *fine*

6. Mt 11:30
7. Mt 10:41
8. Ps 73:7
9. Ps 62:10
10. Ti 2:12
11. Cf. Jdg 19:22
12. Mt 11:21

linen and purple.[13] Besides, we have been taught by Scripture that on that day *when the sons of God took their place before the Lord, Satan was also among them.*[14] And so from the beginning there was in the Church no lack of just persons who were improving themselves and of wicked persons who were putting them to the test.

Perceiving that he would get nowhere by correcting them and that in disregarding the observance of the Rule and customs, *each of them was following the base desires of his own heart,*[15] the man of God decided to leave them. He was afraid that while he labored in vain for their spiritual profit, *he might lose his own soul.*[16] When dissension broke out among them, therefore, he left them and went to a place called Auz, having heard that there were brothers living there, serving the Lord in a humble spirit.

When he arrived among them he was warmly welcomed by them and lived among them a while, working with his own hands so as to be able to have the means of giving something to anyone in need. He served God tirelessly, persevering uninterruptedly in vigils and prayers. And although he excelled all the others in holiness, he made himself everyone's servant and considered himself the least of all of them. So before long they elected him abbot, and he took pains to govern them with complete modesty, showing special concern for the sick and encouraging the healthy,[17] *not as though lording it over those in his charge, but becoming an heartfelt example for his flock.*[18]

ROBERT IS RECALLED TO MOLESME

The monks of Molesme, moved to repentance at the thought of having offended the man of God and having somehow driven him away by their disobedience, nervously rued their moral as well as their economic loss. They discovered in the event that the Lord had bestowed temporal prosperity on them because of blessed

13. Lk 16:19
14. Job 1:6
15. Jer 16:12
16. Mk 8:36
17. Cf RB 2.24–25
18. 1 Pt 5:3, cf. RB 2.11–12

Robert's merits. After soul-searching discussions[19] therefore, they approached the supreme pontiff[20] and, bolstered by his authority, they recalled the man of God to Molesme. There, unflaggingly intent on fasting and prayer, he was *envied* so much by his subjects *with a godly envy*[21] that in no time he had reformed them to monastic discipline.

Among them there were four men unusually robust in spirit, that is: Alberic and Stephen and two others who, after learning the rudiments of claustral discipline, aspired to the solitary struggle of the wilderness. Leaving the monastery of Molesme, they arrived at a place called Vivicus. After they had dwelt there for a while, they were threatened—at the instigation of the monks of Molesme—with the sentence of excommunication by the venerable Josserand bishop of Langres[22] unless they returned home.

Forced to abandon the aforesaid place, they arrived in a certain forest called Cîteaux by the inhabitants. Here they built a chapel in honor of Blessed Mary, Mother of God and Virgin. Nor could they be recalled by threats or by pleas from their set purpose of *serving the Lord day and night*[23] indefatigably and in fervor of spirit.

ROBERT TRANSFERS TO CÎTEAUX

Hearing of their holy way of life, blessed Robert went out to them, taking twenty-two brothers with him, that he might share in and contribute to their holy purpose. Received by them with the highest respect, he led them for a while with fatherly consideration, instructing them according to the Rule in their way and manner of life and providing them with an example and a model of religious observance and upright life.

19. Cf. 1 Pt 12:19
20. Urban II, 1088–1099
21. 2 Cor 11:2
22. The hagiographer is either writing retrospectively or confusing this separation with a later parting of the way. Josserand (Gauceran) became bishop only in 1110. The bishop of Langres from c. 1085 (possibly 1077) to 1110 was, in fact, Robert I. See *Gallia Christiana* 4:566–569.
23. Lk 2:37

from it neither to the right nor to the left. Let us earn our food and clothing by the work of our own hands and let us give up wearing trousers and shirts and animal skins, in accordance with the Rule. Tithes and offerings let us relinquish to the clergy who serve the diocese, and in this way let us persevere zealously in running after Christ in the footsteps of the fathers.'

With these statements the community of monks did not agree. In fact they argued against these excessive novelties by appealing to the example and institutes of their predecessors whose lives manifestly glowed with conspicuous miracles and to the well trodden paths of well respected men. 'Up until now we have observed the way of life which was followed long ago in France by our holy fathers in monastic life, whose miracles bore witness to a holiness pleasing to God in life and after burial, and we choose to continue in it in all its particulars until death. On the matter on which we are rebuked by you, reverend father—that we stray from the strictness of the monastic rule and do not walk along the harsh path of the Egyptian fathers who dwelt in olden days among barbarians in the Thebaid and Scete and Nitria—consider with close attention the compelling reasons.

'No guide compels the faithful by law to suffer in peacetime everything the holy martyrs were forced to bear during pagan persecutions, for before they were assaulted by the ungodly, not even they bore the things which they later of necessity endured in fighting for the faith. This the Lord clearly explained when he said to Peter, 'When you were young you girded yourself and walked where you wanted. When you grow old, however, you will hold out your hands and another will gird you and lead you where you do not want to go.'[7] Examine carefully, according to the precepts of divine law, how it is your responsibility discreetly to lead along God's way those who, drawn of their own free will from worldly wickedness, have chosen to embrace a life of amendment under your guidance. How can you conceive that you should forcefully banish to the hideaways of Paul or Anthony the very persons who want to change their wickedness into goodness? They fled their

7. Jn 21:18

own homes, in fact, for fear of being killed by their relatives. A far-sighted physician treats a sick man with moderate medication for fear of killing the patient he undertook to cure by causing pain through an inappropriate medication. No prudent person loads an insupportable burden on an invalid, for fear that the porter, weary or oppressed by the burden, may perish along the way.'

To the monks who openly opposed him this way, abbot Robert then said, 'I mention the imitable life of the Egyptian fathers to let you know what is good, but no brutal demand has been placed on you in connection with it; instead a wholesome proposal is being made to you. I am inviting you to keep, in every particular, the Rule of Saint Benedict, which I realize has been put to the side on many points to which you sincerely made profession. Therefore I stand in dread of the reproof of the heavenly judge, lest he condemn us as guilty of transgression in the last great judgement.'

To this the monks replied, 'Our blessed father Benedict, as we all know, sent to Gaul his prior, blessed Maur, whom he had raised from childhood in his own monastery.[8] And with him he sent to the Franks a manuscript of the Rule which the man of God had written with his own hand, along with a pound of bread and an hemina of wine. Made welcome by King Theodobert,[9] Maur remained in Gaul until his death and with the help of Florus, the king's adviser, he built a monastery and there, at a place called Glanfeuil, he instructed a hundred and forty monks in the Rule. Yet this prudent father Maur did not imitate the customs of the Egyptians who forever burn in the heat of the sun. Instead he took the trouble to learn the ways of the Gauls, who often shiver in the icy blasts of the west—something he had carefully been taught by his spiritual master. For Saint Benedict says, "Clothing shall be given to the brothers according to the conditions and climate of the place they

8. This tradition derives from a ninth-century *Life of Saint Maur* by Odo, abbot of Glanfeuil, who attributed the work to Faustus to give it greater antiquity and therefore authority The *Vita sancti mauri abbatis* is found in the *Acta Sanctorum* January 1:1042; on the forgery, see L. Halphen, 'La *Vie de saint Maur*: exposé d'une théorie de M. Auguste Molinier', *Revue historique* 88 (1905) 287–295.

9. Theodebert, king of Austrasia, died 547.

live, for more is needed in cold regions and less in hot. This decision rests with the abbot".[10] In the same way he arranges and adjusts food and drink and all the human necessities of monastic life, so that all things may be done in moderation on account of the weak[11] and so that there will be no complaining.[12]

'He especially warns the abbot to take thought for everyone's weakness.[13] He orders him to assign to weak and delicate brothers such tasks or handicrafts that they not be idle or oppressed by the hardship of the work and run away.[14] Paul and Anthony and many others who first sought out a hermitage and built monasteries for themselves in secluded desert places chose that very harsh life because they were driven there by fear of the pagans, as we pointed out earlier, and by God's grace they turned necessity into choice.[15] Then, by their praiseworthy example the number of those fleeing the world vastly increased and because of the differences of place and human customs this gave rise to various ways of doing things. Yet all within the one faith; as Pope Gregory says, differences of custom do not divide the one holy Church.[16]

'Most people in hot regions do without trousers and wear long loose tunics, like women. There, in the cradle of monasticism, monks do not look down on this custom but accept it. In the western clime everyone wears trousers and never do without them both because of the cold and for decency's sake. And for these same reasons this is the custom in our order, nor do we choose to give it up, because it is both useful and modest. The learned teachers who have gone before us in the holy habit have handed down reasonable answers in similar cases. In Italy and Palestine and in other places where there are lots of olives, those who use its fruit in cooking their various dishes do not need lard, which has mercifully been allowed to us here, where there is no olive oil.

10. RB 55.1–2
11. RB 48.9
12. RB 40.9
13. RB 48.25
14. RB 48.1, 9, 23–25
15. Jerome, *Life of Saint Paul*, 5.
16. Bede, *History of the English Church and Nation* 1.27

24

'Because we do not work with our hands every day, we are
subjected to many people's criticism, but we dare point to the
honest work we do in divine worship, something we learned from
authentic teachers well and long experienced in the observance
of divine law. King Dagobert[17] and Theodoric and the Emperor
Charlemagne[18] and other kings and emperors piously founded
monasteries and from their own resources bestowed generous grants
towards feeding and clothing the servants of God. And they introduced a crowd of retainers to take care of all the external duties and
installed monks to concentrate on reading and their holy prayers for
all their benefactors and the divine mysteries. From that time on, by
the institution of princes and long custom, it has been the practice
in Gaul for peasants to do field work as suits them and for serfs to
discharge the menial ministry. But monks, who have voluntarily
left the vanities of the world behind to fight for the King of kings,
live quietly in claustral enclosures like the daughters of kings. They
persevere in studying the hidden secrets of sacred law and continue
gladly meditating in silence. They guard their lips from vile and idle
speech, they chant David's hymns and other mystical songs day and
night to the Creator, and they concentrate every day on carrying
out other pure and fitting activities, as commonsense demands in
accordance with the precepts of our forebears. In the west monks
have done these things until now and everyone knows and attests
that this should be their sort of undertaking. God forbid that rustics
grow lethargic in idleness and waste time in boistrous laughter and
inane sport when their proper lot is to be engaged in hard work.
Still less that respectable knights and gifted philosophers and learned
scholars, if they have renounced the world, be forced to take part
in servile and unsuitable endeavors and work like common serfs
for their own food. The tithes of the faithful and offerings are, by
general authorization, granted to clergy and the ministers of God;
as Paul the Apostle says to the Corinthians: "Those who are work
in divine service eat what comes from divine service. Those who

17. Dagobert, son of Lothair and last of the strong merovingian kings,
ruled 629–639.
18. King of the Franks, crowned Holy Roman Emperor in 800.

serve the altar share in the altar."[19] So, too, the Lord ordained that those who proclaim the Gospel live by the Gospel. By order and by office, we are clerics and we offer a clerical service to the High Priest who entered heaven[20] so we may, by his help, obtain a place in the heavenly inheritance. Ecclesiastical benefits, therefore, we claim by right and we are determined to hold on to them always by common privilege. This, reverend father, should, beyond question, be well known to Your Holiness. We have learned these things, which have been observed by earlier cenobites who followed a monastic routine, and as heirs of the order and its privileges, we hold to them. And as long as the monks of Cluny and of Tours[21] and other men under rule preserve them, we shall not abandon them. Nor do we want to be condemned far and wide by our brothers as rash innovators of novelties.'

While the monks were still rehearsing these and many other similar arguments, the abbot, quite set in his opinion, withdrew from them with twelve likeminded brothers who had decided to keep the Rule of Saint Benedict strictly to the letter, as the Jews keep the law of Moses, and for a long time he looked for a suitable place for himself and his companions. At length Duke Odo, the son of Henry of Burgundy, took pity on them and granted them a manor at a place called Cîteaux, in the diocese of Chalons. There abbot Robert, after he had lived in the wilderness with his chosen brothers for a while under very harsh conditions and had begun to build a cenobitic monastery, within a short time had many who imitated his holiness.

19. 1 Cor 9:13
20. Heb 4:14
21. Monks in the tradition of Saint Martin, the proto-monk and one of the patron saints of France.

Robert Returns
to Molesme

Orderic Vitalis' Account

fter a while the monks of the monastery at Molesme, once they had begun to miss their pastor and were being regarded by neighbors and friends as somehow contemptible because of the departure of the man of God well known for his virtue, approached Pope Urban as suppliants and directly asked his advice and assistance, after describing the tangled series of events I have related above. He heard both sides with fatherly affection. He ordered the abbot, on apostolic authority, to return to his former monastery and to rule it according to the Rule, lest it decline; and at the other he had founded later to put in his place some suitable person from among its monks. Then by a strict sanction he decreed that everyone was to choose at the outset which way of life he preferred and hold to it unremittingly his whole life long.

So this very ingenuous pope promulgated an helpful decree on the matter, saying, 'Above all we must be on guard that loathsome schism not be fostered in the house of God, and swamp or invade it to the ruination of many; but also that what is good, that is, divinely inspired for the salvation of souls, not be culpably snuffed out. For everyone's benefit, therefore, we make provision in a fatherly manner and also on apostolic authority enjoin that the monks of Molesme who choose the general customs of monks keep them unwaveringly and not later leave their house to transfer to other customs. But the monks at Cîteaux who commit themselves to keeping the Rule of holy Benedict in everything may not ever return to those customs which by their own free will they now abandon. Stability in community and perseverance in whatever is good are to be stressed and steadfastly observed, because this is acceptable to the Creator, who demands even the tail of the victim in sacrifice,[1] and it is fittingly pleasing to people who are moved to the summit of virtue by seeing an example of holiness.

Constrained this way, abbot Robert trudged back to Molesme and there commendably contended for God until the end of his life. Alberic, a man of great monastic fervor, he appointed to take his place in the work at Cîteaux and he made him abbot of Cîteaux over John and Hilbod of Arras and the twenty-two other brothers. Alberic spent ten years in great privation and struggled very hard with his companions for God, from whom he confidently expected the inestimable reward.

The Life of Robert

ROBERT IS RECALLED TO MOLESME

The monks of Molesme took being abandoned by such a pastor badly, however, and betook themselves to the sovereign pontiff [to demand] that the man of God, blessed Robert, be ordered to return to the church of Molesme which he had originally founded. Yet the sovereign pontiff, hearing that the new plantation at Citeaux was firmly rooted in Christ, *was extremely glad*[2] to discover that they were going strong in utter integrity of monastic custom and that, formed by the example of blessed Robert, they were more than ordinarily fervent in observing the Rule of Saint Benedict. Seeing however that ruin lowered over the monks of Molesme if they were deprived of the presence of the man of God, he wrote to the archbishop of Lyon[3] that once another abbot had been blessed for the monks at Citeaux, he was to compel blessed Robert to return to Molesme.

1. Lev 3:9
2. Lk 23:8
3. Hugh of Romans or of Burgundy, Bishop of Die 1073–1083, Archbishop of Lyon 1081/82–1106, and Papal Legate to France 1075–1085 and 1093–1099. It was Hugh, as Papal Legate, whom Robert had petitioned in 1099 for permission to settle at Molesme (*Gallia Christiana* 4:106).

Once he learned of this, blessed Robert, knowing that *obedience is better than sacrifice*[4] and that *not to acquiesce amounts almost to the sin of idolatry,*[5] and having arranged everything that pertained to the observances of the new institution, appointed as abbot over them a worthy man of God named Alberic, who had been one of the first monks at the church of Molesme. And once everything had been beneficially arranged, he returned to the monastery at Molesme which he had himself founded in honor in blessed Mary. When Alberic died two years later, Stephen succeeded him, installed as abbot for the monks at Cîteaux by blessed Robert.

And so the man who is considered the founder of that new plantation, because the well being of both monasteries—Molesme and Cîteaux—was due to his will, returned with two monks to Molesme. The monks of Cîteaux were grieved at his departure but the monks of Molesme rejoiced at his return. . . .

4. Qo 4:17
5. 1 Sam 15:22–23

The Archbishop of Lyon Releases Robert from the New Monastery

HUGH, servant of the Church of Lyon, to his well beloved brother Robert, bishop of Langres: Greetings. What we decided, at the meeting held recently at Port d'Anselle, in the matter of the church of Molesme we have deemed necessary to notify Your Fraternity. There came before us there monks of Molesme, with your letters, pointing out the destruction and desolation to their place that followed upon the removal of Abbot Robert and petitioning strenuously for his return to them as their father.

In no other way did they hope to have peace and quiet restored to the church at Molesme, or the vigor of the monastic order recalled to its earliest state. Also there in our presence was Brother Geoffrey, whom you ordained as abbot in that church [Molesme], claiming that he would willing give place to this Robert as to his own father, should it please us to send him back to the church of Molesme. After having listened to your petition and to that of the brothers of Molesme, and having re-read the letter on this matter sent to us by the Lord Pope, and having then taken the advice of a number of religious men, bishops as well as others who were present with us in council, we acquiesced to your pleas and to theirs, and decreed that he should return to the church at Molesme in this manner: that before he returns, he should go to Chalon to return the [abbatial] staff and the abbey's charge into the hand of our brother, the bishop of Chalon, to whom, following the custom of many abbots, he made profession; and that the monks of the New Monastery who made profession to and promised obedience to him as their abbot, he is to release, free and clear, from that profession and obedience. And in this way he will be released by that same bishop from the vow he made to him and to the church at Chalon. We also grant licence to all those brothers of the New Monastery who choose

30

the follow him when he leaves the New Monastery to return with him to Molesme, on this condition: that never again shall either [community] presume to solicit or to receive [members of] the other, except in accordance with what Blessed Benedict laid down on the reception of monks from a known monastery . . .

On the chapel furnishings of the aforesaid Abbot Robert and of the other things which he took with him when leaving the church of Molesme, and with which he presented himself to the bishop of Chalon and at the New Monastery, we order this: that all these things remain intact with the brothers of the New Monastery, except for a certain breviary which they shall keep to transcribe until the feast of Saint John the Baptist, with the permission of the monks of Molesme.

Exordium parvum

Víduata suo pastore

Alberic Becomes Abbot of the New Monastery

Viduata igitur suo pastore cisterciensis ecclesia convenit, ac regulari electione quemdam fratrem, Albericum nomine, in abbatem sibi promovit, virum scilicet litteratum, in divinis et humanis satis gnarum, amatorem regulae et fratrum, quique prioris officium et in molismensi et in illa diutius gerebat ecclesia, ut ad illum de Molismo transmigrarent fratres locum, et pro hoc negotio multa opprobria, carcerem et verbere perpessus fuerat. . . .

Praefatus Albericus, cura pastorali, licet multum renitens, suscepta, cogitare coepit veluti vir mirabilis providentiae, quae tribulationum procellae sibi creditam donum aliquando concutientes vexare possent, et praecavens in futurum, cum consilio ratrum, transmisit monachos duos, Iohannem et Ilbodum, Romam, comum papam Paschalem per eos exorans, ut ecclesia sua sub apostolicae protectionis alis quieta et tuta ab omnium ecclesiasticarum seculariumve pressure personarum perpetuo sederet.

Widowed therefore of its shepherd, the church of Cîteaux assembled and through a regular election elevated a certain brother by the name of Alberic to be its abbot. He was well versed in both divine and human letters and a lover of the Rule and the brethren. For a long time he had held the office of prior in the monastery of Molesme as well as here, and he had labored much and long for the brethren to move from Molesme to this place, for which endeavor he had had to suffer many insults, prison and beatings . . .

The aforesaid Alberic, albeit after much resistence, accepted the pastoral charge. As a man of remarkable forethought, he began to ponder what squalls of tribulation might sometime or another batter and disturb the house entrusted to him. Taking precaution for the future, with the consent of the brothers, he sent two monks, John and Hildebod, over to Rome. Through them he petitioned the lord Pope Paschal [II] that their church might nestle under the wings of apostolic protection, peaceful and safe from the pressure of all persons, whether ecclesiastical or lay . . . .

Exordium parvum[1]

1. Chapters 9–10.

Viduata Suo Pastore

A BRIEF NOTE

Chrysogonus Waddell, OCSO

IDUATA IGITUR SUO PASTORE, cisterciensis ecclesia convenit . . . A number of readers will recognize here the opening words of Chapter 9 of the *Exordium Parvum*—that remarkable collection of official acts, historical narrative, and commentary which records for us the early history of Cîteaux. This chapter marks a critical point in the saga of the New Monastery. The year is 1099; the month is probably September. The founding abbot, Robert, has just left at the urging of the pope and the insistence of the erstwhile apostolic legate, Hugh, archbishop of Lyons, to take up again the abbatial charge in his former monastery, Molesme. A sizable number of the pioneer monks have returned with Robert to the abbey from which they had so recently departed on the crest of a wave of reform-enthusiasm. Their reform-mindedness had proved short-lived, and the New Monastery is now both shepherdless and depleted of a substantial number of its original members. We know, of course, that the new abbot is going to be 'a certain brother, Alberic by name, a learned man, that is to say, well versed in things human and divine, a lover of the Rule and of the brethren'.[1] Almost every phrase in this chapter of the *Exordium Parvum* gives off resonances of multiple biblical and liturgical sources. Failure to recognize these will in no way deprive us of a basic understanding of the text in question; but the author means to gives us more than just a basic understanding.

The opening words of this chapter are a typical case in point. They reach back into the dim past long before being adapted for

---

1. *Exordium Parvum* 9: ' . . . virum scilicet litteratum, in divinis et humanis satis gnarum, amatorem regulae et fratrum . . .'.

use in the account of the abbatial election of Alberic. Mistranslate
them, and you have deprived us of a significant expression of one of
the ways our Fathers understood the abbatial role. In the translation
used by Louis Lekai, O. Cist., in his invaluable *The Cistercians, Ideals
and Reality*,[2] we read: 'Deprived of its shepherd, the community
of Cîteaux assembled. . . .' This is certainly less problematic than
would be a literal translation respectful of the mixed metaphor of
the Latin: *ecclesia-pastor-vidua*, church-shepherd-widow. After all, it
is the death of a husband, not of a shepherd, that makes a wife a
widow.

*Viduata igitur suo **pastore**, cisterciensis ecclesia convenit*

Deprived of its shepherd, the community of Cîteaux
assembled.

More literal, more problematic, but also potentially richer in meaning would be:

Widowed, therefore of its **shepherd**, the **church** of Cîteaux assembled . . .

That the metaphor is a bit mixed is hardly the fault of the
author of the *Exordium* text, given the earlier history of the formula.
The term 'widowed Church' was probably already ancient when it
appeared in canon 25 of the Council of Chalcedon (451). There
it dealt with vacant episcopal sees: metropolitans were warned to
ordain bishops for such dioceses within three months of their falling
vacant; and it was further noted that the diocesan revenues, during
the vacancy, remained subject to the control of the treasurer or
steward of the **widowed church**. The relevant Latin text is:

. . . verumtamen redditus *ecclesiae **viduatae*** penes
oeconumum integri reserventur.[2]

2. Consult any latin edition of the canons of the Council. Here I
have transcribed the text, not from the more standard Mansi collection,
but from the earlier edition edited by the Jesuits Labbé and Coassart,
Sacrosancta Concilia ad Regiam Editionem Exacta . . . 4 (Paris, 1671) col. 778;
and again, same volume, col. 785.

Slightly more than a hundred years later, Pope Pelagius I (556–560) was dealing with a related problem, that of metropolitans who dillydallied over making their profession of obedience to the Holy See and over asking for the pallium within three months. Until such profession was made and until the metropolitan designate received the pallium, he could not proceed to the consecration of bishops to fill vacant sees of his province. Four times within a relatively brief paragraph the term 'widowed church' recurs:

> . . . ac per hoc episcoporum consecratio *Viduatis eccle-siis* non sine periculo protelatur . . . / . . . sitque licentia metropolitanis aliis . . . *Viduatis ecclesiis* . . . subvenire. / . . . si . . . ultra tres menses *Ecclesia viduata* consistat . . . / . . . si . . . retinuerit *Viduatam ecclesiam*.[3]

Unsurprisingly, both texts were excerpted by compilers of canons, and are to be found in the important collections put together by Burchard of Worms (whose collection is datable 1012–1023), Anselm of Lucca († 1086), Yvo of Chartes († 1117) in both his *Decretum* and his *Panormia*, 'Polycarp' (before 1118), and Gratian (whose *Decretum* dates from around 1150).[4]

None of these texts, however, combines the metaphor 'widowed church' with that of 'shepherd' or 'pastor'. For this we have to turn to Pope Saint Gregory the Great. In Book VII of his Register of letters, Letter 39, dated August of 597, is addressed to Marinianus, archbishop of Ravenna and by that same token metropolitan of the see of Imola, whose bishop had lapsed or apostatized. Archbishop Marinianus has delayed overlong in providing a new incumbent for the vacant see. After referring to the prohibition of the sacred canons concerning a vacancy in excess of three months, Saint Gregory provides the rationale: if the *shepherd* falls, the ancient foe might seize this as a welcome opportunity to attack the Lord's flock: *ne*

3. As edited in E. L. Richter and E. Friedburg, *Corpus Iuris Canonici* 1 (Leipzig, 1879; reprint, Graz, 1959) col. 352.
4. For precise references, see Richter-Friedburg, notes to the corresponding canons, cols. 265–266 (Distinctio LXXV, Pars I, C. II) and cols. 351–352 [Distinctio C. Pars I, C. 1. The text from Pope Pelagius I is also frequently attributed to Pope Saint Damasus (366–384)].

cadente Pastore dominicum gregem antiquuus, quod absit, hostis insidiano dilaniet.[5] He concludes just a few lines later with the summary statement that 'a *church* of God ought not to remain for a long time *widowed* of its own bishop'; *Ecclesia Dei diu viduata a proprio episcopo non debet remanere.*[6] But can we be sure that the author of the *Exordium parvum*—surely Saint Stephen Harding—knew this text by Pope Saint Gregory? Not without further verification. There is a splendid manuscript of Gregory the Great's letters written at the New Monastery during the same period which produced the great collection that dates from the first few decades of the monastery's existence: Dijon, Bibliothèque municipale, MS 180 (*olim* 144).[7] Not having a microfilm or an analysis of the manuscript at hand, however, I am by no means sure that this particular manuscript includes Letter VII. 39. Indeed, I personally would prefer to think that when Stephen Harding began his account of Alberic's abbatial election, he did not have present to his mind Saint Gregory's letter to Archbishop Maurinianus. For had this been the case, we would then have yet another early cistercian text to be added to the dossier put together by J.-A. Lefevre, 'Saint Robert de Molesme dans l'opinion monastique du XIIe siècle'.[8] The texts assembled by Lefevre demonstrate convincingly that, in sharp contrast to later cistercian opinion (which was, in point of fact, responsible for Saint Robert's canonization in 1221/1222), early cistercian opinion about Robert was so negative that Robert, upon returning to Molesme, was even denied his (for us) rightful title as first abbot of Cîteaux. Robert, having put his hand to the plow of a more perfect monastic observance, had looked back and returned to a less perfect way of life. In the line of thought current among early Cistercians (including Saint Bernard), and based on a position formulated centuries earlier by Pope Saint Gregory the Great, such turning back rendered one, in the words of the gospel saying, unfit for the

5. CCL 140:503, Letter VII. 39. In earlier editions, printed as Letter 42 in the same Book or, at times, in Book VI VII.

6. *Ibid.*, lines 9–10, 14–15.

7. C. Oursel, *Miniatures cisterciennes* (1109–1134) (Macon, 1960) 24.

8. See *Analecta Bollandiana* 74 (1956) 50–83.

kingdom of heaven. In such a context, an implicit literary allusion to Gregory's letter to Maurinianus would have been hideously apropos: in one instance, a church widowed because of the lapse of its bishop needs to be given a new shepherd; in the other instance, a church widowed because of the 'lapse' of its abbot–founder similarly needs a new shepherd.

Like Canon 25 of the Council of Chalcedon and like the letter of Pelagius I, Gregory's letter to Maurinianus was also excerpted for insertion into collections of canons.[9] But the citation stops two lines short of the *ecclesia viduata* text. This does not necessarily suggest that the combination *Viduata - Pastore - Ecclesia* must therefore have been derived directly from Gregory's Letter VII. 39. We find the same grouping about the same time in the Life of Oswald, Archbishop of York, written by the monk of Canterbury, Eadmer († c. 1130). In this passage, Saint Dunstan wishes to offer the king advice about the replacement of a pastor in a church that has recently been widowed of its bishop:

> Volens autem idem Pater pro suo officio *Viduatae ecclesiae* consultum ire, regem petit, et consilium, quod salubrius sibi de substituendo *Pastore* occurrit, regi proponit.[10]

The combination of terms was, apparently, in general circulation. There is, however, one medieval chancery-formula which should figure in this survey. An abbot-elect, like a bishop-elect, could not be presented to receive the abbatial blessing without some kind of official statement that he had been elected according to due form by the community in question. In the case of a bishop, the instrument of presentation had to be read in public before the consecrating bishop could proceed to the actual consecration of the bishop-elect. There was even a model provided for this in a number of manuscripts of the twelfth-century Roman pontifical, a kind of ritual containing the texts and rubrics of all the various papal rites and blessings. The formula for the presentation of the bishop-elect,

9. See Richter-Friedberg, p. 181, Dist. L, Pars I, C. XI, with speical reference ot note 112.
10. PL 159:776 C.

printed in M. Andrieu's edition, *Le Pontifical romain au Moyen-Age,*[11] begins, immediately after the opening formula of address:

> Credimus non latere apostolatus vestri celsitudinem quod nostra *ecclesia suo* sit *viduata pastore* . . .

No need to point out how very close the *Exordium Parvum* formula is to this:

> *Viduata* igitur *suo pastore*, cisterciensis *ecclesia* convenit, et regulari electione . . .

The formula of presentation inserted into the Roman pontifical, however, had been preceded centuries earlier by a related text in the tenth-century *Pontificale Romano-Germanicum*, for the consecration of a bishop. This compilation served as the model for most medieval pontificals, and also provided material for monastic rituals. Here the formula which serves as a parallel to the Roman one is:

> . . . haec sancta *ecclesia* metropolis nostra sit *viduata pastore* . . .[12]

An abbot is not the same as a bishop, however, and the various pontificals do not provide a model-formula for the presentation of an abbot-elect. It would be surprising, however, if in chancery practice the formulas used for the presentation of an abbot-elect were not modelled on those used for a bishop-elect.

A further search would possibly suggest that the combination *Viduata-Ecclesia-Pastore* was in even more common currency in the twelfth century than the texts quoted above would suggest. Here, however, the important thing is that we appreciate the theological significance of thise phraseology, especially in the case of a writer who chose his words as carefully as did Stephen Harding.

---

11. Tome I (= *Studi e Testi* 86) (Città del Vaticano, 1938) 139, lines 16–31.

12. From the edition of the instrument of episcopal presentation in C. Vogel, *Le Pontifical Romano-Germanique du dixième siècle* 1 (*Studi e Testi* 226) (Città del Vaticano, 1963) 194, lines 10–11.

If a church becomes *widowed* when the pastor or bishop dies, the metaphor is evident: the pastor/bishop is husband and the church/diocese is wife. It is easy enough to be reminded of the New Testament roots of this concept. 'Husbands, love your wives, as Christ also loved the Church, and delivered himself up for it . . . This is a great mystery: I take it to mean Christ and the Church' (Eph 5:25, 32). It is only natural that the marriage relationship which stands for the relationship between Christ and the Church universal should have been extended to apply to the local church and to its pastor. There is a wonderful expression of this in Roman Ordo 39, a kind of directory concerning ordinations.[13] For many centuries these ordinations were celebrated, by preference and in keeping with early Church practice, on Ember Saturdays. In Rome, there was often a need for a new pastor for a vacant Roman parish church, an *ecclesia viduata*. The man to be ordained had to be 'provided with a title', that is, he had to be attached to a church. The church which was to receive its new priest at the Ember Saturday ordinations at Saint Peter's organized a procession to escort the newly ordained shepherd to his own church. The new pastor was placed on a splendidly caparisoned horse. Two persons appointed by the pope preceded him, each holding the horse's bridle, and shouting out: 'Saint So-and-So [the saint of the titular church] has chosen Such-and-Such as priest' [the priest newly ordained for the service of the church]. Candlebearers and thurifers swelled the procession. And the sacristan of the same church acted as distributor of alms. But, for our purpose, the most interesting role was that of the assistant priest. He was at the side of the newly ordained from the moment the cortege was formed until it arrived at the parish church—indeed, until after Mass was celebrated by the newly ordained in the parish church. This assistant priest was the *paranymphus*. The term comes from the early rites for marriage, where 'paranymphs' were the bridesmen or companions of the groom; and Saint Augustine tells us that their main role was to

13. Critical edition based on Paris, BN ms lat. 974, in M. Andrieu, *Les Ordines Romani du Haut Moyen Age* 4 (Louvain, 1956) 281–286, with introductory notes, pp. 273–280.

lead bride and groom to their nuptial chamber.[14] After arriving at the parish church, the paranymph remained throughout the entire celebration at the side of the new priest, who, by way of exception, was allowed to sit in the chair by the altar otherwise reserved for the bishop and to sing the 'Glory to God'—privileges ordinary priests enjoyed in those days only at Easter and on this important occasion. It was the paranymph, too, who read the gospel. Need it be added that the Mass was followed by a banquet? What we have here is something of a wedding celebration in which the pastor-groom is brought by his paranymph to his wife, the parish church; and the wedding feast of the Eucharist is prolonged by the nuptial banquet of a more earthy sort.

It is highly doubtful that anyone at early Cîteaux was even vaguely aware of the existence of a church-ordo such as Ordo 39. But they did not need to be aware of Ordo 39 in order to grasp the significance of the *Ecclesia suo pastore viduata* metaphor. Transposed from the episcopal to the monastic context, it suggests that the relationship between abbot and community is also a marriage-relationship—though perhaps it would be more accurate to say that it suggests *one aspect* of the relationship between abbot and community. For just as the person and mission of Jesus require expression in numerous titles, each of which suggests a different aspect of that person and mission, so also in the case of the abbot who mediates Christ's presence and action in the community: his role and his relationship to the community and to individuals admit of multiple expressions.

The concept expressed in the *Ecclesia viduata* metaphor is important for our understanding of the abbot's role in early Cîteaux. For this marriage-relationship between abbot and community is just as implicit in the Order's early legislation as it is in the metaphor of a monastic church widowed through the death or removal of its abbot. To be specific, in the Charter of Charity, the abbot is always referred to as abbot-father, while the community is mother. If new foundations are styled 'daughters' rather than 'foundations' or 'dependent houses', this is because the new foundation is thought of in the first instance as the fruit of the relationship between abbot

14. *De civitate Dei*, Bk VI.9.3; Bk XIV.18; PL 41:188 and 426.

and community, between father and mother. It is their mutual love become fruitful that brings forth new life. It is not surprising, then, that the term 'to beget' occurs so frequently in this context. Chapter 8 of the Charter is not entitled 'De statuto inter egressos de Cistercio et suos quos *fundaverint*', but rather, 'De statuto inter egressos de Cistercio et suos quos *generaverint*'. Nor should we be surprised to read, when the same chapter says that a monastery with foundations does not hold its own general chapter, 'Ipsi vero cum his quos *genuerint* annum capitulum non habebunt'. In the eleventh and final chapter of the early version of the Charter of Charity, which treats of the death of abbots and the election of their successors, all the terms relevant to our discusison occur in quick succession within a single sentence:

> In caeteris quoque coenobiis quolibet casu proprio *pastore viduatis*, fratres illius loci convocent illius *ecclesiae* abbatem quae eos *genuit* . . .

> Also in other monasteries *widowed*, in whatever manner, of *their own pastor*, let the abbot of the *church* which *gave them birth* . . .

Here there is a hint, though one of the very vaguest, that the author of the charter, Stephen Harding, may indeed have had floating about in his subconscious the phraseoloy of Saint Gregory's Letter VII.39; here he writes '*Proprio* pastore viduatis' rather than '*Suo* pastore viduatis'—clearly close to Saint Gregory's closing line, 'viduata a *proprio* episcopo'. However this may be, it is hardly surprising to find the identical terminology shared by Chapter 9 of the *Exordium Parvum* and the final section of the early version of the Charter of Charity, since these passages were written by the same person, Saint Stephen Harding.

Please note that I have advisedly referred to the *early* version of the Charter of Charity. Reworked and much amplified towards the middle of the twelfth century, the revised Charter corresponded to the concrete exigencies of an Order that was now international in membership; but in this necessary process of revision nuances from the earlier version were sometimes lost. The few lines under present consideration offer a good case in point:

CC 1 In caeteris quoque coenobiis quolibet casu
CC 2   Si qua domus Ordinis nostri

CC 1 proprio *pastore viduatis,*
CC 2 *abbate* proprio fuerit *destituta,*

CC 1 fratres illius loci convocent illius *ecclesiae* abbatem
                    quae eos genuit . . .
CC 2 maior abbas *de cuius domus illa exivit* . . .

In the revised text, all echoes of early texts concerning the election of pastors for widowed churches have been muted to the point of extinction. Nothing is left that reminds us of the diction of Canon 25 of the Council of Chalcedon, of the letter of Pelagius I, of the letter of Gregory I, of the texts excerpted for use in the great medieval compilations of canons, of the formula for the presentation of bishops—or abbots-elect. For 'pastor' we have 'abbot'; for 'widowed', 'deprived'; for 'church', 'house'; for 'gave birth', 'went forth'. True, the later version of the Charter of Charity uses the verb *genuit* a few lines farther on; but in view of the inconsistency of the revised terminology, one feels that the terms no longer spring from a deeply felt perception of what lay behind the expressions penned by Saint Stephen Harding. We have come a long way in a short time . . . and more's the pity.

Eulogy on the Death of Alberic

Attributed to Stephen Harding

I F, AT THE LOSS of so good a man, grief levels all of us, it will be a feeble comforter who offered no comfort. You have all lost a respected father and guardian of your souls. I have lost not only a father and a guardian, but a companion, a comrade, and an athlete unique in God's warfare—a man whom our revered father Robert raised from the cradle of monastic life within a single household, a singular teaching, and equivalent accountability.

He is gone from us, but not from God. And if not from God then not from us. For this is the characteristic and conspicuous thing about holy persons, that when they depart this life, they leave their bodies behind for their friends and they take their friends with them in their spirit. We have the puny body and singular pledge of our always beloved father, and he has drawn us all along in his spirit by his devoted attachment. And if he, now taken to God, is joined to God by an inseparable love, then he has also conjoined us who are in him.

What more is there to grieve over? A happy outcome, happier still for him whom it has touched this way; happiest of all for us who are borne along to so great a presence. Nothing happier could overtake the athlete of Christ than, having left behind the mantle of the flesh, to fly to him for whose love so many hardships have been endured. The contender receives the prize, the runner snags the reward, the victor attains the crown; our winner offers us the palm—what then are we grieving over? Why are we moaning over someone who is rejoicing? Why are we sniffling over someone who is celebrating? Why are we downcast, complaining with doleful voices to God as if the person who has been carried up the stairway were grieving at this—if the blessed can grieve—the very person who is earnestly pleading for a like end for all of us?

Let us not grieve over our warrior, now safe. Let us grieve for ourselves, still caught up in the battle. And let us raise our sad and melancholy voices in prayer, beseeching our triumphant father not to allow the roaring lion and the raging adversary to triumph over us.

Amator regulae et loci

Stephen Harding
Becomes Abbot of the New Monastery

VIR AUTEM Domini Albericus, in schola Christi per novem annos et dimidium regulari disciplina feliciter exercitus, migravit ad Dominum fide et virtitubus gloriosus, et ideo in vita aeterna a Deo merito beandus. Nuic successit quidam frater Stephanus nomine, anglicus natione, qui et ipse cum aliis de Molismo illus advenerat, quique amator regulae et loci erat. Huius temporibus interdixerunt fratres una cum eodem abbate, ne dux illius terrae seu alius aliquis princeps curiam suam aliquo tempore in illa ecclesia tenerent, sicut antea in sollemnitatibus agere solebant.

YET THE MAN of the Lord, Alberic, having contended cheerfully in the discipline of the Rule in the school of Christ for nine and a half years, went home to the Lord, distinguished by faith and virtues, and therefore deserving to be blessed by God in life everlasting. A brother, Stephen by name, English by ancestry, succeeded him. He too had come here from Molesme with the others and was a lover of the Rule and of the place. It was during his time that the brothers, along with this same abbot, forbade the duke of that land or any other prince to hold his court at any time in that church as they previously been in the habit of doing on solemn feasts.

Exordium parvum. Chapter 17

The New Monastery under Stephen Harding

An English Benedictine Account by William of Malmesbury

I n [Pope Urban II's] day[1] arose the monastic observance of the Cistercians, which now is both reputed and believed to be the very best way of moving along towards heaven. To speak about it does not seem at odds with the work I have undertaken, since it redounds to the glory of England, which produced the worthy man who was the author and agent of that monastic observance. Ours he was, and as a boy served the apprenticeship of his early years in our schools. If we are not stirred by envy, therefore, we will welcome his good deeds the more gratefully the closer we feel to him; likewise, my purpose is to extol his praise because the mind is at its best if you approve in another the good which you do not aspire to in yourself.

He was called Harding among the English, born of not obscure parentage. From childhood he was a monk of Sherborne, but when he reached adolescence worldly nettles gave him an itch and, having come to loathe those threads, he took off first for Scotland and then for France. There, having labored at the liberal arts for several years, he felt the goad of godly love: once mature age had put aside childish fumblings, he set out for Rome with a classmate as his companion;[2] neither the distance nor the difficulties of the journey, nor the scantiness of their resources, even once succeeded in preventing them from chanting the entire psalter every day, both coming and going.

Actually, the mind of this worthy man was already yearning for what he undertook, not much later, by God's grace; now, having got back as far as Burgundy, he shed his curly locks at Molesme, a large, new monastery, and he readily re-learned the first elements of the

1. 1088–1099
2. Peter of Jully; see below, page 63, n. 9.

Rule he had previously seen. But when other observances were put to him, which he had neither read in the Rule nor seen elsewhere, he began—modestly, of course, as becomes a monk—to delve into the reasoning behind them, saying: 'By reason, the supreme Creator has made all things, by reason he governs all; by reason the fabric of the poles revolves, by this same reason even those stars which are called 'shooting' follow their erratic path, by reason the elements are directed; and by reason and by equilibrium our own nature ought also to subsist. But because [that nature] often falls away from reason by sloth, various laws were once upon a time laid down. Last of all, through blessed Benedict, a Rule was divinely promulgated which was to call the flux of nature back to reason; although there are in it things whose reason I am not clever enough to penetrate, I nevertheless consider that its authority should be acquiesced to. For reason and the authority of the holy scriptures, although they may seem to differ, are one and the same: Yet since God has created, or recreated, nothing without reason, what could induce me to believe that the holy fathers, zealous students of God, would ordain anything contrary to reason, as if we were meant to put our faith only in authority? So for those things which you forge, adduce either a reason or an authority. Even though not much credence should be given to something just because some human reason can be alleged—since it can be undermined by an equally persuasive argument. Wherefore, give examples from the Rule which are supported by reason and authority, inasmuch as it was dictated by the spirit of all the just.[3] Because if you cannot do this, you vainly profess its preeminence when you scorn to follow its teaching.'

Opinions of this sort, wending from one [person] to others, as happens, quite properly move the hearts of God-fearing folk, for they may take fright that they are running or have been running all to no purpose.[4]

This discussion, kept simmering in frequent chapter meetings, therefore, came to this conclusion: the abbot himself approved of the opinion that only the pith of the Rule was to be studied in depth,

3. Gregory the Great, *Dialogues* II.8.8; SCh 260:166.
4. Cf. Gal 2:2

and accretions to it were to be set aside. So there were elected two brothers in whom knowledge of letters squared with monastic observance, who by vicarious consultation were to investigate the intention of the author of the Rule and propose what they found to the others. The abbot worked assiduously to bring the entire community to consensus, but because rooting out from human minds something which has long been ingrained is no easy task— because they spew out unwittingly what they imbibed at their first gulp—nearly all of them refused to accept the new things because they loved the old.

Only eighteen [monks], among them Harding—who [was also called] Stephen—tenacious in their holy stubbornness, left the cenobium with their abbot; declaring that they could not keep the purity of the Rule in a place where a congestion of wealth and indigestion of foodstuffs were choking even the resistant mind. They came therefore to Cîteaux, formerly a very forested area but now, by the monks' oft repeated activities, so open to light that it is not undeservedly thought of as an intimate of the very Godhead. There, with the support of the archbishop of Vienne, who is now the apostle,[5] they took up the task memorable and venerable to all the world.

And certainly many things seemed harsh,[6] but especially these: they wore no fur or linen, not even that finely spun woollen fabric we call linsey-woolsey; they never wear trousers, except when sent on a journey, and these they return, cleaned, when they come home. They have two tunics with cowls,[7] and wear no extra in winter, though in summer, if they choose, they may lighten it.[8]

They sleep in their clothes and belts,[9] and never at any time return to the beds after Vigils: but they so adjust the hour of Vigils that the light comes up before Lauds; so protective are they of the Rule that they would never think of passing over a single jot or tittle

---

5. Calixtus II (1119–1124)
6. RB 58.13
7. Cf. RB 55.10–11
8. Cf. RB 55.1–5
9. Cf. RB 22.5

of it. Immediately after Lauds they sing Prime; after Prime they go out to work for the appointed hours; anything to be done or sung they complete during the day, without artificial light.[10] No one is ever absent from the day hours, nor anyone from Compline— except the infirm; the cellarer and the guestmaster, after hearing Compline, wait on the guests, while scrupulously observing the silence.[11] The abbot permits himself no dispensation beyond the others: he is everywhere present, everywhere shouldering his care for his flock. Only at meals is he not present, because his table is always with the pilgrims and paupers.[12] Nevertheless, wherever he may be, he is sparing of verbiage and victuals; for neither to him nor to the others are more than two dishes served,[13] and never lard or meat, except to the infirm.[14]

From the Ides [13th] of September until Easter, no matter what the festival, they never break their fast save once a day, except on Sundays.[15] They never leave the enclosure except on work assignment; neither there nor elsewhere do they ever speak to one another, except to the abbot or prior. The canonical hours they keep up tirelessly, adding no extras extrinsic [to the Rule], except for Vigils of the Dead. At their divine offices, they use Ambrosian chants and hymns, insofar as they have been able to learn these from Milan. While taking good care of guests and the infirm, they apply insupportable crosses to their own bodies as a restorative for their souls.

These things abbot [Robert] himself was doing and urging on the others during that first great flush, but with the passage of time this delicately reared man came to think better of it, and ill bore such scantiness of daily food. Coming to know what he wanted (whether by word of mouth or by letter is uncertain), the monks still living at Molesme, applying pressure to a willing [subject], bundled

10. Cf RB 41.9
11. Cf. RB 42.10
12. RB 56.1
13. Cf RB 39.1,3
14. Cf RB Cf RB 36.9
15. Cf RB 41.6

him back to that monastery by an obedience cleverly wrested from the pope. As if he were worn down by the imprudence of those entreating him,[16] he left the confining walls of paupers and again took up his expansive [abbatial] throne. All those who had come with him followed him out of Cîteaux, except for eight. These, few in number but many in merit, made one of their company, a certain Alberic, abbot and Stephen prior. The former did not linger in this life more than eight years before being gathered happily up by sovereign decision.

Then, doubtless at the divine nod, Stephen, although absent, was elected abbot, the erstwhile leader of the whole undertaking and the special and banner ornament of our generation; the greatness of his merit is attested to by the sixteen abbeys now established by him, and seven [more] under way. So he, God's resounding trumpet, guides those ranged about him toward heaven, now by a word, now by example; doing nothing short of the precept [rule]: affable in speech, pleasant in appearance, always cheerful in the Lord in outlook. From this comes the joy of an overtly handsome countenance; from this, covertly, [comes the joy] of a permeating dew; for, weary of this dwelling place, he longs with unflagging love for the homeland.

He is held in high regard by everyone because God generously pours into the human mind a love for men whom he loves. Wherefore any resident of that territory who gives his money to God through that man's hand counts himself blessed. He has received a good many things; but what with his meager expenses for his own and his [brethren's] needs, he quickly disburses the rest on the needy and in building monasteries. Stephen's pouch is, in fact, the public treasury for all needy persons. An indication of his abstinence is that there, unlike at other monastic houses, you will never see things shining with gold, glistening with gemstones, or sparkling with silver; now, as the pagan says, 'What is gold doing in a holy place?'[17] We all consider something in sacred vases trifling unless the enrichment of stones encases the base metal shell—or the blaze of topaz

16. Cf Lk 11:8
17. Persius, *Satyricon* II.v.69

or the violet of amethyst or the herbal glow of sapphires; unless the priestly vestments dance in gold; unless the walls sparkle with polychromed paintings and coax the sun into the nooks and crannies. But they, holding in second place what mortal men falsely esteem as first, put all their efforts into adorning their way of life. They love resplendent minds more than golden vestments, knowing that the very best payback for benefactors lies in the fruit of a pure conscience.

Whenever the compassion of this praiseworthy abbot either wants, or acts as if he wants, to bend a bit of the rule's yoke, they argue him out of it: saying that they have a life not so much ahead of them as behind them: that they hope to persevere in their resolve and as an example to those who come after them, who, if they themselves were to become lax, would fall into sin. And indeed this would happen in no time because of human weakness; whose everlasting rule is that nothing brought to birth with excruciating labor can last very long. But, let me summarize everything which is said, or can be said about them: the Cistercian monks today set the standard for all other monks; [they are] a mirror for the diligent, a gad-fly for the indolent.

Deeds of the Kings of England, Book IV

Quidam frater Stephanus Nomine, anglicus natione

THE ENGLISH BACKGROUND
OF STEPHEN HARDING[1]

H. E. J. Cowdrey

'ACERTAIN BROTHER Stephen by name, English by nation': thus a perhaps late passage of the EP (17.2) referred to the man whom modern historians call Stephen Harding. The debate that for the past forty

1. Bibliography and Abbreviations—The earliest cistercian documents are best studied in *Les plus anciens textes de Cîteaux*, edd. J. de la C. Bouton and J. B. Van Damme (Achel, 1985); they are abbreviated as follows: EP: *Exordium Cisterciensis Coenobii (Exordium Parvum)*; CCP: *Carta Caritatis Prior, followed by the* Privilegium Calixti; EC: *Exordium Cistercii, Summa Cartae Caritatis* (SCC), *et Capitula*. To them are added: Stat(s): The *Statuta* 'of 1134', in *Statuta capitulorum generalium Ordinis Cisterciensis*, ed. J.-M. Canivez, 8 vols. (Louvain, 1933–1941), 1. 12–32; EM: *Exordium Magnum Cisterciense, sive Narratio de initio Cisterciensis Ordinis auctore Conrado*, ed. B. Griesser (Rome, 1961). Bede's *Ecclesiastical History* and *History of the Abbots* are edited in *Bædae Historia Ecclesiastica gentis Anglorum: Venerabilis Bedae opera historica*, ed. C. Plummer, 2 vols. (Oxford, 1896); the *Eccles. Hist.* is also edited in *Bede's Ecclesiastical History of the English People*, edd. B. Colgrave and R. A. B. Mynors (Oxford, 1969). Other abbreviations used are: Auberger: J. B. Auberger, *L'unanimité cistercienne primitive: mythe ou réalité?* (Achel, 1986); Laurent: *Cartulaire de Molesme* (916–1250), ed. J. Laurent, 2 vols. (Paris, 1907–1911); Marilier: *Chartes et documents concernant l'abbaye de Cîteaux (1098–1182)*, ed. J. Marilier (Rome, 1961); PL: *Patrologia Latina* ed., J. P. Migne; Załuska: Y. Załuska, *L'enluminure et le scriptorium de Cîteaux au XIIe siècle* (Cîteaux, 1989).

This paper was stimulated by my participation in the *Colloque Saint Bernard* at Lyons and Cîteaux, 5–9 June 1990. My special thanks are due to Frère Auberger and Mme Załuska for their papers, and to Père Dominique Bertrand for his invitation to attend.

58

years has gathered about Cistercian origins has done nothing to reduce his stature as a leader of the early Cistercians. He was one of the group of twenty-one under Abbot Robert of Molesme who in 1098 left that abbey for Cîteaux; during the abbacy of Alberic (1099–1108) he was prior of Cîteaux, and he was abbot from 1108 until failing health compelled his resignation in 1133, the year before his death. The latest appraisal of Stephen's work, by J. B. Auberger, has emphasized the distinctiveness of his rule at Cîteaux as compared with Saint Bernard's at Clairvaux. Auberger's hypothesis of two traditions in early cistercian monasticism is an arresting one which, if open to debate and reconsideration, suggests many lines of further inquiry. The purpose of this paper is to raise just one consequential question: is it possible that Stephen's monastic outlook and achievement may have owed more to his English background than has hitherto been appreciated?

Since Auberger's work is not well known amongst English historians, four of its leading conclusions may be indicated, all of which impress the present writer as being basically well founded. The first is that the early cistercian documents provide evidence for two distinct traditions: an 'official' tradition maintained at Cîteaux which was intended to inform new recruits to the cistercians about how the Order had come to be as it was (EP Prol.), and an 'unofficial' record emanating from Clairvaux which was concerned not so much to inform as to educate and edify. In terms of the sources, Auberger departs from the conclusions of J. A. Lefèvre, for whom (in the simplest terms) the EP was late, tendentious, and unreliable, while the EC disclosed the mind of Stephen Harding.[2] Rather, so far as events up to 1134 are concerned, the 'official' record from Cîteaux is mainly to be found in (1) EP *caps* 1–10 and 14; (2) CCP, of which caps 1–3 date from the foundation of its first 'daughter' at

2. For a list and discussion of Lefèvre's articles, see D. Knowles. *Great Historical Enterprises. Problems in Monastic History* (London, etc., 1963) pp. 198–222. Subsequent work before Auberger's is discussed by K. Hallinger, 'Die Anfänge von Cîteaux', in: *Aus Kirche und Reich: Studien zu Theologie, Politik und Recht im Mittelalter. Festschrift für Friedrich Kempf,* ed. H. Mordek (Sigmaringen, 1983) pp. 225–235.

la Ferté (1112/13), and *caps* 4–11 were a gradual response to the foundations as well in 1114 and 1115 of Pontigny, Morimond, and Clairvaux, the whole being confirmed by Pope Calixtus II in his *privilegium* of 1119; and (3) Statutes 1–27 of the Statutes 'of 1134'. The 'unofficial' Clairvaux record began to take shape at about the time of Bernard's *Apologia to Abbot William of Saint-Thierry*, dated to 1123/4; its documents are the EC with the accompanying SCC and Capitula.

Secondly, the difference between the 'official' and 'unofficial' records can be epitomized in two adverbs, *artius* and *altius*: should the Rule of Saint Benedict be followed 'more strictly', or is the keynote 'more highly'? According to the Cîteaux tradition, at Molesme the Rule had been followed with culpable laxity—*tepide ac negligenter*; henceforth it should be followed *artius . . . atque perfectius*, and the Lord should be served *salubrius atque quietius* (EP 2.3–4). In the Clairvaux tradition, on the other hand, the hardships of the reforming party at Molesme before 1098 (EP 9.39) had not been directly experienced. Molesme was a praiseworthy monastery— *fama celeberrium, religione conspicuum*; but some of its members who aspired more highly (*altius intelligentes*) and were lovers of virtues took thought about how they could better themselves under a regime of fertile poverty (*paupertas foecunda*) and serve the better as *milites Christi* (EC 1). For the one tradition, the change was from bad to good, but for the other from good to better.

Thirdly, so far as Stephen was concerned, his association was, therefore, with the aspiration to live *artius*. Even so, as abbot of Cîteaux his outlook and style of rule developed as the Cistercians multiplied and diversified. Initially, as ruler of only one house, his concern was to foster in perpetuity a strict observance within his own community there; only with the multiplication of new foundations did he become concerned with authenticity and unanimity throughout a Cistercian family. His wider concern is first expressed in the foundation charter of Pontigny (1114), in the reference to a *carta caritatis et unanimitatis* between Cîteaux and its daughters (in the plural) which is generally accepted to be found in CCP *caps.*

1–3.[3] As settled by *c.* 1119, the CCP was extended to make sophisticated provision for visitations and general chapters. Stephen's constitution-making was a prolonged process which involved major developments in response to the expansion of the Order.

And fourthly, as scholars have for some time appreciated, the earliest documents of Stephen's abbacy indicate that he at first exercised strong personal, even monarchical authority—a veritable *paternalisme abbatial.* In his *Monitum* concerning the Bible (1109), he could write that 'we prohibit by the authority of God and of our congregation . . .'. In his encyclical letter on the chant, probably of the same date and, significantly, addressed *successoribus suis,* he declared that 'by God's authority and our own we enjoin that you never presume by your levity to change or root out the integrity of the holy regulation (*integritatem sanctae regulae*) which you see that we have worked out and established in this matter by no small labor'.[4] It has long been recognized that CCP 1–3, the so-called 'primitive' *Carta Caritatis,* is distinctively expressed in the first person plural as an expression of the abbot's authority. Even so late as the CCP, some of the plural verbs, like *si aliquid constituerimus aut permutaverimus* (8.4), still read like expressions of Stephen's own authority.[5] Stephen's persistent, if diminishing, exercise of the abbot's powers must be borne in mind, no less than his constitutionalism.

What, then, may Stephen's English background have contributed to his part in shaping cistercian monasticism, especially if these four points are borne in mind?

There is only a little evidence for Stephen's life in England and elsewhere before he entered Molesme—though there is rather more than historians seem currently to appreciate. To begin with what is familiar, that master of digression, William of Malmesbury, made a digression about the Cistercians which was prompted by

3. For the Pontigny charter, see Marilier, p. 66, no. 43.
4. Auberger, p. 327, no. I/1a, b; Załuska, pp. 274–275.
5. *Ibid.,* p. 31. For the abbot's authority, see L. J. Lekai, *Histoire de l'Ordre cistercien* (Paris, 1957) 37–45; also the comments of L. Moulin, 'Note sur les particularités de l'Ordre cartusien', in *Historia et spiritualitas Cartusiensis: Colloquii quarti internationalis Acta,* ed. J. De Grauwe (Destelbergen, 1983) 283–288.

the approximate synchronism of their foundation in 1098 with the death of King William II (1087–1100).[6] He gloried in Stephen's English birth, and exaggerated his part in the separation of the Cistercians from their confrères at Molesme: 'It redounds to the glory of England, that it produced such a man who was both the author and the promoter of this way of monastic life' (*cap.* 334, cf. 335). William wrote at an early date, for he referred to the archbishop of Vienne, Guy, whose papal name was Calixtus II (1119–1124), as the reigning pope when he wrote (*cap.* 335). It was not until 1128 that the first cistercian house, Waverley (dioc. Winchester), was founded in England; one suspects that William gained his information through the foundation from Cîteaux in 1121 of Waverley's parent-house, l'Aumône (dioc. Chartres). Though William's facts were not always full or correct he was remarkably well informed, although there is no evidence that he had seen the EP or the CCP in any form. As regards Stephen's English background, only William records that, until he adopted this name, he was called Harding (*caps.* 334, 335). Born to parents of middling social rank, he was a child oblate at the cathedral priory of Sherborne and was evidently professed there: he was *a puero monachus*, and at Molesme he easily resumed the elements of the religious life with which he had once been familiar. But he had tired of monastic life at Sherborne, and had wandered first to Scotland and then to France (*cap.* 334). Familiar English sources make it possible to say a little more about Sherborne. It is not known when Harding became an oblate there, but since he died an old man in 1134 it is likely to have been soon after the Norman Conquest of 1066—probably in the 1070s or 1080s. Materially Sherborne was probably fairly prosperous, for the Domesday evidence suggests that it suffered little from the Norman Conquest.[7] Ecclesiastically, Sherborne had been made a cathedral priory *c.* 993 by its then

6. William of Malmesbury, *De gestis regum Anglorum libri quinque*, iv. 334–337, ed. W. Stubbs, 2 vols. (London: Rolls Series, 90, 1887–1889) 2:380–5.

7. *Domesday Book*, vol. i, f. 77ab; see M. M. C. Calthrop, 'Sherborne', in: *Victoria County History of the County of Dorset*, ed. W. Page, 2 (London, 1908), p. 63.

bishop, Saint Wulfsin (*c.* 993–1002). Bishop Alfwold (1045–1058) had rebuilt the monastery and translated the relics of Saint Wulfsin and of the Cornish Saint Juthwara. The see and priory further benefitted from the return to England in 1058 of Bishop Herman of Ramsbury, who from that date held the sees of Ramsbury and Sherborne and established himself at the latter place. He had recently himself become a monk of Saint-Bertin (dioc. Arras), whence he brought the monk and hagiographer Goscelin who seems to have spent some time as a monk at Sherborne. There, in 1077/8 Goscelin was to write a Life of Saint Wulfsin,[8] which incidentally shows the night office being faithfully performed (*cap.* 19) and Saint Wulfsin being vigilant to safeguard the bishop's rights against royal officials (*cap.* 20). All this points to there having been a fair standard of monastic observance and study in the Sherborne that Harding knew. But in 1075 the Council of London decreed the transfer of Herman's see to Salisbury; only in 1122 was the priory raised to the status of an abbey. Goscelin's Life of Wulfsin shows that it was ruled by priors of English name—Wulfric under Bishop Herman (d. 1078) (*Pref.*) and Aelfric under Bishop Osmund of Salisbury (1078–1099) (*cap.* 21). The bishop-abbots' withdrawal and the sole rule of a prior may have had a permanently unsettling effect which might help to account for Harding's departure.

According to William of Malmesbury, when Harding reached France he spent some years studying the liberal arts before experiencing spiritual compunction. Then he journeyed to Rome with a clerk who had been a fellow-student; whatever the difficulties of the journey they persisted in the daily recitation of the whole Psalter. Upon his return to Burgundy, Harding became a monk at Molesme, 'a new and great monastery' (*cap.* 334). Important light is thrown upon these events by another, largely neglected source for Stephen's English connections which discloses who was Stephen's companion

8. C. H. Talbot, 'The Life of Saint Wulfsin of Sherborne by Goscelin', *Revue Bénédictine* 69 (1959) 68–85. For Goscelin, see also Talbot, 'The *Liber confortatorius of Goscelin of Saint Bertin*', *Analecta Monastica*, 3ᵉ sér., edd. M. M. Lebreton, J. Leclercq, and C. H. Talbot, *Studia Anselmiana* 37 (Rome, 1955) 1–117, esp. pp. 1–22.

upon his journey to Rome.[9] He was another Englishman, named Peter, who died in 1136 two years after Stephen, and whose Life was written between *c.* 1160 and *c.* 1185 from a strongly Molesme standpoint. His career interlocked with Stephen's for many years. According to the Life, he was born in England of noble parents; in the course of a devout childhood he studied the liberal arts.[10] But, like Stephen, he left England for France;[11] one wonders how many more Englishmen may have reacted to the Norman Conquest in this way. In France, Peter determined to live *peregre*, that is, to live the wandering life of a stranger and pilgrim upon earth, 'like another Abraham', said his Life, 'travelling from his land and kindred, and from his father's house'.[12] Peter's wanderings brought him to Burgundy, where he met Stephen, 'a man of most chaste life'; Stephen's religious amendment to which William of Malmesbury referred seems to have predated their meeting. Peter and Stephen became friends, and Peter's Life confirms William of Malmesbury's record by saying that they used daily to recite the whole Psalter, saying alternate verses.[13] In due course they journeyed to Rome, where they together spent a time of rigorous devotion and penance. Then they returned to Burgundy, and both of them became monks at Molesme.[14] The Life depicts Peter at Molesme as an exemplary monk. His friendship with Stephen continued, but since a monastic regime did not permit their continuing to say the Psalter together daily as they had been accustomed, they divided it between them

9. *Vita sancti Petri prioris Juliacensis puellarum monasterii et monachi Molismensis*, PL 185:1255–70; see G. Mathon, 'Pietro de Jully, beato', *Bibliotheca Sanctorum*, 10 (Rome, 1968) 704. William of Malmesbury's account of the journey to Rome is repeated by Herbert of Clairvaux, writing *c.* 1178: *De miraculis libri tres*, 2.24, PL 185.1333D, whence EM 1.21. See also H. E. J. Cowdrey, 'Peter, Monk of Molesme and Prior of Jully' in Michael Goodich, Sophia Menache, Sylvia Schein, edd., *Cross Cultural Convergences in The Crusader Period* (New York et al.: Peter Lang, 1995) 59–73.
10. 1257B–58C.
11. 1260A, cf 1261A, 1258D–59A.
12. 1260A, 1258D.
13. 1259BC.
14. 1259D–60A.

and said half each.[15] It is to be observed that the Life always referred to Stephen by this name, with the implication that he adopted it long before his entry into Molesme. Peter's own name is an unlikely one for him to have received from his parents, since it was introduced into England by the Normans. The possibility must be entertained that both Peter and Stephen discarded their original names in favor of those of the prince of the apostles and of the New Testament protomartyr, as part of the dissociation from the past that went with the *vita peregrina*.[16]

The Life of Peter said nothing about him between his entry into Molesme and Stephen's election to be abbot of Cîteaux. However, his religious strictness and his friendship with Stephen raise the question whether he was not the Peter who was named in the EP in company with Stephen, Abbot Robert of Molesme, and four other monks in the text of the letter which the papal legate, Archbishop Hugh of Lyons, wrote in late 1097 to the monks of Molesme. Hugh confirmed the purpose of the abbot and his companions to follow the Benedictine Rule more strictly and perfectly elsewhere than at Molesme (2.5). If so, Peter must have been one of those who in 1099 returned with their abbot from Cîteaux to Molesme, for his future was wholly bound up with the latter abbey. The EP documented the steps whereby, through Archbishop Hugh's good offices, a *modus vivendi* was established between Molesme and Cîteaux so that the two abbeys henceforth lived in peace and in freedom from mutual claims (*in pace et libertate*) (7). It is remarkable that Peter could live as strictly at Molesme as Stephen did at Cîteaux, and that their spiritual friendship should have persisted, at least on Peter's side; there is no evidence of any kind on Stephen's.

At the time of Abbot Alberic of Cîteaux's death, Peter's abbot had sent him to one of Molesme's cells, at Useldingen in Luxemburg (1260A, cf. 1261A).[17] Possibly Molesme gave its more eremitically inclined members an opportunity to fulfill their aspirations by thus

---

15. 1259D–60A.

16. Although Peter took a continuing interest in English affairs; in his last illness he warned Count Theobald of Blois and Champagne that it was not God's will that he should seek the English crown: 1266AB.

17. For Useldingen, see Laurent, 1.236–7, no. 47, and 2.175, no. 194.

directing them to the solitude of its cells. Molesme's relations with Cîteaux seem to have been sympathetic. The Life referred to it kindly, as 'that new plantation of Cîteaux which fled the tumult of the peoples and the storms of the world, and sought in solitude to serve God alone' (1260A).[18] When Cîteaux lost its abbot, it sought the prayers of its mother (Molesme); upon the advice of godfearing men it elected Stephen as its abbot. Peter persisted in his bond of prayer with Stephen: knowing how busy an abbot must be, he now adopted the custom of reciting both halves of the Psalter daily on his own and Stephen's behalf.[19] The spiritual friendship of the two expatriate Englishmen was indeed, enduring and significant. It was possible for two equally rigorous monks, bound by lasting spiritual friendship, to be equally at home in Molesme and Cîteaux. The 'unofficial' Clairvaux presentation of Molesme as *religione conspicuus* (EC 1.2) was evidently not without foundation.

In the light of the Life of Peter, it was also explicable. For Peter was eventually sent to be claustral prior of its house for women, Jully-les-Nonnains (dioc. Langres), established there in 1113.[20] The Cistercians were for long reluctant to make provision for women who wished, or who were under pressure, to become nuns, and it was Jully that two of Bernard of Clairvaux's closest female relatives entered—Elizabeth, the wife of his eldest brother Guy who became a monk of Clairvaux, and his younger sister Hombeline who, after a spectacular conversion from a worldly life, secured her husband's permission to enter religion.[21] Both women became prioresses of Jully. Given this link with Bernard, it is easy to understand why, if the EC is to be associated with Clairvaux, it should be characterized by a favorable view of Molesme.

18. '*novella illa Cisterciensis plantatio, quae populorum tumultum et saeculi turbinem fugiens in solitudine soli Deo vacare contendebat*'; for the vocabulary, cf. EC 1.7, 2.11.

19. 1260B.

20. 1263C–64C.

21. For Jully, see Laurent, 1.253–6. For Bernard's relatives, see William of Saint-Thierry, *Sancti Bernardi abbatis Clarae-Vallensis vita et res gestae* (*Vita prima*) 1.3.10, 6.30, *PL* 185:232–3, 244–5; *Secunda vita sancti Bernardi abbatis auctore Alano*, 3.9, *PL* 185:474; *Vita sancti Petri* (as n. 8), cap. 10, *PL* 185:1264D–5B.

The Life of Peter thus offers invaluable evidence to the student of early cistercian history. For the question principally raised in this paper, whether Peter's friend Stephen's monastic outlook and achievement owed more to his English background than has been appreciated, it may be helpful to reflect further upon the *peregrina vita* that Peter embarked upon and shared with Stephen. It was, of course, anything but a novel commitment: ever since the columbanian mission to the continent of Europe in the late sixth century, the celtic mission to England in the seventh, and the anglo-saxon missions to the continent in the eighth, it was a familiar way of religious self-devotion. It may be that the two men adopted it simply as a well established custom of the Christianity in which they had been brought up. Yet both were educated men; Stephen, at least, had had access to a monastic library at Sherborne. Therefore they may have read of the *peregrina vita* in Bede's *Ecclesiastical History*, where it was presented in memorable terms. One thinks especially of Egbert, one of Bede's central characters, who lived in exile in Ireland for the sake of Christ (3.4). There, he had as a companion Ethelhun; both caught the plague, and Ethelhun's death frustrated their hope that they might enter into eternal life together. The survivor, Egbert, took a vow so to live as a pilgrim (*peregrinus*) that he would never return to Britain, and in addition to the canonical psalmody he would daily recite the whole Psalter to the praise of God (3.27). Egbert had earlier lived a similar life with Chad, the future bishop (4.3), and later had missionary companions; he thought of himself preaching to the heathen on the continent or of going as a pilgrim to Rome (5.9). However he ended his life with a stay of thirteen years in the monastery of Iona which he taught to observe the Catholic Easter (5.22). There is no positive evidence that Peter and Stephen were moved by Egbert's example, yet Bede's account of him could have put into their heads so many features of their own life as *peregrini*. And if there is much in Bede that may have inspired Stephen the *peregrinus*, it is worth asking whether Bede may not also have inspired Stephen, the monk and abbot.

In the late eleventh century Bede's *Ecclesiastical History* is widely attested both in England and on the continent; in the England of King William I it was keenly studied, not least in connection with the revival of northern monasticism in Bedan sites, including Bede's own monastery of Wearmouth-Jarrow.[22] In his Life of Saint Wulfsin, Goscelin of Saint-Bertin cited the *Ecclesiastical History*, in all likelihood from a copy which he saw at Sherborne.[23] If William of Malmesbury was right about Stephen's journey to Rome, he was probably also right about his journey to Scotland. This may have taken him to Durham, where the books which Bishop William of Saint Carilef (1080–1096) gave to the library of his cathedral priory included Bede's *Ecclesiastical History*; early in the twelfth century Bede's *History of the Abbots of Wearmouth and Jarrow* was added to the manuscript.[24] Even at a time when *pueriles ineptiae* were obscuring his true vocation, Stephen may have been sufficiently interested in the revival of northern monasticism to read the Bedan works that were available at places like Durham. He is certainly more likely to have gained any knowledge of them that he may have had in England rather than on the continent; it is not known whether Bede was included in the early libraries of Molesme and Cîteaux, although later in the twelfth century Cîteaux possessed a copy of the *Ecclesiastical History* and *Life of Saint Cuthbert* which still survives.[25]

The earliest cistercian documents, and especially those which, upon Auberger's construction of them, are to be associated with Cîteaux rather than with Clairvaux, are notoriously barren of

22. For the manuscript tradition of the *Ecclesiastical History*, see the edition of Colgrave and Mynors, pp. XLII–LXIV. For its influence in Stephen's lifetime see R. H. C. Davis, 'Bede after Bede', in *Studies in Medieval History presented to R. Allen Brown*, edd. C. Harper-Bill, C. J. Holdsworth, and J. L. Nelson (Woodbridge/Wolfboro, 1989) pp. 103–116.

23. (as n. 8), cap. 9.

24. For the manuscript tradition of Bede's *History of the Abbots*, see Plummer's edition of Bede, I.CXXXII–CXL, CXLIV. For the Durham MS of Bede, *Cathedral Library*, B.II.35, see R. A. B. Mynors, *Durham Cathedral Manuscripts* (Oxford, 1939) pp. 41–42, no. 47.

25. Dijon, *Bibliothèque Municipale*, MS 574; Załuska assigns a date in the third quarter of the twelfth century; pp. 244–245, no. 54. She also lists the following of Bede's works amongst Cîteaux's later twelfth-century MSS: *In librum beati patris Tobiae, De tabernaculo, De templo Salomonis, Expositio in Evangelium Lucae, Expositio in Epistolas catholicas*: pp. 232–233, 235, 237, 238–239, 246, nos. 29, 34, 38, 41, 59.

indications, whether express or implicit, of sources from the past which may have helped to shape them. Simple and practical, they focused upon immediate and particular problems rather than upon general principles, and especially upon the Rule of Saint Benedict and how it should be interpreted and lived. Auberger has made clear that there is no reason for thinking that, at the Cîteaux which Stephen knew, anyone had in mind the monasticism of the Desert Fathers; the cistercian attraction to their writings was a mark just a little of the early Bernard of Clairvaux, but mainly of later generations.[26] Nor is there evidence that in the early years of Cîteaux there was antagonism, express or implied, to Cluny.[27] Not only did the cluniac pope Urban II seek to ease the tension between Molesme and Cîteaux by encouraging Abbot Robert to return to Molesme (EP 6), but at the subsequent successful negotiations over which Archbishop Hugh of Lyons presided at *Portus Ansillae*, the cluniac papal chamberlain Peter was approvingly present (EP 7.12).[28] Yet if the early Cistercians were neither inspired by the Desert Fathers nor in reaction against the Cluniacs but concerned with their own particular and immediate problems, they are not likely to have proceeded in a total vacuum. There are three connections in which it may be worth posing the question whether seventh-century northumbrian monasticism as exhibited by Bede may not have been in Stephen's mind, perhaps already as a monk at Molesme and more strongly as abbot of Cîteaux: the concept of a *carta caritatis et unanimitatis*; the role of the abbot of Cîteaux, especially in relation to the Rule of Saint Benedict; and Stephen's agenda as abbot of Cîteaux, especially in his early years.

First, the concept of a *carta caritatis et unanimitatis*.[29] No one reading Bede's account of the double monastery of Wearmouth and Jarrow in his *History of the Abbots* with the Cistercian CCP

26. Auberger, pp. 123, 133, 159, 167, 173–174, 319, 323.
27. *Ibid.*, pp. 8, 59.
28. For Peter, see *Imprecatio beati Hugonis abbatis*, in 'Memorials of Abbot Hugh of Cluny', ed. H. E. J. Cowdrey, *Studi Gregoriani*, 11 (1978), 174–175.
29. For the phrase, see the foundation charter of Pontigny, as n. 2.

in mind can fail to be struck by the comparability of the two situations. There was a similar need to maintain constitutional unity and monastic uniformity amongst related communities that were set at a distance from each other. Wearmouth-Jarrow was not, of course, a blueprint that Stephen could have merely copied, if only because of the multiplication of cistercian houses. Yet Bede, who was himself a monk of Wearmouth-Jarrow from 679/80 until 735 under the abbots of whom he wrote, penetrated to the heart of how, in the earliest days of the Rule of Saint Benedict in England,[30] its earliest followers so applied it that plurality was balanced by unity, and unanimity was preserved. In this light, the *History of the Abbots* might almost be called a *Carta caritatis et unanimitatis*.

The early development of Wearmouth-Jarrow was as follows. In 674, Benedict Biscop founded Wearmouth, dedicating it to Saint Peter; in 681 he founded Jarrow, some ten kilometers to the north, dedicating it to Saint Paul, thus already invoking the heavenly unanimity of the martyred princes of the apostles. Benedict Biscop, abbot of both houses, soon afterwards departed upon his sixth journey to Rome, having appointed Ceolfrid to be abbot of Jarrow and Eosterwine of Wearmouth. As Bede pointed out, this produced the situation, which called for a defense, of one monastery with two abbots (1.7). Before Benedict Biscop returned, Eosterwine died; on arrival Benedict was glad to find that Eosterwine had been replaced by Sigfrid. However, in 689 and 690 respectively, both Benedict Biscop and Sigfrid died; Bede wrote a moving account of their fraternity during their last illnesses (1.11–13). Ceolfrid became abbot of both monasteries until he resigned through old age and infirmity in 716; he was then replaced by Hwaetbert.

---

30. It is unlikely that the Rule of Saint Benedict was the sole Rule of the early communities at Wearmouth-Jarrow, since Benedict Biscop spoke of the seventeen monasteries upon which he drew: *History of the Abbots*, 1.11. But Bede laid emphasis upon the Rule of Saint Benedict: 1.11, 2.16, and was at pains to associate Benedict Biscop with Benedict of Nursia: 1.1. Eleventh-century readers would certainly have regarded the communities as benedictine. For the problem of the Rule followed by them, see P. Wormald, 'Bede and Benedict Biscop', in: *Famulus Christi*, ed. G. Bonner (London, 1976) pp. 141–145.

Bede commented at length on the bonds between Wearmouth and Jarrow. At the beginning, Benedict Biscop established as the guiding principle (*ratio*)

> that between the two places a single peace and concord, the same familiarity and goodwill, should be perpetually observed; and that just as, for example, the body cannot be sundered from the head through which it breathes, and the head cannot forget the body through which it lives, so no one should seek by any device to divide from each other the two monasteries which are joined in the fraternal society of the chief apostles.

Bede rounded off his comments with the example of Saint Benedict of Nursia, who found it convenient to set twelve abbots over his disciples 'without detriment to charity—nay, to the increase of charity' (1.7).[31] A very similar thought concluded what is generally taken to be the primitive *Carta Caritatis*: there must be a single usage in customs, chant, and liturgical books, 'so that in what we do there may be no discord, but we live by one charity, one rule, and like customs' (CCP 3.2; cf. Prol. 3–4, Stats. 2–4). As dedication to Saint Peter and Saint Paul joined Wearmouth and Jarrow, because Molesme and Cîteaux were dedicated to the Blessed Virgin, all cistercian houses were to be so dedicated (Stat. 18). Perhaps a similar situation generated a similar response; but perhaps when Stephen considered the specific problems of Cîteaux and her daughters, Bede's model was present in his mind.

The earliest evolution of the cistercian general chapter further suggests that this cannot be excluded. Both before and after the dying Benedict Biscop concluded that, after his death, it would conduce to peace, unity, and concord if a sole abbot ruled both houses (1.13), the collaboration of the two monastic chapters in abbatial elections provided a significant model. When Eosterwine died in Benedict Biscop's absence, the Wearmouth chapter met

---

31. Bede referred to Gregory the Great, *Dialogues* 2.3.13, edd. A. de Vogüé and P. Antin, 3 vols. *Sources Chrétiennes*, 251, 260, 265 (Paris, 1978–1980) 2.148–151.

with his co-abbot Ceolfrid of Jarrow to elect Sigfrid—in Benedict's retrospective opinion, an admirable step to have taken (1.10). In due course, Hwaetbert was elected abbot of both monasteries by all the Wearmouth monks together with many of the seniors of Jarrow. 'Fit una concordia, eadem utrorumque sententia', Bede commented (2.18). There is an interesting similarity to the earliest general chapters at Cîteaux under Stephen as reflected in the CCP, where abbots of other houses at first assembled with the conventual chapter of Cîteaux, only gradually reserving business to themselves (7.3, 8.2). Perhaps again, Stephen was acting along lines which he recalled from Bede, until Cîteaux's distinctive arrangements became fully established.

A comparison with Molesme may serve to underline the special nature of the arrangements which developed at Cîteaux under Stephen's guiding hand as abbot. In 1097, by a charter written by a Stephen who may have been the future abbot of Cîteaux, Abbot Robert of Molesme, assisted by his prior Alberic, constituted its dependent cell at Aulps (dioc. Geneva) an abbey with its own abbot. Aulps had been established early in the 1090s by monks from Molesme who, in a phrase anticipating the Cistercians, aspired to hold to the precepts of Saint Benedict *arcius*. But in 1097, relations between the two abbeys remained largely within those familiar in monastic confraternity agreements. In 1107, Aulps founded its own dependency of Balerne (dioc. Besançon). A dispute quickly arose between Aulps and Balerne which Robert of Molesme settled in an adjudication of 1110 which sought to establish *pax et concordia* between them. In a remarkable anticipation of the primitive Cistercian *Carta Caritatis* (CCP 1), neither Aulps nor Balerne was to make any material exaction from the other. But, overall, Balerne was simply made subject to Aulps under Molesme's general superiority.[32]

32. For the documents, see Laurent, 2.7–8, 150–151, nos. 4, 158; reprinted with indication of parallels in CCP, by Bouton and Van Damme, *Textes*, pp. 129–131. For further comment, see H. E. J. Cowdrey, 'Legal Problems Raised by Agreements of Confraternity', in: *Memoria. Der geschichtliche Zeugniswert des liturgischen Gedenkens im Mittelalter*, edd. K. Schmid and J. Wollasch (Munich, 1984) pp. 233–254, esp. pp. 250–254.

On the one hand, the Molesme documents show that, after the composition with Cîteaux (EP 7) and with the good relations between Molesme and Cîteaux that seem to have prevailed when Stephen was elected abbot,[33] Molesme anticipated a major cistercian principle; yet, on the other hand, the development at Molesme seems to have been arrested there. In the second decade of the twelfth century, it did not accompany Cîteaux down the path that led to general chapters as provided for in the CCP. As abbot, Stephen seems to have had a powerful and individual vision of how mother and daughter abbeys might be bound together which his recollection of Bede could have induced.

Secondly, his recollection of Bede may have suggested to Stephen at least some features of his role as an abbot who sought himself to live strictly according to the Rule of Saint Benedict and to guide his monastic family in a common fidelity to it. For there is much in Bede's depiction of his *History of the Abbots* of the abbots under whom he lived that can be paralleled in Stephen's government. Thus, Bede commended abbots who attended sedulously to their true monastic business—Ceolfrid, with his peerless and unfailing diligence in prayer and psalmody (2.16), and Hwaetbert, who deserved election as abbot because from boyhood he had not only been brought up to the observance of regular discipline but had also been zealous in writing, singing, reading, and teaching (2.18); at Cîteaux, Stephen was *amator regulae et loci*, a model of observance and stability

33. See above, p. 328–329. On Stephen's custom of referring to himself as the second, not the third, abbot of Cîteaux, see the encyclical letter on the chant (Auberger, p. 327, no. I/1b), EP 17.1, is perhaps best understood as a courteous and conciliatory gesture to Molesme. The contrast between such good relations and the sharp criticism of Molesme in the EP (see above, pp. 323–324) presents a difficulty. However, there is a similar contrast in Saint Bernard's attitude to Cluny, with on the one hand his strictures as in the *Apologia ad Guillelmum abbatem* and, on the other, the mutually good relations that ultimately prevailed between him and Abbot Peter the Venerable—good relations that are surely more comprehensible if Peter were the 'reformer' and his predecessor Pontius the 'traditionalist' (H. E. J. Cowdrey, 'Abbot Pontius of Cluny (1109–22/6)', *Studi Gregoriani*, 11 [1978] 177–268) than if, as Auberger suggests (pp. 276–277, 320), the roles were reversed.

(EP 17.2). Bede's abbots shared in all the work of the monastery, particularly manual labor—Eosterwine was an especial exemplar (1.8); so at Cîteaux the abbot and monks shared in performing 'the ecclesiastical and all the precepts of the Rule' (EP 15.1–4), and a story in the EM displayed Stephen at manual labor with his monks (1.22, p. 80/35–81/3). Abbot Ceolfrid, who in so many respects suggests himself as a model for Stephen, was frugal in food and drink and wore coarse clothing, all to a degree which Bede noticed as being unusual among those in authority (2.16); at Cîteaux, Stephen would have nothing in the house of God that smacked of pride or superfluity, or that damaged poverty, the guardian of virtues (EP 17.5, cf. EM 1.21,27). Ceolfrid's decision to resign as abbot when extreme old age (*impedimentum suppraemae aetatis*) unfitted him for zealous leadership (2.16) remarkably resembles Stephen's resignation in 1133 when he was *longo senio confectus*, in spite of the presumption of the Rule of Saint Benedict that an abbot was appointed for life.[34] The example of the Ceolfrid as a very early benedictine abbot may well have satisfied Stephen that resignation was a proper course to take.

Underlying such particular features of Stephen's abbacy, Bede's presentation of an abbot's duty in relation to the Rule of Saint Benedict also shows perhaps significant parallels. Bede wrote of Ceolfrid that he resigned 'after an abundant schooling in regular observance which, as a provident father, he brought to bear by the authority of his predecessors alike upon himself and upon those subject to him', and that 'he sought to exhibit a proper pattern of spiritual duty alike by his teaching and in his own life' (2.16). Stephen expressed himself remarkably similarly when, in the primitive *Carta Caritatis*, he required a like interpretation of the Rule in all cistercian houses: as Ceolfrid appealed to the *priorum auctoritas*, probably meaning earlier abbots since Saint Benedict of Nursia of whom Bede regarded Benedict Biscop, founder of Wearmouth-Jarrow, with special honor (1.1), so Stephen instructed

---

34. CCP 9 already provided for the enforced resignation of an unworthy abbot. For Stephen's resignation, see Herbert, *De miraculis*, 2.24, PL 185:1334A, whence EM 1.31.

his subjects everywhere to construe the Rule 'as our predecessors (*antecessores*), the holy fathers—I mean the monks of the New Monastery [Cîteaux]—understood and held it and as we ourselves today understand and hold it' (CCP 2.2–3). The common appeal to the *auctoritas* of those best qualified to judge in matters of the Rule amongst whom the founding fathers were pre-eminent, is complemented by a common appeal to critical thought. As the *History of the Abbots* gave a *ratio* of relations between associated houses (1.7) while Ceolfrid sought to exhibit 'a proper pattern of spiritual duty', so the EP recalled how at Molesme before 1098 there was earnest debate about the Rule and how it should rightly be kept (3.6).[35] Again, the example of Ceolfrid comes to the mind of the student of Stephen and the writings of his time as abbot.

Thirdly, several items of his agenda as abbot of Cîteaux may recall Bede's account of Wearmouth-Jarrow. This is particularly the case with Stephen's early years, when Cîteaux was in straitened circumstances, in terms both of the number of its monks and of the sufficiency of its resources to support them (EP 16.2–4, 19.9). One of the greatest achievements of Ceolfrid was the making of three copies of the 'new translation' (i.e. the Vulgate of Jerome) of the whole Bible, to be added to a copy of the 'old translation' which Ceolfrid had himself brought from Rome. Ceolfrid left a copy of the 'new translation' to each of his monasteries at Wearmouth

35. Auberger's hypothesis of a late date for EP 3.6 (pp. 73, 116) may be questioned in the light of William of Malmesbury's admittedly artificial reconstruction of debates at Molesme (cap. 334). For all the artificiality, writing as early as *c.* 1125 William could envisage debates in which Stephen was involved as turning upon how the Rule should be interpreted in the light of tradition and reason. There is no inherent anachronism in EP 3.6, as a résumé of the debates upon which William embroidered. For William's account, see esp. C. Waddell, 'The Origin and Early Evolution of the Cistercian Antiphonary: Reflections on Two Cistercian Chant Reforms', in: *The Cistercian Spirit: a Symposium in Memory of Thomas Merton*, ed. M. B. Pennington (Cistercian Publications, 1973) 190–223, at pp. 202–204, and 'The Reform of the Liturgy from a Renaissance Perspective', in: *Renaissance and Renewal in the Twelfth Century*, edd. R. L. Benson and G. Constable (Oxford, 1982) 88–109, at pp. 104–105; G. Constable, 'Renewal and Reform in Religious Life: Concepts and Realities', in: *Renaissance and Renewal*, 37–67, at pp. 61–62.

and Jarrow; he took the third—the *Codex Amiatinus,* now in the Laurenziana at Florence—on his last journey to Rome, intending it to be a present for Pope Gregory II (2.15).[36] Stephen's *Monitum* of 1109 recorded his concern to establish a corrected biblical text. The so-called 'Bible of Stephen Harding', now Dijon, *Bibliothèque municipale,* MSS 12–15, embodies the result of his endeavors.[37] Again, Benedict Biscop had been greatly concerned to establish in his monasteries the order of chanting, psalmody, and conducting divine service which was current at Rome (1.6), and part of the experience in such matters that Hwaetbert brought to bear as abbot was acquired in Rome (2.18). Stephen looked to less than fortunate sources in his quest for authentic models—to Metz for the Roman chant and to Milan for hymns.[38] But what matters in the present connection is the fact of a comparable quest for authentic material, with an emphasis upon Roman models, at both Wearmouth-Jarrow and Cîteaux. There are points of contrast as well: Bede made much of Benedict Biscop's bringing home from Rome pictures to adorn his churches (1,6,9), while for the early Cistercians, most decoration of churches was forbidden (CCP 17.6–8, Stats 13, 20); yet the earliest cistercian manuscripts showed a variety and elaboration of illumination that probably owed much to Stephen's English past and familiarity with the anglo-saxon artistic tradition.[39]

In constitutional matters, the Cîteaux of Stephen from its foundation until his death had several features in common with the Wearmouth-Jarrow of Bede's early abbots. They had been anxious to receive the blessing of their local bishop at the time of their election; Benedict Biscop charged his monks always to summon the

36. For the *Codex Amiatinus,* see R. Loewe, 'The Medieval History of the Latin Vulgate', in: *The Cambridge History of the Bible,* 2: *The West from the Fathers to the Reformation,* ed. G. W. H. Lampe (Cambridge, 1969) pp. 116–118-136.

37. Auberger, pp. 190–194; Załuska, pp. 64–111.

38. See the articles by Waddell, cited in n. 35.

39. See Auberger, pp. 183–223. For English influences upon the 'first style' of Cistercian manuscript illustration, see Załuska, pp. 76, 78, 82, 90, 111. [See also Treat Davidson, 'Sources for the initials of the Cîteaux *Moralia in Job,*' in Meredith P. Lillich, ed., *Studies in Cistercian Art and Architecture* 3 (Cistercian Publications, 1987) 46–68–ed.]

bishop to confirm an abbot-elect with the customary benediction (1.11); when Hwaetbert was elected, Bishop Acca of Hexham duly thus confirmed him in office (2.20). The early Cistercians took a similar view in theory and in practice (EP 4.1,7–8, CCP Prol. 2). Yet the protection of papal authority was no less important either for the abbots of Wearmouth-Jarrow (1.6,11, 2.15) or for the abbots of Cîteaux (EP 14, *Privilegium Calixti*). As regards lay donors, Bede's abbots secured sufficient endowments from them, whether from kings (1.4,7) or from lesser men (2.15); but they saw to it that excessive lay demands upon them did not develop in return: Benedict Biscop insisted that temporal considerations should not affect the choice of an abbot (1.11), and Ceolfrid told his monks that he would never accept a gift without giving back as much as he received (2.17); then, no counterclaim could develop. The early Cistercians had received land and material benefits both from local petty lords and from Duke Odo of Burgundy, though under Alberic no new gifts were received, perhaps on account of reduced numbers after Abbot Robert and his companions returned to Molesme. Under Abbot Stephen, in due course gifts became substantial.[40] But under his regime, the monks of Cîteaux forbade the duke of Burgundy or any other prince to hold court at Cîteaux during solemn festivals (EP 17.4).[41] The balance between receiving lands or other gifts and avoiding inappropriate obligations was carefully struck in both the circles that are under consideration, so that it is reasonable to ask whether Stephen may not have reflected upon the practice that Bede put on record.

In conclusion, it cannot be demonstrated that Abbot Stephen of Cîteaux had in mind or drew inspiration and models from Bede's writings such as the *Ecclesiastical History* or the *History of the Abbots*. Yet there is a likelihood that he knew them, at least during his years as a monk and then a traveller in his native England. The

40. See Marilier, pp. 49–51, 52–53, 57–65, 67–77, 79–81, nos. 23, 26, 33–38, 39–41, 46–61, 66–67, and the discussion by Auberger, pp. 135–149.

41. Marilier, pp. 52–53, no. 26, may illustrate the holding of the ducal court at Cîteaux.

sources upon which he drew at Cîteaux remain problematic, and it is unwarranted to read back into his mind or into the earliest cistercian documents the outlook of Saint Bernard or later cistercian leaders and thinkers. It is appropriate to seek other mentors. The similarities between Stephen's work at Cîteaux and the monastic world that Bede depicted are sufficient in number and strength to warrant the question whether Stephen did not owe a major debt to his English background, and whether he may not have been numbered with those Englishmen who found in the pages of Bede a great deal of guidance in renewing the monastic life of the late eleventh and early twelfth centuries. Such guidance, if Stephen indeed sought it, did not take the form of direct copying. It was a matter of finding in abbots who were near to Benedict of Nursia in time and tradition the spiritual orientation and practical discernment with which to provide for the early cistercian family as it began to multiply. One may conclude by asking which of all the sources of guidance that were available to Stephen would have been more useful and appropriate than the works of Bede?

Abbot Stephen
Reforms the Hymnal

BROTHER STEPHAN, second minister of the New Monastery, to his successors: Greetings.[1]

We make known to the sons of holy Church that we have authorized the hymns which it is certain were composed by blessed Ambrose, archbishop of Milan, to be brought to our place here, that is, to the New Monastery, from the Church of Milan where they are sung; and by the common consent of our brothers and our decision we have ordained that from this time forward these and no others are to be sung by us and those who come after us. This is because in his Rule—which we have decreed shall be kept with utmost zeal in this place—our blessed father and teacher, our Benedict, directed that these ambrosian hymns be sung.[2]

Wherefore, by God's authority and ours, we enjoin: never presume to mitigate or by some whim detract from the integrity of the holy Rule which you see we have established by no little sweat in this place. But instead, thinking of yourselves as lovers and imitators and perpetuators of the holy intention of our aforementioned father, keep to these hymns without alteration.

1. Translated from the edition of M. Chrysogonus Waddell ocso, in *The Twelfth-Century Cistercian Hymnal*, Volume 2: *Edition*, Cistercian Liturgy Series, 2 (Gethsemani, 1984) 11–12. This work is dated to between 1108–1112 (see the following article).

2. Cf. RB 9.4, 12.4, 13.11, 17.8

The Molesme
Cistercian Hymnal

Chrysogonus Waddell, OCSO

THE VERY FIRST hymn-repertory in use at the New Monastery (the usual name for Cîteaux until around 1119) was quite simply that of Molesme, the abbey from which Robert, former abbot of Molesme, had departed in early 1098 with some twenty-one monks of the same monastery. The did not arrive empty–handed at the site of their new monastic home. For Robert had brought with him everything needed to ensure the continuance of the celebration of Mass and Office as at Molesme. If the argument from commonsense does not suffice—for how could a group of monks trained in a largely oral chant tradition leave Molesme one day and then, a few days later in the forest of Cistercium, begin chanting Mass and Office in a quite different non-Molesme tradition?—if the argument from commonsense does not suffice, I say, no matter. We have the formal statement of Hugh, archbishop of Lyon and former papal legate, who, when arranging the practical details of Robert's return to his original community at Molesme in 1099, stipulated that the 'chapel' (*capella*, a term which includes liturgical furnishings, vestments, sacred vessels, liturgical books) brought by Robert to Cistercium was to remain with the brethren of the New Monastery, with the exception of a certain *breviarium*, which, with the permission of the monks of Molesme, was to be transcribed at the New Monastery before being returned to the brethren at Molesme.[1]

We need not pause to speculate about the nature of the *breviarium* to which Hugh refers; I think it more likely is a Night Office lectionary than a 'breviary' in the modern sense. Here the important consideration is that, according to the terms of Hugh's decree, the

1. See the Letter of the Archbishop of Lyon above, page 30.

liturgical books of the pioneer community are either books brought from Molesme or else a book or books copied from a Molesme model (the *breviarium*). Later on this Molesme repertory was to be in large measure abandoned: Mass and Office chants from Metz would replace those from Molesme; and the Molesme hymns would give way to hymns from Milan. But all this must have been, in the year 1099, still several years in the offing. For the truly serious and consistent work of reform did not begin, according to the account given by the author of the *Exordium Parvum*, until after the reception of the papal privilege *Desiderium quod* of 19 October 1100. This was the privilege which ensured for the reforms that protection from outside interference thanks to which they could now—and the connecting link in the account is *dehinc*—from this time forth, afterwards, thereupon—implement consistently and in minute particulars their programme of strict observance of the Holy Rule. It is anybody's guess how long it took them to arrive at the decision that their mass and office chants were to be taken from the Metz books, their hymns from the Milanese hymnary; anybody's guess, too, how long it took, once the decision had been made, to obtain copies of the new material, to learn the new repertory, and to adopt it to the utter exclusion to the office chants and hymns familiar to the brethren from their days at Molesme.

Was there anything specifically Cistercian about the Molesme hymn repertory transplanted to the New Monastery? Not really. It was simply a question of the Molesme hymns being changed both at Molesme and at the New Monastery and, as a matter of fact, at a number of other abbeys as well. For this hymn repertory is a highly distinctive one preserved almost intact and with relatively few modifications in a substantial number of monasteries at one time connected directly or indirectly with the pre-Merovingian abbey near Tours, Marmoutier, of Saint Martin of Tours fame. . . .

The office material at Marmoutier travelled in 1038 with a reforming abbot to the small and precariously situated abbey of Montier-la-Celle,[2] the monastery where Saint Robert had lived for so many years, first as a simple monk (from around 1043, if not earlier), and then as prior. It is hardly surprising that the liturgical

2. Or Moutier-la-Celle

tradition of the monastery of Molesme, near Tonnerre, was the same liturgical tradition which flourished at the founder's former abbey close to Troyes. From Montier-la-Celle we have no fewer than three manuscripts which, through relatively late, offer with remarkably few local additions, the identical hymn repertory used at Molesme and Jully.

This remarkably uniform body of hymnody represents a tradition found within a grouping of monasteries considerably larger than the sub-group constituted by Molesme, Jully-les-Nonnains, and Montier-la-Celle. The centre and fountainhead of this tradition is the ancient abbey of Marmoutier, near Tours, whose importance as a catalyst for renewal and reform in numerous monasteries of France during the eleventh century was second only to that of Cluny. There seems little doubt but that the advent of Bernard, or Benard, monk of Marmoutier, as reforming abbot of Montier-la-Celle, in 1038, marked also the advent of the Marmoutier liturgical books—the hymnary included—into the ancient but small and precariously situated abbey of Montier-la-Celle. But the Marmoutier hymnal travelled not only to Montier-la-Celle and to Molesme and its dependencies and even to the New Monastery, but to other monasteries in other parts of France, such as the abbey of Sainte-Trinité de Vendôme, colonized by monks from Marmoutier in 1032. There is no dearth of manuscripts from this Marmoutier milieu; and these manuscripts all contribute to reaffirm the existence of an extremely conservative and homogeneous repertory of hymns all but identical for all these various houses. Where the manuscripts differ is almost exclusively in those formularies which were relatively late in gaining admittance into the monastic books (Saint Mary Magdalene, Trinity Sunday, Immaculate Conception) or those formularies for saints proper to a given house (as Saint Ayoul and Saint Frodobert at Montier-la-Celle). . . .

THE STEPHEN HARDING 'MONITUM'

The why and wherefore of jettisoning the Molesme hymnary in favor of a hymnal fetched from Milan and the creation of the first specifically Cistercian hymnal is nowhere more clearly expressed than in Stephan Harding's introductory *monitum* to the twelfth-century Cistercian hymnal.

The text has survived in but a single manuscript (Nantes, Bibliothèque municipale, MS 9, f. 144r2). The late twelfth-century scribe, having finished copying Rufinus' translation of some of Origen's homilies, proceeded to fill up a partially blank column with a curious text long out of date at the time of his writing.[3] The opening rubric is clearly by the scribe, since Abbot Stephen is styled 'second abbot of Citeaux'—Citeaux being the monastery name which became current only towards 1119.[4] That the *monitum* is to be dated long before 1119 emerges from the text itself, where 'Brother Stephen' refers to himself as the second minister[5]—the language is biblical[6]—of the New Monastery (rather than Cîteaux), and where his address is directed, not to the daughter houses and granddaughter houses of the mother abbey, but simply to Stephen's successors at the New Monastery. Clearly, we are at a time before the New Monastery had embarked on its programme of first foundations, which began with the founding of Pontigny in 1113. Since Stephen's predecessor, Alberic, died early in 1108,[7] Stephen could have written his *monitum* no earlier than 1108; and it is unlikely he would have written it, given its address formula, any time after 1112.

Was the hymnal to which Stephen prefaced his *monitum* already being used at the New Monastery? Or was the *monitum* written

3. For a discussion of the manuscript, see Pierre Blanchard, 'Un monument primitif de la Règle cistercienne', *Revue bénédictine* 31 (1914) 35–44.

4. See J. Marilier, 'Le vocable "Novum Monasterium" ", *Cistercienser-Chronik* 57 (1950) 81–84. Reference to Stephen as the second, rather than the third, abbot of the New Monastery is consistent with early cistercian usage. See note 5, below.

5. On Stephen as second, rather than third, abbot of the New Monastery, see J. Lefevre, "St Robert de Molesme dans l'opinion monastique du XIIe et du XIIIe siècle', *Analecta Bollandiana* 74 (1956) 50–83.

6. Mt 20:26, 23:11 and parallels.

7. See J. Marilier, *Chartes et documents concernant l'Abbaye de Cîteaux 1098–1182*, Bibliotheca Cisterciensis 1 (Rome: Editiones Cistercienses, 1961) 22–23.

to preface a hymnal newly edited under Stephen's own direction, if not by Stephen himself? If the latter were the case, then the Molesme hymns would have been sung at the New Monastery for at least a decade, rather than for just a few years. There is no reason, however, why Stephen could not have appended his *monitum* to a hymnal already long in use at the abbey. The answer to the question is, then: we simply do not know.

The *notificatio* (*filiis sancte ecclesie*) could hardly be more formal, and it might strike more than one reader as being mildly hilarious that a document about a hymnal drawn up for a tiny backwoods community consisting, perhaps, of less than a dozen members, would be called to the attention of all the 'children of Holy Church'. But this kind of public formulation goes with formal acts of a binding nature; the permanent validity of the object of the act is what is here envisaged. This is no temporary decision. Saint Stephen Harding is acting with the full authority of his abbatial office, and he—together with his brothers—are enacting a decision binding on future generations of monks at the New Monastery. This is an official decision, and Stephen means for it to be as official as it can possibly be.

The following lines tell us that the hymns contained in this hymnal had been composed by Saint Ambrose, archbishop of Milan (†397). The statement may well bring a smirk to the lips of knowledgeable readers. We today know full well that scholarly consensus recognizes only a scant fourteen texts as being genuinely by Ambrose, and that a few scholars would like to add an additional four (the traditional hymns of Prime, Terce, Sext, and None) to the ambrosian hymn canon while just as many other scholars would like to reduce the fourteen to an even smaller number.[8] In the early twelfth century the question of which hymns in the Milanese tradition were really by Ambrose was much less problematical. If a hymn was in the Milanese hymnal, it was there because Saint Ambrose had put it there. To have a copy of the ambrosian hymn

8. On this, see A. S. Walpole, *Early Latin Hymns* (Cambridge: Cambridge University Press, 1922; rpt. Hildesheim: Georg Olms Verlagsbuchhandlung, 1966) 16–27.

repertory was to have a copy of Saint Ambrose's *opera hymnica*. In fact, we shall have to wait until the late seventeenth century for a serious attempt at discrimination even to be hazarded, for only then was it that the Maurist editors, J. de Frische and N. le Nourry, tried—not wholly successfully—to separate the genuine hymns from the less genuine for their edition of Saint Ambrose's works.[9]

The text goes on to inform us, by way of historical introduction to the decision about to be enacted, that these hymns had been brought from the church at Milan to the New Monastery, and that by common counsel and decree of the brothers—one could hardly get more official—it had been laid down that these and only these hymns were to be sung from now on, not only by the brethren of that generation, but by the brethren of all succeeding generations. This is, then, no arbitrary decision on the part of Father Abbot; it is a collective decision arrived at with great deliberation, and in the spirit of Chapter Three of the Rule of Saint Benedict, 'On Summoning the Brethren for Counsel'.

But why this astonishing devotion to the Milanese hymnary, to the exclusion, now and forever, of all other hymns? The reason is clearly formulated: it is because, in his Rule, 'our blessed father and teacher Benedict' proposed precisely these ambrosian hymns to be sung at the Divine Office. Anyone who knows the least bit about the place of the Rule of Benedict in the early cistercian enterprise hardly needs to be reminded of the determination which Stephen refers to when he remarks: 'we have decreed to observe it in this place with the utmost zeal'.

But where, we may ask, does Saint Benedict prescribe that his monks sing only hymns composed by the great archbishop of Milan? Nowhere explicitly. But if we take the trouble to examine the vocabulary in Saint Benedict's liturgical code, Chapters 8–20 of the Rule, we find that, although he refers eight times to hymns by the common term *hymnus*, he also uses equivalently the term *ambrosianum* four times:

9.4   *Inde sequitur ambrosianum . . .*

12.4   *Inde benedictiones . . . ambrosianum, versu . . .*

9. Two volumes, published 1686–1690.

13.11   *Post haec . . . ambrosianum, versu . . .*

17.8   *Post quibus . . . ambrosianum, versu . . .*

We may note in passing—this observation will be of importance only at a later stage in the evolution of the cistercian hymnal—that the term *ambrosianum* is used only in those chapters dealing with the Night Office (9.4), Lauds (12.4, 13.11) and Vespers (17.8).

So what, we ask, is an *ambrosianum* according to the mind of Benedict—which is, of course, the only mind about which the first Cistercians here concerned themselves? The most obvious answer is that an 'ambrosian' hymn is a hymn composed by Saint Ambrose. In the centuries preceding the cistercian reform, this was indeed one of the two accepted meanings of the term. Isidore of Seville tells us that, after the time of Hilary, 'Bishop Ambrose, a man of great glory in Christ and a most shining teacher in the Church, is known to have shone more copiously in composing songs of this sort, and these hymns are themselves called *Ambrosiani* after his own name'. [10] To the best of my knowledge, all those who attempt to explain the technical term 'ambrosian' repeat the substance of Isidore's exegesis, though they sometimes suggest yet another meaning. Commenting on the text of the Rule, *Inde sequitur Ambrosianus*, Paul the Deacon explains that this means a hymn; and that 'ambrosian', derived from *ambrosia*, means that it is divine or heavenly—that is, divinely inspired. But Paul redeems himself in his fanciful etymology of *ambrosianum* by admitting that 'others prefer to derive "ambrosian" from the master of hymnody, Ambrose'. [11]

Paul's exegesis passed word for word into Paul's emulator, Hildemar, and into the much more widely circulated commentary by Smaragdus, abbot of St-Mihiel († after 826). [12] 'Ambrosian' from 'ambrosia' strikes us as imaginative, and it doubtless had the same

10. *De ecclesiasticis officiis*, Book 1, Chapter 6; PL 83:743B.

11. Pauli Warnedrifi, *In sanctam regulam commentarium* (Monte Cassino, 1980) 232.

12. A. Spannagel and P. Engelbert, edd., *Smaragdi abbatis Expositio in Regulam S. Benedicti*. Corpus Consuetudinum Monasticarum 8 (Siegburg, 1974) 197.

effect on the first Cistercians, who tended to take the Rule noway if not literally.

The practical upshot of all this is spelled out clearly in the four-word *dispositio* clause of Stephen Harding's text: 'hold on to these hymns—inviolably'. It is preceded by six lines filled with terms redolent of the love and even passion these reformers felt whenever the Rule was at issue—the Rule for the observance of which they had shaped up and legislated at the cost of 'no little sweat'. Never was this integrity—we would probably speak in terms of 'integral observance'—to be changed or uprooted by any of Stephen's successors. Those who came afterwards were to be lovers of the programme formulated by 'our holy father', imitators or followers of it, and even its propagators.

This is a remarkable text. And Stephen Harding, seconded by this brothers, meant every word of it. The practical consequences for Stephen's successors were to be considerable.

T. *uenarabili abbati scireburnie et Congregationi sibi a deo com-*
misse, frater Stephanus, cistertiensis Ecclesie seruus: christum
3 *cum dilectione timere, et cum timore diligere.*
EPISTOLARE *offitium est alloqui absentes quasi presentes, et*
coniungere per caritatis contubernium quos interualla locorum ab
6 *inuicem decludunt. Vnde quia os nostrum et caro nostra estis, com-*
moneo uos ut me pauca scribentem patienter sufferatis.[a] Ego monachus
uester fui, et in baculo meo mare transiui, ut in me omnium uestrum
9 *minimo, nullius momenti apud uos, dominus diuitias misericordie sue*
demonstraret, et uos ad emulandum me prouocaret. Vas enim uacuum velut
uiuus fons, sicut uoluit, impleuit, ut uos qui meliores sanctissima
12 *parentela eratis, religionem fortiter tenere, et de domino presumere*
auderetis. Nunc enim qui solud de terra mea et pauper egressus sum,
diues et cum quadraginta turbis uiam, universe carnis letus ingredior,
15 *securus expectans denarium operariis fideliter in uinea laborantibus[b]*
repromissum. Vnde uestram cohorter dilectionem, ut bonam famam que
de uobis ad nos usque manauit profectui uirtutum applicare satagatis;
18 *ut de bono in melius proficientes, et uere religioni firmiter inheren-*
tes, castitatem, humilitatem (?), studiis parsimonie cum caritate inser-
uientes corde et corpopre useque ad morterm tenere non desistatis, ut
21 *deum deorum uidere mereamini. Amen.*

---

a sufferatis *1st hand correction, above line, of* erudiatis
b laborantibus *1st hand correction (with expunction dot) of* larborantibus

A Letter from Abbot Stephen Harding to Abbot Thurston of Sherborne

TO THURSTON, venerable abbot of Sherborne and the congregation entrusted to his care by God. Brother Stephen, servant of the Church at Cîteaux. Fear Christ, but with love; and love him, but with fear.

THE FUNCTION OF A LETTER is to address those absent as though they were present, and to bring together through a union of charity those separated by long distances. And so, because you are our bone and our flesh, I admonish you to bear patiently with me as I write these few words. I was your own monk, and with my staff I passed over the sea, so that in me, the least of all of you and of no importance whatever when I was with you, the Lord might show forth the riches of his mercy and provoke you to emulation of me.

For, living fountain that he is, he filled the empty vessel: for so he willed, that you, who were so much better by reason of the holiness of your family-line, would have the courage to hold fast and strong to monastic observance, and to presume on the Lord. For I, who was all alone when I went forth from my country, and poor, am entering upon the way of all flesh, happy, rich, and with forty bands, looking forward with confidence to the penny promised to the laborers who work faithfully in the vineyard.

And so I exhort your love to strive to make the good repute you have, and which has reached from you even as far as us, the occasion for [further] progress in virtues, so that, progressing from what is good to what is better and cleaving firmly to true monastic observance, you may never cease to observe chastity and humility, submitting [yourselves] to the zealous practice of frugality together with charity even unto death that you may see the God of gods. Amen.

An Exegesis of Stephen Harding' Letter to Sherborne

Chrysogonus Waddell, OCSO

ETTERS BY SAINT STEPHEN Harding are not easily come by. The *registrum* of his official correspondence disappeared from Cîteaux so completely and at so early a date,[1] that not even a Manrique or a Henriquez—geniuses in the art of retrieving *deperdita*—were able to find so much as a few authentic fragments to incorporate into their mammoth collections of *cisterciana.* A few authentic texts by Saint Stephen can be classified, at least in loose terms, as 'letters': the *monitum* dated from Christmas Eve of 1109 and written for the celebrated Bible-manuscript which today so rightly goes by the name the 'Stephen Harding Bible';[2] or the similar *monitum* which prefaced the early Milanese-Cistercian hymnal.[3] There are, however, two *bona fide*

1. For a brief history of the archives of Cîteaux, with abundant bibliographical references, see Abbè J. Marilier, *Chartes et documents concernant l'abbaye de Cîteaux 1098–1182* (Rome, 1961).
2. Frequently edited, as in Mabillon, *Opera Sancti Bernardi* (edition of 1719) 1: p xii; PL 166:1375–1376; Marilier, p. 56, Document 32. The best edition is that by Charles Oursel, *Miniatures cisterciennes* (1109–1134) (Macon: Protat Frères, 1960) unpaginated introductory loose folio.
3. Also frequently edited, but not without inaccuracies, as in P. Blanchard, 'Un monument primitif de la règle cistercienne' in RB 31 (1914) 35–44; Othon Ducourneau, *Les origines cisterciennes*, p. 106, note 3 [=*Revue Mabillon* 23 (1933) p. 102 note 1]; S. Marosszéki, 'Les origines du chant cistercien' in *Analecta SOC* 8 (1952) 9 (a particularly inaccurate transcription); C. Waddell, 'The Origin and Early Evolution of the Cistercian Antiphonary. Reflections on Two Cistercian Chant Reforms' in M. B. Pennington, ed., *The Cistercian Spirit: A Symposium in Honor of Thomas Merton*, CS 3 (1970) 206, but with discussion and bibliographical references, pp. 204–206; finally, Marilier, p. 55, Document 31. See above, pages 77-86.

letters with Saint Stephen's name in the superscription, the one addressed to Louis the Fat, the other to Pope Honorius II. But the first of these is written in the name of Stephen, the assembly of cistercian abbots, and the brethren of Cîteaux; while the second specifies as senders, along with Stephen, Hugh of Pontigny and a certain abbot of Clairvaux called Bernard. Since both letters have come down to us only through their inclusion in collections of Saint Bernard's letters,[4] the presumption seems to be that the first abbot of Clairvaux ghost-wrote them both. There is, however, one letter, a single letter, which is both a real letter and a letter indubitably written by Saint Stephen Harding himself.

It is a remarkable letter. The text has been printed on three different occasions, but in two different transcriptions. In an article of 1936, 'An unpublished letter of Saint Stephen,' C. H. Talbot shared with readers of *Collectanea O.C.R.* his recent exciting discovery.[5] While working with the Rievaulx manuscripts at the Jesus College Library, Cambridge, he had come across, in a collection of varia, a copy of a letter by one *frater Stephanus cisterciensis ecclessiae servus* addressed to *T. venerabili abbati scireburniae*. He identified the text, 'written in a small neat hand' and dating, it would seem, from the 'end of the XII century'[6] as a letter from the third abbot of Cîteaux to Thurstan, abbot of the community at Sherborne in Dorset. Ancient as Sherborne was, the community had no abbot of its own until 1122. Till that time the abbey had been united with the bishopric, so that the bishop of Sherborne (and, from 1075 onwards, the bishop of Old Sarum) had also been the abbot of Sherborne. The dissociation of offices had taken place in 1122; and since the first abbot serving under the new arrangement was in office from 1122 till around 1142, and since his name was Thurstan, the two immediate emergents were these: 1) Stephen's letter must

4. SBOp 7:133–134 and 7:14–141 for Letters 45 and 49 respectively; PL 182:149B and 157B.

5. Father Hugh Talbot, 'An Unpublished Letter of St Stephen' in *Collectanea OCR* 2 (1936) 66–69.

6. Talbot, p 66.

have been written between 1122 and 1134, the date of his death; 2) the addressee was Abbot Thurstan.

Two further details enabled C. H. Talbot to suggest tentatively an even more specific date:

1) Stephen refers to the existence of forty *turbae* or communities of Cistercians; if Stephen is precise in meaning forty rather than 'about forty,' and if Janauschek is correct in his chronology of cistercian foundations, then Neuberg in Alsace is abbey number 40,[7] and the date we are looking for is 1131. If Stephen is using more-or-less numbers, however, then we should be a bit more vague, and settle for something like 1129–1134.

2) Stephen mentions yet another helpful circumstance: he is soon to go the way of the flesh; and this would suggest a date closer to 1134 than to 1122. All in all, 1131, give or take a year or two, is then the likely date. But why was the letter written? 'Under what circumstances the letter was written, it is not easy to surmise,' writes Talbot; and he continues: 'The history of Sherborne is so fragmentary that I have been unable to discover any particular event with which it might be connected.'[8] He notes, too, that the text of the letter 'adds nothing in particular to our knowledge of the Saint or of the Order.'[9]

A quarter-century later the letter was printed in a quite different transcription with a title all but identical as that of the earlier article by Talbot: 'An Unpublished Letter of Saint Stephen Harding' by D. L. Bethell. It appeared in the 1961 autumn issue of *Downside Review*[10] with fewer helpful introductory notes and in a less accurate transcription than was the case of the earlier *Collectanea* version. But at least this later publication brought the letter to the attention of a new circle of readers.

7. L. Janauschek, *Originum Cisterciensium*, I (Vienna: A. Hölder, 1877; rpt 1964) p. 18.
8. Talbot, p 6.
9. *Ibid.*
10. Pp. 349–350. Mr Bethell had attended school at Sherborne, in the same location where Saint Stephen had learned the first elements of reading and writing more than eight-hundred and fifty years earlier.

In the same year, 1961, the abbé Jean Marilier reproduced the Talbot transcription in his own *Chartes et documents concernant l'abbaye de Cîteaux 1098–1182*.[11] He summarized the text as a 'letter of Abbot Stephen Harding to T[hurstan], abbot of Sherborne; he reminds him that he himself had been a monk of Sherborne before crossing the sea [to the tombs of the apostles at Rome, and before entering Molesme] and he exhorts the religious of his former monastery to virtue.'[12]

Thus far the printing-history of the letter. What has been its impact on the scholarly world? Nil, so far as I can determine. Writers interested in things cistercian have, of course, referred to the text in connection with Saint Stephen and early Cîteaux. But there seems to be an understandable though tacit disappointment that the text sheds so little specifically new light on the life and mission of Saint Stephen. Expunge our document from the dossier of Stephen Harding source material, and it would make no real difference to what has been written about him in the last four decades. It would seem that C. H. Talbot was right: the letter 'adds nothing in particular to our knowledge of the Saint or of the Order. . . .'

The purpose of the brief notes which follow is chiefly to call attention anew to a text which, bland and minuscule though it seems to be, has much to tell us about the experience and inner life of one of the most remarkable of all Cistercians. Convinced at last that the best way of ensuring the serious exegesis of the text at some future date, by a scholar more competent than myself, would be to provide a preliminary study, I offer the reader the following notes.[13] The reader is forewarned of the provisional and sketchy nature of them.

In his recension of D. L. Bethell's presentation of the letter, Father C[harles] D[umont] suggested that, though there were now

11. Marilier, p. 91, Document 88.
12. *Ibid.*
13. [The editor of the present volume has diminished the author's caution and humility by changing the title and removing the next sentence: 'If I cannot honestly adopt as the title of this study, "The Exegesis of a Letter by Saint Stephen Harding," I can at least settle for "Notes *towards* the Exegesis of a Letter by Saint Stephen Harding" '].

94

two different transcriptions of the text in print, perhaps a third would not be superfluous in view of the important divergences between the two transcriptions.[14] We have begun, then, with the third transcription. A phrase-by-phrase commentary will follow. By way of summing up, the English version used in the commentary has been pieced together and revised as a first draft of a translation.

NOTES ON THE TRANSCRIPTION

The volume in which our unique text is found is a commonplace book from Rievaulx which includes among other things a catalogue of the abbey library, the cistercian *Consuetudines*, Saint Bernard's Prologue to the reformed antiphonary and the treatise *Cantum quem*, and even some notes on prosody. All this material is datable to the twelfth and thirteenth centuries and an analysis of the manuscript—MS 34 (Q.B. 17)—may be found in M. R. James, *A Descriptive Catalogue of the Manuscripts in the Library of Jesus College, Cambridge* (Cambridge, 1895) pp. 43–56. The manuscript was given to Jesus College Library by Thomas Man, Fellow of the College (B.A. 1674, M.A. 1678, M.Div. 1687) and later vicar of Northallerton, where he collected a sizable collection of mediaeval manuscripts. We do not know where the Rievaulx manuscript was between the dissolution of the monasteries and the time it came into Man's possession.[15]

The end of the twelfth–century date proposed by C. H. Talbot seems more likely than the mid-twelfth century date suggested by D. L. Bethell.[16] I am not sure, however, that I would describe the hand, as does Talbot, as 'neat'. In spite of the preliminary tracing of lines in dry-point, the lines of the written text run crooked; letters are unevenly spaced; and the general impression is that of a competent but somewhat undisciplined scribe whose style was a bit on the nervous side. He was, however, very much an Englishman.

14. *Collectanea O.C.R.* 25 (1963) 404.
15. This information was communicated to me in a personal letter dated 22 January 1962, from the Assistant Librarian of Jesus College Library, Isobel Keith.
16. Talbot, p. 66; Bethell, p. 350.

No expatriate monk from across the Channel would use the long-tailed *r* and the kind of *s* that soars high above the line and curls determinedly below (though the same scribe inconsistently uses a different form of *s* in a few instances). Though we are clearly moving away from the romanesque, we are far from having arrived at the gothic, and the letters are virtually unclubbed. The abundance of abbreviations suggest that the scribe may have had experience in a chancery, and this seems even more likely when we note in line 10 of the manuscript text the form of *de* with the *e* astraddle the ascender—a typical chancery trick. But honesty forces us to face the fact that the other three instances of *de* are written in the usual way.

If we are correct in accepting a date roughly towards the end of the twelfth century, the inference is that we have before us not a copy of the original, but a copy of a copy of the original. Otherwise, it would be difficult to envisage a late twelfth-century copy being made directly on the original letter delivered to Sherborne around 1131. We could, of course, imagine that a monk of Rievaulx copied the text in the course of a visit to Sherborne; or that a monk brought the original to Rievaulx for copying. But this is far-fetched indeed. Far less imagination is needed to surmise that when the colony of cistercian founders of Rievaulx arrived in 1132,[17] they brought with them, in a packet of other letters meant for distribution to various parts of England (including Waverly and Tintern, neither very far from Sherborne, a letter addressed to the abbot and community of Sherborne Abbey. Though written, to all appearances, in somewhat vague and general terms, the Sherborne letter touched at least obliquely on the strained relations between monks of the standard observance and cistercian radicals. It was just as well, then, that a copy of the letter be kept at Rievaulx for future reference. I suggest, then, that our scribe filled up part of a blank folio of his manuscript using as his model a copy of the letter made decades earlier, and probably removed from the abbot's *registrum* as no longer serving any useful purpose. Still, a letter by so holy an

17. The traditional foundation date is 1132; but preparations for the foundation would have involved a number of Cistercians in cross-channel travelling for a considerable period prior to the official foundation date.

old-timer as one of the founders of Cîteaux was interesting if only as a curio. Why not use it, then, to fill up an empty space of some stray folio?

Since norms vary so much from editor to editor, I have followed my own preferences in my transcription. I have extended abbreviations and suspensions, and I used modern punctuation. But I prefer to follow the scribe in matters of spelling and capitalization (in most instances, non-capitalization). One further concession to current *praxis*: I adopt the standard letter-format, and even type in caps the initial word of the body of the text.

COMMENTARY

1. *T. uenerabili abbati scireburnie*: 'T.' for T[hurstino] or T[hurstano] or some other form of the name of Thurstan, first abbot of Sherborne Abbey in Dorset. Sherborne's importance as a monastic and ecclesiastical establishment antedated Thurstan by many centuries. When the West Saxon see of Dorchester was divided around 705, Sherborne was made the seat of a bishopric comprised of the counties of Wilts, Dorset, Berks, Somerset, Devon, and Cornwall. Later territorial divisions eventually left Sherborne with no more than the county of Dorset. Secular canons staffed the cathedral church until 998, when King Ethelred gave Bishop Wulsin a charter authorizing the replacement of the canons by a community of monks living *secundum institutionem sancti patris Benedicti*,[18] and designating the bishop as *abbas et pater* of the monastic community. As in the case of other monastic cathedrals the acting head of the community was the prior. In 1076 the see of Sherborne was translated to Old Sarum or Salisbury, in alleged conformity with the ordinance of the Council of London of the preceding year, which decreed that bishops' sees be removed from obscure places to towns of the greatest note in their dioceses.[19] It is true that William of Malmesbury expressed

18. The material on Sherborne Abbey is particularly rich in William Dugdale, *Monasticon Anglicanum*, (London, edition of 1817) pp. 331–341. King Ethelred's charter and Saint Wulsin's character are both reported in full, pp. 337, Nums. II and III.

19. All recent authors I have seen give the translation date as 1075, so I write under correction. But Dugdale, whom I here follow, gives the date

astonishment that Sherborne, being so tiny a place—*viculus*, he calls it—could have perdured for so many centuries as the seat of a bishopric,[20] but he also describes Old Sarum as more of a castle than a town.[21] At any rate, after 1076, the office of prior continued at Sherborne until sometime around 1122, when Roger of Caen, Bishop of Salisbury, separated the office of bishop from the office of abbot. Sherborne was erected into an independent abbey, and Thurstan (around 1122 to around 1142) was blessed as its first abbot.[22] There can be no reasonable doubt as to the identification of 'T., Abbot of Sherborne.'

1–2. *et Congregationi sibi a deo commisse*: 'and to the Congregation entrusted to his care by God.' This is specifically Holy Rule language. Pick up any concordance of the Holy Rule, and look at the entries under *congregatio*. Clearly this is one of Saint Benedict's terms of predilection for his community, the 'flock' (*grex*) that has been brought together (*con-*). More precise Rule-resonance results, however, from the juxtaposition of *Congregatio sibi* and *commissa*. Only a reader unfamiliar with the Holy Rule will fail to catch an echo of Saint Benedict's *non solum detrimenta* **gregis sibi commissi** *non patiatur* (RB 2.32) and *Abbas non conturbet* **gregem sibi commissum** (63.2). With the very opening words, then, Saint Stephen strikes a 'benedictine' note that will be sustained through the course of the entire letter.

---

of the London Council as 1075, and assigns the implementation of the decision, in the case of Bishop Hereman, to 1076. See Dugdale, 1:333.

20. *De gestis pontificum Anglorum*, Lib. II, De episcopis Schireburnensibus, Salisburiensibus, Wiltunensibus: 'Schireburnia est viculus, nec habitantium frequentia, nec positionis gratia suavis, in quo mirandum, et pene pudendum sedem episcopalem per tot durasse saecula'. PL 179:1533C.

21. *Ibid.*: ' . . . tribunal suum transtulit [Hermannus] a Schireburnia Salesberiam, quod est vice civitatis castellum locatum in edito. . . .' PL 179:1538C.

22. Dugdale, 1:334. The author gives Thurstan as the first known abbot of Sherborne, but wrongly presupposes that between 1075 and 1122 other abbots had preceded and resided at Sherborne. During this period the abbot of the place remained the bishop, presumably in residence at Old Sarum; and the chief functionary at the abbey was the claustral prior who, for most (but not all) practical purposes functioned as would an abbot.

98

We note, too, that this letter is addressed, not to Abbot Thurstan only, but to Abbot Thurstan together with his community.

2. *Frater Stephaus. cisterciensis Ecclesie servus*: 'Brother Stephen, servant of the church at Cîteaux.' No room here even to touch on the twelfth-century understanding of the monastery as a local church, as the Church present in and through a given monastic community. It was standard usage for the Fathers, however, to refer, not to the monastery of Clairvaux or the abbey of Cîteaux, but to the *church* at Cîteaux (or Clairvaux). And 'Brother Stephen', relative to the church at Cîteaux, takes the role of the servant, *servus*. Elsewhere, in his *monitum* to the early Cistercian Hymnal, he refers to himself as the *minister* of the New Monastery, *Frater Stephanus Novi Monasterii* **minister**.[23] At the time of writing, Saint Stephen is still in office, otherwise he would hardly style himself *servus*. Since he renounced his abbatial office in 1132, this gives us a convenient *terminus ante quem* for dating the letter.[24]

2–3. *Christum cum dilectione timere, et cum timore diligere*: 'Fear Christ, but with love; and love him, but with fear.' Possibly *timere* would be better rendered by 'reverence'; but the terms combined in this greeting are clearly meant to express something of a paradox, and the intent of the author is probably better served if we use 'love' and 'fear'—terms at first blush irreconcilable with each other. For a moment we have the impression that the phrase must have been excerpted from the Holy Rule, and we think straightway of Chapter 72. But though all the terms are present, they are present in different combinations. We are dealing with a traditional *topos*: the dialectic between love and fear that provides the dynamism of the monk's ascent of the degrees of humility in Chapter 7 of the Rule. But rather than situate this salutation in the context of the Rule as exegeted with the help of Cassian's three kinds of 'fear' or Saint Augustine's 'chaste love,' we shall here simply note that Saint

23. See Note 3, above, for references to the *monitum*.
24. On the chronology of the first abbots, see Marilier, p. 26; but for a more detailed presentation, see the same author's article, 'Catalogue des abbés de Cîteaux pour le XIIᵉ siècle' in *Cistercienser-Chronik* 55(1948) 1–11.

Stephen introduces into his greeting-formula a theme important for our understanding of the final lines of his letter. We might note in passing, too, that the object of our love-fear, fear-love, is not simply 'God', but specifically Christ.

4–6. *Epistolare offitium est alloqui absentes quasi presentes, et coniungere per caritatis contubernium quos interualla locorum ab inuicem secludunt.* 'The function of a letter is to address those absent as though they were present and to bring together through a union of charity those separated by long distances.' The opening formula is a splendid one, and has a ciceronian air. I suspect that if I knew more than I do about the classical epistolary literary genre, I would be able to point to half-dozen variations on this particular introductory formula. I am more interested, however, in the content of the phrase. If you find the translation toned down from the latin original, you are probably right. The vocabulary is a bit 'intense'; but it is an insoluble problem, when working with mediæval texts, to judge just how 'used up' an originally colorful word has become after centuries of general usage. *Coniungere* can be strong: to join, to unite in a nuptial bond; and *contubernium* originally meant tent-fellowship. At its strongest, then, the phrase means that a letter ought to bring together in close communion, and under the roof of charity, people separated from one another by geographical distance. *Contubernium* can also mean 'kinship', people living together as one family in the same tent. From Cîteaux to Sherborne, then, is quite a distance; but Saint Stephen meant this letter to bring sender and receivers together in the family-bond of a love unhindered by limitations imposed by geography. The theme seems to have been a constant with Saint Stephen. In his own words, the purpose of the *Carta caritatis* was to provide the bond of charity by means of which monks 'scattered in body throughout abbeys in diverse parts of the world, should be indissolubly joined together in spirit,' *monachi . . . per abbatias in diversis mundi partibus corporibus divisi animis indissolubiter conglutinarentur.*[25] This is even more 'intense' diction than in the

25. J. de la Croix Bouton and J.-B. Van Damme, edd., *Les plus anciens textes de Cîteaux.* Cîteaux: Commentarii Cistercienses, Studia et Documenta 2 (Achel, Belgium: 1974) 89. Translation by Bede K. Lackner, taken

100

letter to Abbot Thurstan and brethren (especially since 'joined together' stands for 'glued together,' 'cemented together'); but the greater intensity is here justified by the closer communion among brethren of the same family within the *ordo monasticus* at large.

6. *Vnde quia os nostrum et caro nostra estis*: 'And so, because you are our bone and our flesh. . . .' The biblical point of reference is not the 'bone of my bone and flesh of my flesh' (*os ex ossibus meis, et caro de carne mea*) of Genesis 2:23, but rather Laban's joyful recognition of his nephew, 'who, when he heard that Jacob his sister's son was come, ran forth to meet him; and embracing him, and heartily kissing him, brought him into his house. And when he had heard the causes of his journey, he answered: Thou art my bone and my flesh': *Os meum es et caro mea* (Gen 29:13–14). Since the Jacob-story is to supply a yet more explicit point of reference just a few words later in the letter, we can be fairly certain that the 'our bone and our flesh' comes from this recognition-scene where Laban and the pilgrim Jacob celebrate the family kinship.

6–7. *commoneo uos ut me pauca scribentem patienter sufferatis*: 'I admonish you to bear patiently with me as I write these few words.' This line has a 'feel' of biblical diction, and even without a preliminary glance at a concordance we can turn to 2 Corinthians 11:19 on the strength of *sufferatis* (which the scribe first wrote as *erudiatis*). We remember that the pauline text about suffering fools gladly introduces his extraordinary account of his apostolic ministry; and here, in our own letter, this sentence introduces Stephen's own summary of his *curriculum vitae*. Contextually, the phrases are concordant. But when we look at the actual latin text, points of verbal resemblance—the choice of words and the word order— are practically nil: *Libenter enim suffertis insipientes. . . .* Perhaps it is the earlier verse one of the same chapter that we are reminded of, 'Would to God you could bear with some little of my folly; but do bear with me.' Unfortunately, the Vulgate text fails to bear us out: *Utinam sustineretis modicum quid insipientiae meae, sed et supportate me.* Instead of 'I admonish' (*commoneo*), we find 'Would to God'

from Louis Lekai, *The Cistercians. Ideals and Reality* (Kent State University, Ohio: Kent State University Press, 1977) 462.

(*utinam*); instead of 'some little of my folly' (*modicum quid insipientiae meae*), '[bear patiently with] me as I write these few words [or things]'. As for the *sufferatis*, this appears (in a different grammatical form) in verse nineteen, but with *libenter* for its adverbial modifier, rather than *patienter*. There is, however, another possible pauline point of reference. In Acts 26, Paul gives King Agrippa an account of his life, conversion, and calling. He begins by saying how happy he is to be able to address his defense to someone who knows 'both customs and questions that are among the Jews.' He then summarizes his life-work and experience, introducing all this with the remark: 'Wherefore I beseech thee to hear me patiently' (Acts 26:2), *Propter quod obsecro, patienter me audias.* The context is *ad rem*: Paul is about to make his *apologia* before one who knows both customs and questions that are among the Jews; Stephen is about to make a similar *apologia* addressed to a community well aware of the customs and questions that are among monks.

Whether he is writing in 1131 or a bit earlier, it is a time when tempers of monastics are flaring high, and controversy over customs and questions that are among monks is the order of the day.[26] Relations between communities of *status quo*-minded Benedictines and communities of cistercian radicals are not always remarkable for their cordiality. The wide circulation of the abbot of Clairvaux's *Apologia* has added fuel to the flame; and in some quarters, the conflagration has reached the proportions of a forest fire out of control. To make matters worse, it is precisely at this period that the english invasion of the White Monks begins. First comes Waverley, in Surrey and the diocese of Winchester, in 1128. Waverley had been founded in 1120 as a benedictine house; but in 1128 it turned cistercian and entered the filiation of Cîteaux, with l'Aumône as its mother-house. Tintern comes next, in 1131. Located in Monmouthshire on the banks of the Wye, it too is a foundation of l'Aumône, and

---

26. The literature about the feud between Cîteaux and Cluny is extensive. For a fairly recent treatment of the topic, with helpful survey of the more serious scholarly contributions to the discussion, see A. H. Bredero, 'Cluny et Cîteaux au XIIᵉ siècle: les origines de la controverse' in *Studi Medievali* 12 (1971) 135–175.

therefore has the abbot of Cîteaux—a certain Stephen Harding, formerly of Devonshire—as head of its filiation. If we look at a map of monastic southern England, we shall find Sherborne roughly equidistant from Waverley on the right and Tintern on the left; and though these are not precisely next door neighbors of Sherborne, they are uncomfortably close. I, myself, am quite sure that, had I been a monk of Sherborne Abbey at the time, I would not have viewed these incursions of a foreign monastic body into my own monastic neighborhood without a real concern. My emotional response would have been further heightened by my realization that this enormously successful new observance that was about to turn England into cistercian territory had had among its founders, and now had as its leader, a monk who had abandoned *my* own community in circumstances which were not particularly edifying. Stephen had been a monk of Sherborne, and he is explicit about it:

7–8. *Ego monachus uester fui*: 'I was your own monk.' Stephen's youthful departure from Sherborne has always been a source of embarrassment for his biographers. The only account of it came from the pen of William of Malmesbury, who can hardly be accused of anti-cistercian or anti-Stephen prejudice. Quite the contrary, William has nothing but praise for his compatriot monastic reformer. Yet it is the sympathetic William who candidly tells us that the first stage of Stephen's monastic odyssey terminated with his apostasy from Sherborne.

> He had been a monk from childhood; but when then
> the prurience of the world began casting its allurements
> on the youngster, he came to loathe those [monkish]
> weeds, and so struck out first for Scotland, then for
> France . . . [27]

In his wonderfully informative article, 'Saint Etienne Harding mieux connu,'[28] Father Jean-Baptiste Van Damme, developing ideas proposed by Charles Oursel in a conference given in 1962,[29] situates

28. *Cîteaux: Commentarii Cistercienses* 14 (1963) 307–313.

29. Published as a pamphlet, Charles Oursel, *Saint-Etienne Harding, abbé de Cîteaux* (Dijon: Bernigaud et Privat, 1962).

Stephen's departure from Sherborne in a rather different context. The Hardings were an important family in the area. Stephen's uncle or grandfather, Elnod, had been steward to King Harold. But after the Battle of Hastings, Elnod played the turncoat and rose high in the service of the norman invader, William the Conqueror. In 1069 we find him suppressing rebellions in Dorset, Somerset, and Devon. Elnod the Quisling was so hated in this region that—so the hypothesis goes—the entire Harding family became *personae non gratae* in Devonshire. Because of the political turmoil, then, the young Harding boy, who had been an oblate at Sherborne from an early age, was constrained to cross the Channel by way of Scotland, the preferred route of English expatriates at this troubled period of history. The hypothesis is fascinating. If I personally hesitate in accepting it, I do so because Stephen, upon leaving Sherborne for family and political reasons, did not head for another monastic community, but spent a number of years getting his education in a non-monastic milieu on the Continent. Whether Stephen was still an oblate when he left Sherborne, or whether he was a professed monk, he was enough a member of the community to be able to write in his old age, *Ego monachus vester fui*, 'I was your own monk.' And again, whether he left Sherborne simply because the call of the world was too strong to be gainsaid, or because his presence had become a problem for himself and for the community by reason of his politically compromised family, his departure from Sherborne was surely not attended by happy memories. We are, of course, in the realm of pure hypothesis the moment we disclaim the probative value of William of Malmesbury's account of Stephen's inglorious departure. If I am going to hypothesize, I think I should try to do so in a way that would take account of both William's reportage and the recently proposed exile-with-honor interpretation. Since I have known more than one monk who has left his community because of aspirations to a higher form of spiritual life, but who has somehow failed to reach his destination because of involvements along the way, I would have no problem in envisaging the situation in this way: A youngster in his mid-teens, raised from childhood in the monastery, and now a bit restless, like any normal adolescent, is constrained to leave his community because of difficulties occasioned by family connections. Since the problem would be the same for Stephen in almost any English monastery after 1066, he must perforce find his new monastic home on the continent. He proceeds thither by the preferred escape route, Scotland. But before eventually finding a new monastic home, he cannot resist the opportunity of seeing a bit more of life outside the cloister. In point of fact, we find him in something of a university milieu. William states specifically that he spent some years at his studies in France, and that he finally went on pilgrimage to Rome in the company of a fellow student, who was a cleric.[30] The *Vita Sancti Petri, Prioris Iuliacensis Puellarum Monasterii et Monachi Molismensis*,[31] is devoted to this fellow student, himself another Englishman by the name of Peter. It has them strike up a close friendship in Burgundy, where Stephen, still a young man—but a young man of the utmost moral probity (*continentissimae vitae*)—is at his studies.[32] It would seem that Stephen, upon leaving England, had betaken himself to a region where the current Anglo-Norman fray posed less immediate personal danger for him. Quite possibly, then, the 'allurements of the world' to which our Stephen succumbed temporarily were less the brawling pleasures of the tavern than the heady joys of dialectics. I shall return to this discussion later. Here we need only insist that he thought of himself as having once been a monk of Sherborne, and that he expected his former brethren to recognize the fact that, Yes, he had once been a monk of theirs; and that between Sherborne

30. *De gestis regum, ibid.*: 'Ibi [France] aliquot annis litteris liberalibus exercitus, divini amoris stimulos accepit: namque cum pueriles ineptias robustior aetas excluderet, Romam, cum consorte studiorum clerico, profectus est.' PL 179:1287B.

31. PL 185:1257–1270. The pertinent texts about Saint Stephen Harding are found in c. II, col. 1259B-D. See H. E. J. Cowdrey, 'Peter, Monk of Molesme and Prior of Jully', in *Cross Cultural Convergences in the Crusader Peirod. Essays Presented to Aryeh Grabois*, edd. Michael Goodich, Sophia Menache, Sylvia Schein (New York: Peter Lang, 1995) 58–73.

32. ' . . . Burgundiae partes subintrans, quemdam continentissimae vitae reperit adolescentem, natione Anglicum, Stephanum nomine qui eodem desiderio ductus quo et Petrus, in hanc se contulerat regionem; cuius vitam, et mores videns, et approbans Petrus, sese ei coniunxit familiarem et socium.' PL 185:1259B.

and Molesme he had tarried an unconscionably long time on the way, seizing the occasion to further his mastery of the liberal arts.

8. *et in baculo meo mare transivi*: 'And with my staff I passed over the sea.' This is only a slight adaptation of Genesis 32:10b: *In baculo meo transivi Iordanem istum.* What makes this brief phrase exciting is the context to which it refers us. Once again we have a text from the Jacob-story. It immediately precedes the episode of Jacob's night-long wrestling with a mysterious 'man', and is part of the prayer Jacob addresses to God in his anguish over his coming encounter with his alienated brother, Esau. He had left his home and his indignant brother under the most painful circumstances; he had sojourned and prospered mightily in a distant land, and now he was returning in the company of his wives and children. 'Deliver me from the hand of my brother Esau,' prays Jacob, 'for I am greatly afraid of him: lest perhaps he come, and kill the mother with the children' (Genesis 32:11). Is Saint Stephen suggesting by his use of this biblical text that just as Jacob, a *persona non grata*, had once crossed the Jordan on his way to foreign parts, so also Stephen had once crossed the sea on his way to foreign parts, a *persona non grata*? And that he was now returning, so to speak, in the company of his family acquired across the sea (Tintern and Waverley, with foundation-plans for Rievaulx already laid)? And that he wanted to be sure that his brethren of former times would not be hostile to the family begotten by the former exile?

8–10. *ut in me omnium uestrum minimo, nullius momenti apud uos, dominus diuitias misericordie sue demonstraret, et uos ad emulandum me prouocaret*: ' . . . so that in me, the least of all of you, and of no importance whatever when I was with you, the Lord might show forth the riches of his mercy, and provoke you to emulation of me.' The several pauline allusions discernible here are not accidentally juxtaposed; they are brought together in a contextual unity which has to be meditated upon to be appreciated. *In me omnium vestrum minimo*, 'in me, the least of all of you,' has two possible points of reference. In Ephesians 3:8, Paul expresses his wonderment that, 'To me, the least of all the saints (*mihi omnium sanctorum minimo*), is given this grace, to preach among the Gentiles the unsearchable riches of Christ.' The immediate context is the justification of Paul's

very special apostolate. He is not a maverick apostle; he is not
the leader of a splinter group; he has a special mission to bring
into the Church a whole category of Gentiles deemed by some as
ineligible for salvation. 1 Corinthians 15:9 provides us with a similar
context: *Ego enim sum minimus apostolorum*, 'For I am the least of the
apostles. . . .' The risen Lord had appeared to Cephas, then to the
Eleven . . . and last of all to Paul, as to one born out of due time,
unworthy, by reason of his persecution of the Church, to be called
an apostle. For all that, it was Paul who labored more abundantly
than all the others; and it was Paul who was the privileged herald
of the Gospel for the Gentile world.

    Ut . . . Dominus divitias misericordiae suae demonstraret: 'so that . . .
the Lord might show forth the riches of his mercy.' Here there is
no doubt about the *locus biblicus*, Romans 9:23: *ut ostenderet divitias
gloriae*. We may as well discuss at the same time the next phrase, *et
vos ad aemulandum me provocaret*, which is a re-working of Romans
11:14, *si quomodo ad aemulandum provocem carnem meam*, 'if, by any
means, I may provoke to emulation them who are my flesh'. Paul's
discussion begins, at the start of chapter nine, with his love and
concern for the Jews; but he shows that God's election is free
and not confined to one nation only. For even the Gentiles are
to receive God's mercy and show forth the riches of his glory. It
is not without significance, perhaps, that where Saint Paul speaks
of 'riches of his *glory*', Saint Stephen, paraphrasing freely, speaks of
'riches of his *mercy*'. ('What do you seek? a novice is asked, and
he replies, 'The mercy of God and of the Order. . . .') At any rate,
against the Romans context, the thought of the former monk of
Sherborne becomes unmistakably clear. If Stephen, for reasons still
not entirely known, had dissociated himself from the community
at Sherborne and from their impressive tradition, it was to the end
that a new monastic family might enter into the fullness of the great
tradition. That God would choose so unlikely an agent as Stephen,
and that his election would be operative outside the mainstream of
the standard observance exemplified at Sherborne and elsewhere—
all this is yet another instance of how God reveals the riches of his
mercy in the most unexpected ways. Further, the rise of a new and
prodigiously successful reform was not without positive meaning for

the community at Sherborne. For just as the fulfillment of God's promises in the midst of the gentile world was meant to make Israel emulous, and so lead to the consummation of God's plan of salvation for Jew and Gentile alike, so also the astonishing vitality and spread of the cistercian communities was meant, not just for Cîteaux, but for other communities of traditional observance; for these were now being encouraged, by the way God was working with the White Monks, to live to the full their own monastic ideals.

It would be nonsensical to press the analogy too far. All Saint Stephen does is to weave together with utter freedom, but with consummate artistry, pauline fragments helpful for our grasping of the real meaning of the phenomenon of Cîteaux for the *ordo monasticus* at large; and helpful, too, for insuring positive rapport between the community of Sherborne and their cistercian neighbors.

9–10. *Vas enim uacuum uiuus fons, sicut uoluit, impleuit.* 'For, living fountain that he is, he filled the empty vessel: for so he willed.' The vessel-theme might make us think that we are still with Saint Paul in chapter nine of Romans, in the passage about vessels of wrath, vessels of mercy, and about the utter gratuitousness of God's election. But the point of reference is much more interesting in that the passage is one unlikely to come spontaneously to mind. We turn to Jeremiah 14:2, where the word of the Lord comes to Jeremiah concerning the words of the drought, and:

> The great ones sent their inferiors to the water: they come to draw, they found no water, they carried back their vessels empty . . .

The Bible abounds in references to vessels; but this is the only one, so far as I know, where *vasa* is juxtaposed to *vacua: Maiores miserunt minores suos ad aquam: venerunt ad hauriendum, non invenerunt aquam, reportaverunt **vasa** sua **vacua**.* If the *maiores - minores* has a familiar ring, it may be because of Saint Stephen's reference to himself in the preceding line: *omnium vestrum **minimo**, nullius momenti apud vos. . . .* Stephen is the *minor*, indeed, the *minimus* sent by the 'great ones', the community of Sherborne, to draw water for a Judæ plunged in mourning, for a Jerusalem whose cry is gone up. According to the Prophet, the 'inferior' finds no water and has to carry back his vessel empty; 'and for the destruction of the land, because there came no rain upon the earth, the husbandmen were confounded, they covered their heads.' In the case of Stephen, all this has been reversed. The 'inferior', the least of all, has been sent by his betters to look for water; and amid the reeds and marshlands of Cîteaux, God has not only filled his empty vessels, but filled them with himself, the living Water. The 'words of the drought' have been reversed; those who are the least of all are carrying back, not empty vessels, but vessels filled with living waters. Stephen must have pondered long and hard over Saint Jerome's exegesis of these words of drought. That he was familiar with the commentary *In Hieremiam Prophetam* is quite certain; for it was at his request during his visit to Flanders in 1124 that Osbert, the scribe of Saint-Vaast at Arras, wrote a copy of the *expositio*, including a note about the visit and the request on folio 103ᵛ of the manuscript.[33] As Saint Jerome sees it, it was 'the *maiores* who ought to have gone to draw the water; but they send the *iuniores*, who lack the grey hairs of wisdom. So they come to the wells, but find no water such as, Scripture tell us, the patriarchs once found. So the *iuniores* carry their vessels back empty: not because there was no water, but because they could not find it.'[34] But if God filled the empty vessel that was Stephen, it was because of no wisdom on Stephen's part, but simply because this is what God so willed: *sicut voluit*. The verb *velle* occurs in Scripture hundreds of times, but only twice, I think, in close connection with a *sicut*. 'And that which thou sowest, thou sowest not the body that shall be', we read in 1 Corinthians 15:37; 'but bare grain, as of wheat, or of some of the rest. But God giveth it a body as he will'—*sicut vult*. There is, then, no proportion between Stephen's poverty and the living waters that have sprung up through him. But here the tense of the verb is 'wrong', and the context not quite natural. If

<hr/>

33. Reproduced in Marilier, p. 84, Document 75.

34. *In Hieremiam*, III.xxvii: 'Maiores quoque, qui deberent ipsi pergere ad hauriendas aquas, mittunt iuniores, in quibus cani non sunt sapientiae, et idcirco veniunt ad puteos et non inveniunt aquas, quas patriarchas invenisse narrat historia. Reportant vasa sua vacua, iuniores videlicet, non quo aquae non fuerint, sed quo illi invenire non potuerint.' CCL 74: 137, 6–11.

now I, who was all alone when I went forth from my country, and poor. . . .' We easily catch the allusion to the Lord's command to Abram: 'Go forth out of thy country, and from thy kindred, and out of thy father's house, and come into the land which I shall show thee', *Egredere de terra tua* . . . (Gen 12:1).

14. *diues et cum quadraginta turbis viam uniuerse carnis letus ingredior*: 'am entering upon the way of all flesh, happy, rich, and with forty bands. . . .' Biblical and liturgical allusions accumulate and are inextricably interwoven here. Actually, the word *pauper* has to be included here from the preceding phrase to which it is grammatically attached. Starting with *pauper*, then, and combining with it *dives* and *laetus ingredior*, we have the key-words of a text which occurs several times in the Cistercian Mass and Office for Saint Martin of Tours (November 11): *Martinus Abrahae sinu laetus excipitur; Martinus hic pauper et modicus caelum dives ingreditur, hymnis caelestibus honoratur*, 'Happy, Martin is received into Abraham's bosom. Martin, who here was poor and lowly, enters heaven rich, and is honored with heavenly hymns.' The text occurs in this form as the antiphon for None and also as the body of the eleventh Night Office responsory. A truncated form of the text serves for the Mass Alleluia; but since the omitted words include *laetus*, which figures in Saint Stephen's phrase, I take it that the saint's point of reference was either the antiphon or the responsory. The text itself ultimately derives from Sulpicius Severus' *Epistola 3 ad Bassulam*.[37] And what a wonderfully cistercian note this reference to Saint Martin gives! In his characteristically perceptive article on 'Saint Martin dans l'hagiographie monastique du moyen âge,'[38] Father Jean Leclercq gives a survey of the pertinent texts in chronological arrangement, showing that even in monastic circles Saint Martin was presented in the first instance as a worker of mighty miracles—until the advent of the Cistercians. For them, Saint Martin is above all the *pauper et modicus* monk-bishop, who personifies, as a good monk should, all the beatitudes.

37. *Epistola III Ad Bassulam socrum suam*: 'Martinus Abrahae sinu laetus excipitur; Martinus hic pauper et modicus, coelum dives ingreditur . . .' PL 20:184C.
38. In *Studia Anselmiana* 46 (1961) 175–187.

In its own way, this single fragment from Saint Stephen's letter is as eloquent as the Saint Martin sermon preached by Saint Bernard before the abbots assembled in chapter at Cîteaux—one of his longest sermons.[39] Again, who could possibly read the *fioretti*-like vignettes about Saint Stephen in the *Exordium Magnum*,[40] without instinctively thinking of Saint Martin, with all his poverty of spirit and unpretentiousness?

While clearly modelling himself on the Saint Martin antiphon (or responsory), Saint Stephen obviously cannot write **caelum laetus ingredior**. So he substitutes instead a phrase familiar to us all, *viam universae carnis*, 'the way of all flesh.' The expression is apparently derived from Joshua 23:14, or from 1 Kings 2:2, the former dealing with the final testament of Joshua, who had succeeded in bringing the Chosen People into the Promised Land, and the latter dealing with the final testament of the dying King David to his son and heir, Solomon. But the reference is only indirect, for the Vulgate reading in either instance is *ingredior viam universae* **terrae**. The fact is, however, that long before Saint Stephen's time, the variation, 'way of all flesh', had become as much a stock-phrase in Latin as it is in English.[41] It is symptomatic, perhaps, that although the translator of the Douai version kept to the Latin in his version of Joshua 23:14 ('I am going into the way of all the earth'), traditional usage got the better of him in the case of I Kings 2:2 ('I am going the way of all flesh'). I hope that someone will one day trace the history of this expression, which features in so many funeral inscriptions, and is used as a synonym for dying in so many hagiographical accounts. Even though the expression had become an overworked *cliché* by Saint Stephen's time, and enjoyed an existence independent

39. SBOp 5: 399–412; PL 183:489–500.

40. Ed. B. Griesser, *Exordium magnum cisterciense*. Series Scriptorum S. Ordinis Cisterciensis 2 (Rome: Editiones Cistercienses, 1961) Distinctio I, cc. 21–28 and c. 31, pp. 74–86 and pp. 88–89. Parallel texts in PL 185:1012–1016 and col. 1013, but with a different chapter-numbering.

41. Unfortunately, by at least the seventeenth century the expression had taken on a new twist in English. Samuel Butler (1935–1902) has immortalized the term as the title of his posthumous novel (1903), which reflects the Anglo-Saxon obsession with the sex-taboo.

of its biblical *locus*, I still prefer to relate Saint Stephen's use of the expression to the biblical context of the stalwart old and moribund leader giving us his final spiritual testament.

Four words remain: *et cum quadraginta turbis*: 'and with forty bands'—or 'throngs' or 'troops' or what have you The Jacob-story is still present to Saint Stephen. And, almost surely, the scribe has miscopied the important word, giving us *turbis* instead of *turmis*. I have left the text uncorrected, however, since *turba* renders approximately the same sense. The context is, once again, Jacob's return to his original home. His family, servants, and retainers form a sizable entourage; and so he divides them into two 'companies', saying 'If Esau comes to one company and destroys it, the other company that is left shall escape' (Gen 32:8); ' . . . with my staff I passed over this Jordan; and now I return with two companies' (Gen 32:10). The latin word corresponding to 'companies' is *turmae*. Stephen's family, however, has grown hugely, and is now divided into no less than forty *turmae*, that is to say, daughter or grand-daughter houses. In an earlier paragraph I have already alluded to the importance of this number in determining the date of the letter. Here let me remark only in passing that we must be cautious when speaking of a particular house as the twelfth in the order of foundation, or the twenty-seventh, or the fortieth. The chronology of foundation of the early houses is often tangled; and we have to take into account houses that had only an ephemeral existence. Finally, I am not sure that C. H. Talbot is quite accurate in referring to Neuberg, founded in 1131, as the fortieth abbey founded.[42] It is true that Janauschek lists Neuberg under the Roman numeral XL.[43] But Cîteaux itself counts as I. According to this reckoning, La-Bussière, founded also in 1131, by Cîteaux, and quite close to the mother-house in the (present-day) diocese of Dijon, would be the fortieth foundation to derive, directly or indirectly, from Cîteaux.[44] Of course, Saint Stephen could possibly be including Cîteaux itself

42. Talbot, p. 67.
43. Janauschek, p. 18.
44. *Ibid.*, p. 19.

among the *turmae*, in which case Neuberg would be the fortieth 'company', but only the thirty-ninth foundation.

15–16. *securus expectans denarium operariis fideliter in uinea laborantibus repromissum*: ' . . . looking forward with confidence to the *denarius* promised to the laborers who work faithfully in the vineyard'. We are already familiar with Saint Stephen's use of the parable of the workers in the vineyard (Mt 20:1–16) in the Prologue to the *Exordium Parvum*.[45] In the Prologue, however, Saint Stephen is combining the biblical text with allusions to Saint Gregory the Great's homily on that same pericope assigned to Septuagesima Sunday.[46] Here Saint Stephen combines his workers-in-the-vineyard material with an allusion to another liturgical text that is so lightly touched upon that I hesitate to draw attention to it. But I will. The first two words of the phrase under study, *securus expectans*, point at least vaguely in the direction of the classical collect for the Vigil of Christmas. Let me insist that the verbal connection is tenuous; and I am not suggesting that, in Saint Stephen's mind, this particular allusion was consciously thought out. Further, if you feel an *a priori* discomforture at a Christmas formula providing a nuance to an eschatological theme, you would do well to look at the formula in question, which I here transcribe as it appears in the earliest extant cistercian sacramentary:

> Deus qui nos redemtionis nostre annua expectatione
> letificas, presta ut unigenitum tuum quem redemptorem
> leti suscipimus, uenientem quoque iudicem securi uide-
> amus: dominum nostrum ihesum christum filium tuum
> qui tecum.[47]

This formula from the *Hadrianum* may be a Christmas formula, but its major theme is that of the Second Coming and of judgment. In the cadence of the first clause, *expectatione laetificas*, the word *expectatione* provides some of the syllables needed for the *cursus velox*

---

45. Bouton and Van Damme, *Les plus anciens*, p. 54.

46. *Homilia in Evangelia*, Lib. I, Hom. 19, in PL 76:1153–1159. The pertinent texts are found in n. 3, cols. 1155–1156.

47. Paris, Bibliothèque nationale, MS latin 2300, f. 10r (pre-1147).

cadence; and in the climactic termination of the third clause, *securi videamus*, the word *securi* occurs in an equally emphatic position, as part of the *cursus trispondaicus* ending. In the prayer, then, the three word-groups that tend to stick in one's mind are: *expectatione laetificas - laeti suscipimus - securi videamus*. I suggest, then, that as Stephen directs his gaze towards his fast approaching face-to-face encounter with the Master of the vineyard, a distant, barely perceptible resonance of the Christmas Vigil collect is evoked in his subconscious memory. But, once again, the association I am suggesting is so tenuous that I in no way wish to insist on it.

16. *Vnde uestram cohortor dilectionem*: 'And so I exhort your love. . . .' The expression strikes us as a bit odd; but it is simply a conventional epistolary form of address to be found in Augustine, Jerome, Gregory the Great, and still others, as a glance at the corresponding entry in Albert Blaise's *Dictionnaire Latin-Français des Auteurs Chrétiens* will show.[48]

16–17. *ut bonam famam que de uobis ad nos usque manauit profectui virtutum applicare satagatis*: 'to strive to make the good repute you have, and which has reached from you even as far as us, the occasion for [further] progress in virtues. . . .' I am skating on thin ice, and am far from being sure I understand the structure of this sentence. C. H. Talbot, in his own transcription of the letter, suggested that the scribe mistakenly wrote *profectui* instead of *profectu*;[49] but I do not find this 'correction' particularly helpful in construing the phrase. Taking the elements in their logical order, the sequence seems (to me) to be: Saint Stephen urges you 'to strive' (*ut . . . satagatis*) 'to apply' (or some related word: *applicare*) 'the good repute' (*bonam famam*, direct object of *applicare*) 'to progress' (*profectui*, indirect object of *applicare*). If we fill in the modifiers now, the *bona fama*, the good repute', is described as a repute 'which has reached, or—more literally—flowed' (*quae . . . manauit*) 'from you as far as even us' (*de uobis ad nos usque*). The use of *de* instead of *ex* or *a* will make the classical scholar squirm, but Saint Stephen is here in good company,

48. Turnhout, Editions Brepols SA.: 1954, p. 273, under the word *dilectio* towards the end.
49. Talbot, 69.

for even Ambrose, Jerome, and Augustine sometimes follow late Latin usage with respect to *de*.[50] Rather more idiosyncratic is the final position of the adverb *usque* in the expression '[even] to us', *ad nos usque*. So far as I can determine, then, Saint Stephen seems to be exhorting his Sherborne brethren to make the good renown they enjoy the starting point for still further progress in virtue. 'People speak well of you; we hear about you even here in Burgundy. But do not rest on your laurels. Make your excellent reputation serve as a spring-board for soaring still higher in your progress in the life of virtue.' If it strikes us as a bit extraordinary that the fame of Sherborne Abbey as a school of sanctity was being talked about as far away as Burgundy, we are doubtless justified in feeling a certain reserve. But all Saint Stephen says is that the good repute of the brethren has reached 'even as far as us', that is to say, even as far as Cîteaux. Long-term preparation for these foundations and their actual execution, must have given Saint Stephen numerous occasions of hearing a bit of news about his old monastery of boyhood days, about the translation of the bishop's seat to Old Sarum not long after his own departure, and about the still recent separation between the office of bishop and the office of abbot.

18. *ut de bono in melius proficientes*: ' . . . so that, progressing from what is good to what is better. . . .' This has the 'feel' of an implicit citation, but so far I have had no luck in tracking it down. Should someone ever identify the source, I am prone to believe that the text will either be part of a commentary on Psalm 83:8, or else will use this psalm-verse in a prominent way. 'They shall go from virtue to virtue: the God of gods shall be seen in Sion', *ibunt de virtute in virtutem*, **videbitur Deus deorum in Sion**. The last part of the verse is used for the finale of the last line of the letter; and the theme of section we are now studying is *profectus virtutum*. I think almost automatically of Cassian's Conference Eleven, where Abba Chaeremon discourses in his initial conference about perfection, *De perfectione*. Especially pertinent is Chapter 12, on the various degrees of perfection, *De diversitate perfectionum*; and it is in this

50. Blaise, *Dictionnaire*, p. 238: 'dans la latinité postérieure, *de* s'emploie avec n'importe quel verbe et tend à remplace *a*, *ex*.'

section, as a matter of fact, that we find Psalm 83:8 quoted.[51] But the entire conference is structured on the dialectic between fear and love, between *timor* and *caritas*. It deals with the journey of the monk from craven fear to the perfect love that casts out all fear, from a state of slavery to the state of the adoption of sons, in which the progress is from one perfection to another, *de virtute in virtutem, et de perfectione ad aliam perfectionem*. Augustine's treatment of the same progress in his *Enarratio* devoted to Psalm 83 is especially fine. He gives a special twist to verse eight, however, by using a translation that has us going from 'virtues' in the plural to 'virtue' in the singular, from the virtues whose *raison d'être* is bound up with the present ephemeral order of things, to that virtue which alone abides forever. And what is that virtue? The virtue of contemplating. Contemplating what? *Apparebit Deus deorum in Sion*: we shall contemplate Christ when he appears in all his glory; and this is that virtue to which all others are directed.[52]

18. *et uere religioni firmiter inherentes*: ' . . . and cleaving firmly to true monastic observance. . . .' Most of us will doubtless tend to equate *religio* with 'spirituality' or devotion or some related and deeply interior reality. 'Monastic observance' can by no means be separated from what is 'deeply interior'; but it takes in everything. It is simply the monastic way of life, with all the practices associated with it. It includes the satisfaction made by the monk who stumbles on a word in choir as well as the interior humility, reverence, and love that give the outward ritual gesture its true meaning. Translators, failing to understand the technical meaning the term has in mediaeval monastic literature, can easily confuse the meaning of a text. Thus, when we read in the mini-customary of the abbey of the Paraclete, *Religionis erat de cultu terrarum et labore proprio vivere, si possemus*,[53] we would be wrong if we were to translate it as, 'It pertains to the virtue of religion to make our living from farming and our own work, and we would if we could.' Rather, 'Earning

51. E. Pichery, ed., *Conférences VIII–XVII*. SCh 54 (1958) 113–115.
52. N. 11 in the *Enarratio in Psalm 83*—the divisions being the same in all accessible editions of the *Enarrationes*.
53. PL 178:314D–315A.

our living from farming and our own work is part of monastic observance, and we would do so if we could'. Saint Stephen, then, is exhorting the Sherbornites simply to hold fast to an authentic monastic observance. He specifies at least some of the constituent elements of this observance in the phrase which follows—a phrase which has evidently been partially mutilated by a nodding scribe.

19–20. *castitatem, humilitatem, studiis parsimonie cum caritate inseruientes corde et corpore usque ad mortem tenere non desistas*: ' . . . you may never cease to observe chastity [and] humility, submitting [yourselves] to the zealous practice of frugality together with charity even unto death. . . .' The Latin, as I have already suggested, has become snarled; and I realize that the translation has done little to unsnarl it. Perhaps it will help to go through the phrase, as before, in logical order, beginning with the verb that governs the whole convoluted period. *Tenere non desistas*: 'you may not cease to observe (or hold to)'. The only possible object of *tenere* is a word or words in the accusative case; and here we have two such words in immediate succession: *castitatem humilitatem*. For the latter word, I have to take the word of C. H. Talbot and D. L. Bethell, for on my microfilm and enlarged photo, all I can see for the last part of the word is a dark blob caused by ink seepage from the reverse side. But if the Talbot-Bethell reading is correct, then either there is an *et* or *-que* missing for 'chastity' and 'humility', or else these two virtues should be followed by yet a third: *castitatem, humilitatem, et obedientiam*, or something similar. This gives us the essential of the phrase, that is to say, the main verb with its infinitive ('may you not cease to observe') and the object ('chastity-humility'); all the other elements are modifiers of one kind or another, of which there are three: (1) submitting yourselves (or some related word) to the zealous practice (literally, 'zealous practices') of frugality (or parsimony) along with charity; (2) in heart and in body; (3) even unto death. Having divided, I am not sure we have conquered, but at least the main articulations of the period are a bit clearer. We are dealing with typical Rule-talk—with apparently one exception. *Studiis parsimoniae* . . . *inservientes* (note that *inservire* usually takes the dative rather than the accusative, which is why I have construed this participle with *studiis* rather than with *castitatem-humilitatem*). The closest the vocabulary of the Holy Rule comes to *parsimonia* is in the phrases *servata in omnibus parcitate* (c. 39:10) and *non usque ad satietatem bibamus, sed parcius* (c. 40:6). I have translated the word as 'frugality' rather than as 'parsimony', since the latter term so often smacks of 'stinginess' in ordinary usage. Given Saint Stephen's known passion for poverty, one might expect him to have urged the brethren of Sherborne to a zealous practice of evangelical poverty. Instead he uses a word that carries with it practically no resonance of the Holy Rule. I suggest, however, that in the choice of this one word, Saint Stephen reveals himself in all his gentle thoughtfulness and delicacy of feeling. 'Poverty' would be, perhaps, an unrealistic ideal in a cathedral-community structure and life-style much affected by the very nature of an episcopal minister. And though things may have changed somewhat since the separation of bishop's seat from abbey, we have no indication that much of a re-orientation did take place. 'Poverty' was a word that could cause hurt in such a context; a word that might suggest that Stephen was urging them to the same poverty that shone with such radiant simplicity and quiet splendor at Cîteaux. Poverty at Sherborne? To urge it would have been unrealistic, perhaps unkind. So we read, 'giving yourselves to the zealous practice of *frugality*'; and always, of course, *cum caritate*. We all know what austerity can become, where there is no charity. *Corde et corpore* is also the language of the Rule, though it occasionally occurs outside the Rule (Saint Gregory sometimes uses the expression). In our present context, we think instinctively of the twelfth degree of humility in chapter seven, where the humility of the monk is 'not only in his heart', *non solum corde*, but naturally and spontaneously finds expression, no matter where he is and what he is doing, outwardly, 'in his very body'. *Usque ad mortem* is also from the Rule, towards the very end of the Prologue, where we are exhorted to persevere in the monastery in God's teaching 'even unto death'. But before we can grasp the depth of what this means, we must turn again to the chapter on humility, chapter seven, and find in the third degree of humility the paradigm of all humility, of all obedience, of all monastic observance: the Lord himself, who was obedient *usque ad mortem*. These three words were found, too, in the promise of obedience made by all twelfth-century benedictine and cistercian monks in connection with the rite of monastic profession: 'Father, I promise you obedience according to the Rule of Saint Benedict, even unto death'. Which brings us to the final phrase of the letter, the phrase towards which all the preceding has been leading us—

20–21. *ut deum deorum uidere mereamini. Amen.* ' . . . that you may see the God of gods. Amen.' We end, then, with a fragment from Psalm 83:8 that for Saint Stephen and for the monastic tradition he represents stands for the goal of all ascetic striving, of all monastic observance, the face-to-face vision of God for all eternity. Those of us long familiar with the psalm-verse may wonder why Saint Stephen failed to include the two words of the Latin text, *in Sion.* But read over the final clause a few times and try inserting *in Sion* (which, according to cistercian usage at the time would have had the accent on the final syllable of the Hebrew undeclinable *Sión*). No matter where you put it, the music and the strength of this final phrase turn flabby.

If this, then, is a sample of Saint Stephen's correspondence, we can rightly weep all the more bitterly over the total disappearance of his *registrum* of letters. One of the most striking features of his literary style is his use of implicit citations from Bible and liturgy. Not once does he quote a text word for word. He has interiorized the texts and made them so much his own that he spontaneously, and obviously without forethought, rephrases them according to the exigencies of the music of the line and the nuance to be brought out. More remarkable, perhaps, is the sure instinct he seems to have for drawing his subtle allusions from contextually significant *loci.* Not once does he draw an apt expression from a biblical context foreign to the substance of the thought he is expressing. Indeed, the full meaning of his thought becomes all the richer when we replace this word or that in the context of the passage from which it has been borrowed. On the strength of this one brief letter, copied hastily and written inelegantly on a stray empty folio of a Rievaulx manuscript, we can recognize in Saint Stephen a genius at the art of conveying more, hugely more, than the words taken singly could possibly convey. Despite the tangled state of the final part of the text, we can feel too a musicality of expression that in no way depends on his consistent and conscious application of the rules of the rhythmic *cursus.* There is magic in a line like *Vas enim vacuum vivus Fons, sicut voluit, implevit.* There is an accumulation of no less than three *ut*-clauses from line 16 to the end: bad style, surely; but we have only to read the text aloud (snarled though line 19 is), and let ourselves be carried along by the momentum of the rhythm to realize that the thrust of the ideas leading to that final *Amen* is paralleled by a musical phrase that soars to the same point of arrival and fulfillment.

What really overwhelms me is the gentle courtesy and delicacy of feeling of this simple, profound, and noble man. Sherborne territory was being invaded by a new and foreign breed of monks. More colonies were soon to follow. The perpetrator of this great White Plague was none other than a former monk of Sherborne Abbey, a monk who had left the community in not particularly pleasant circumstances. Moreover, profound differences in the concrete living out of monastic ideals had already led to such a pitch of animosity on the continent that certain irate communities did not balk at recourse to violence. Had you or I had to write a letter of reassurance to the brethren of Sherborne, asking for tolerance and understanding as our colonies of monks gained a foothold across the Channel, how would we have expressed ourselves? Not once does Saint Stephen use an offensive word, a blunt expression. Not once does he disparage the Sherborne observance in his joy at what God has wrought through him. His letter is a sustained celebration of gratitude in which he invites his brethren to take heart and to live to the full their own monastic observance.

One particular point. I raise again the question of Saint Stephen's alleged 'apostasy' from Sherborne. In the light of the letter we have been studying, I have considerable difficulty in accepting at face value William of Malmesbury's presentation of Stephen's break with Sherborne in terms of a temporary succumbing to the wiles of the world. Had Stephen been an apostate in any such sense, his letter would have been couched in quite different terms: 'I was your monk. Yet, blind and sinner that I was, I threw off the sacred garb to wallow in the cess-pool and the mire, till the change of God's right hand etc.'. Had this sort of thing really been Stephen's experience, his celebration of his own poverty and God's wholly gratuitous mercy would have been quite the same; his point of reference, however, would not have been the Jacob-story, but the parable of the Prodigal Son or some other biblical figure of a converted sinner. Instead, Stephen has cast himself in the role of an errant pilgrim, exiled because of family troubles, but the founder of a new family: in brief, Stephen is Jacob. At this point, then, the hypothesis that Stephen's departure from Sherborne was occasioned by his dangerous family connection seems rather attractive.

But if Stephen's problematic leave-taking involved no true abandonment of his monastery for unworthy reasons, why does his great admirer, William of Malmesbury, state the contrary? I honestly do not know, at least not with any degree of certainty. I rather incline to think, however, that William included so disedifying an episode in his pen-portrait of the English hero as monk reformer because he was convinced that it was true. And since so many details in his wonderful description of early Cîteaux are details such as only an eye-witness could record, the tale of Stephen's apostasy was doubtless told William by the great 'apostate' himself. 'So you were a monk of Sherborne before coming to Molesme?' 'Indeed I was'. 'But why did you leave?' Long pause—after all, we could hardly expect Stephen, even forty years after the event, to volunteer the information that his quisling uncle's local unpopularity had made his own presence at Sherborne not only embarrassing but dangerous for himself and for the community. At last, a quiet smile, and— 'Why did I leave? Oh, it was the world, the flesh, and the devil'. And he would not have been all that wrong. After all, he had tarried long enough in France to finish the equivalent of college studies before finally, *tandem aliquando*, finding his way to a monastery in politically neutral territory. His years spent in the guise of a cleric in a university milieu meant a foreswearing of his monastic identity at least temporarily; and there must have been times when the confused but earnest young man had all but decided to remain in the world. He may not have been an apostate when he left England for Scotland and then for France. But what was he during the years in Burgundy when he passed himself off as a young cleric pursuing his course of higher studies? 'Why did I leave? Oh, the world was just too strong for me. . . .'

All of this is no more than a hypothesis spun out, possibly, with too much imagination and in no way demonstrable. Still, this is the one hypothesis which, so far as I know, brings into harmony the data drawn from William of Malmesbury, from the *Vita* of Peter of Jully, and from recent investigations into Stephen's family connections in the immediate aftermath of 1066. It is this hypothesis, too, which seems best to accord with Stephen's remarkable letter to Abbot Thurstan and Community.

Rectitudo regulae

The Straight Path of the Rule

DEHINC abbas ille et fratres eius, non immemores spon-
sionis suae, regulam beati Benedicti in loco illo ordinare et
unanimiter statuerunt tenere, reicientes a se quicquid regulae
refragabatur . . . Sicque rectitudinem regula supra cunctum
vitae suae tenorem ducentes, tam in ecclesiasticis quam in caeteris observationibus regulae vestigiis sunt adaequati seu conformati. Exuti ergo veterem
hominem, novum se induisse gaudebant.

THE ABBOT and his brothers, not unmindful of their pledge, unanimously ordained that they would establish and keep the Rule of blessed Benedict in that place, putting away from themselves anything that infringed the Rule. . . . Applying the straight path of the Rule over the whole manner of their life, to the observances of the community as well as to all other things, therefore, they matched or accommodated their footsteps to the tracks of the Rule. Having put off the old man therefore, they rejoiced to have put on the new.

Exordium parvum[1]

1. Chapter 15.

Liturgical-Patristic Resonances of the Straight Path

Chrysogonus Waddell, OCSO

CHAPTER FIFTEEN in the *Exordium Parvum* has a special importance. It purports to be a description of the 'Institutes of the Monks of *Cistercium* Coming from Molesme'. Let the reader be warned: according to the pronouncement of J.-A. Lefevre, echoed by other writers, we are dealing with fraudulent material. 'The crucial "institutes" of Alberic', Louis Lekai writes, 'lack the marks of authenticity'.[1]

> Constant references to the Rule of Saint Benedict particularly in the 'Institutes', were made with the obvious purpose of creating an allusion of rigid legality . . . They [the first Cistercians] invoked and applied [the Rule] when it suited their purpose; they ignored or even contradicted it when it could not be fitted to their concept of monasticism . . . [2]

Unlike many of the other sections of the Exordium, in which official acts are reproduced *in extenso*, Chapter Fifteen is purely narrative. It does not quote official texts, but gives a description of some of the more striking decisions made by the monks of the New Monastery shortly after Pope Paschal II had taken the recently founded community under the special protection of the Holy See in late 1100. The nature of these 'institutes' can be better appreciated, perhaps, if we look at an important study by Jacques Dubois, OSB, 'Les Ordres religieux au XIIe siècle selon la cure romaine'.[3]

1. Lekai, *The Cistercians. Ideals and Reality* (Kent State University, 1977) 22.
2. *Ibid.*, 32.
3. *Revue bénédictine* 78 (1968) 282–309, here p. 308.

The Gregorian reform had re-invigorated the two forms of religious life which had found their definitive shape in the heyday of the Carolingian Empire, the canons and the monks. On these latter the Rule of Saint Benedict was imposed with such vigor that it admitted of no discussion; and it is only by way of concession to usages of an earlier time that mention of the Rule of Saint Basil was introduced [in papal privileges] for a few monasteries in southern Italy.[4]

But the Rule of Benedict was never sufficient in itself. Always it had to be supplemented and adapted and interpreted. As Dubois writes:

No community of religious was able to invoke the protection of the Holy See unless it proved faithful to its ideal. In order to keep this ideal from being imaginary or confused, the papal bulls themselves defined the ideal by naming the Rule and the *institution* which were supposed to be normative for the life of those religious. This distinction soon became standard, for it was in keeping with the legislation of the new Orders founded in the twelfth century, such as the Cistercians or Premonstratensians, who claimed to observe the traditional Rules strictly, but who would have been unable to do so without completing them and making them more explicit with the help of carefully prepared juridical texts. . . . [5]

The Rule, then, was the Rule; but the Rule had to be determined and interpreted in further detail. Cluny and Cîteaux both had the same Rule; but what distinguished them was their *institutio*. This is the meaning of such clauses in papal documents as: *secundum Deum et Benedicti Regulam et **normam** cluniacensis monasterii* . . . or *secundum Deum et beati Benedicti Regulam et **Institutionem** cisterciensium fratrum.* . . . [6] *Instituta* or *institutio* simply referred to particular

4. *Ibid.*
5. *Ibid.*
6. Many examples of the different variations on this formula are given throughout the article.

monastic observances characteristic of the manner in which a given monastery or group of monasteries lived its Rule in the concrete. Chapter Fifteen of the *Exordium Parvum* describes some of these observances.

The historical context is important. Robert and a number of the original pioneers—perhaps even the larger number—have returned to Molesme. The papal privilege of 1100 has assured the reform-minded community of the protection it needs to carry out effectively and without outside interference its program of monastic renewal. The basic principle of integral observance of the Rule had already been formulated long before the departure from Molesme in 1098, but now this principle has to be reduced to some sort of consistent practice. This is what Chapter Fifteen is all about.

The chapter is too long to reproduce in full, and we shall be concerned with only a single sentence from it; but that sentence should be situated within the context of the structure of Chapter Fifteen. The chapter is divided into two main parts. Chapter 15.2–4 of the Van Damme-Bouton edition forms the first major section; and Chapter 15.5–14[7] forms the second major section. Between these two sections lies an important difference. The first concerns points of observance which, it may be argued, follow quite directly from a literal reading of the Rule, matters dealing with clothing, bedding, food and drink. Chapter 15.3 formulates the operative reform-principle—and this is the text we wish to study.

> *Sicque rectitudinem regulae supra cunctum vitae suae tenorem ducentes, tam in ecclesiasticis quam in caeteris observationibus regulae vestigiis sunt adaequati seu conformati.*

The close of this section is indicated by a summary statement which would seem, at first reading, to come straight from Saint Paul: *Exuti ergo veterem hominem, novum se induisse gaudebant*: 'Having put off the old man, they rejoiced at having put on the new'. Surely this is an adaptation of Ephesians 4:22: *deponere vos secundum pristinam conversationem veterem hominem . . .* and Ephesians 4:24: *et*

---

7. Divided wrongly, I think, into two separate paragraphs in *Les plus anciens textes de Cîteaux* [PATC], pp. 46, 48.

induite novum hominem . . . It is indeed an adaptation of the pauline text, but only indirectly; for the text underlying EP 15.4 is the formula spoken by the abbot when, at the solemn profession of the novice—which in former times followed directly upon the end of a one-year novitiate—he removes the candidate's secular garb with the words, *Exuat te Dominus veterem hominem*. He then clothes him in the monastic habit with the words, *Induat te Dominus novum hominem*. The *exuere/induere* of EP 15.4 is closer to the *exuere/induere* of the monastic profession rite than to the *deponere/induere* of the Ephesians text. Nor should the irony of this line escape us. The author is saying that, having taken measures to reduce the Rule to actual practice, the monks of the New Monastery are only now fulfilling the terms of their monastic profession. What had been promised but only imperfectly realized at Molesme has now been accomplished at the New Monastery. It is this vague allusion to a text from the monastic ritual which provides a better understanding of the implications of Chapter 15.4.

The second part of the chapter begins at EP 15.5 and extends to the end of the chapter. It treats matters dealt with less explicitly by the Rule, matters touching on means of livelihood, sources of revenue, business administration, contacts with society and the business world. The decisions here are more corollaries to the principle of the integral observance of the Rule than applications of specific norms formulated in the Rule. This distinction is touched on fairly clearly in Callistus II's privilege of 1119, when the pontiff writes: . . . *quadam de observatione regulae beati Benedicti* [matters in the first part of Chapter Fifteen] *et de aliis nonnullis quae Ordini vestro et loco necessario videbantur* [matters in the second part], *capitula statuistis* . . . [8]

And now our crucial text:

> 3 *Sicque rectitudinem regulae supra cunctum vitae suae tenorem ducentes, tam in ecclesiasticis quam in ceteris observationibus regula vestigiis sunt adaequati seu conformati.*

The text looks easier than it is. If I begin by checking it against Father Bede Lackner's translation, I do so, not because I wish to

---

8. *PTAC*, p. 104, *Privilegium Domini Papae*, 4.

132

criticize a translation much better than others I have seen, but because such a comparison makes us aware of some of the problematic points which need clarification. Father Bede translates:

> Making thus the rectitude of the Rule the foremost concern of their life, they followed or conformed to the pathway of the Rule in ecclesiastical as well as other observances.[9]

'Rectitude of the Rule' certainly seems adequate for *rectitudinem regulae*. All the usual meanings of 'rectitude' seem to fit the context: straightness, moral integrity, righteousness, correctness of judgment or procedure. But what about that participle *ducentes*? Does *ducere rectitudinem* mean 'making the rectitude of the Rule . . .'? *ducere* is a word rich in shifting meanings; but 'to make' is not one of them. *Ducere* sometimes means 'to consider, to reckon, to esteem', so one could simply emend the translation slightly: 'Considering the rectitude of the Rule the foremost concern of their life. . . .' But this runs afoul of the Latin text on two scores. The verbal form is not a simple *ducentes*, but *ducentes **supra***. *Supra* is a proposition here governing the accusative *tenorem*, or, more fully, *supra vitae suae tenorem*. How on earth does one *ducere* rectitude on top of or over the *vitae suae tenorem*? And, to compound our discomfort, why is *vitae suae tenorem* translated here by 'the foremost concern of their life' when *tenor vitae* has already been translated, and well translated, in the 'Prologue', as 'their manner of living. 'In ecclesiastical as well as other observances' does well for *tam in ecclesiasticis quam in ceteris observationibus*, but only if we take 'ecclesiastical' in the sense of 'all that pertains to the monastic community'. Remember that throughout the *Exordium Parvum*, *ecclesia* generally means 'monastic community', the church formed by this particular community of monks. The customary of the Cistercian Order is styled, strictly speaking, *Ecclesiastica officia*; and the one hundred twenty-one chapters of the final recension contain material pertaining not only to the church and liturgy, but to work, refectory reading, meals, the cooks, times for shaving, times for being bled. 'Ecclesiastical observances'

9. Lekai, *The Cistercians*, 459; also quoted in part, p. 30.

means everything pertaining to the observances of the monastic community. So 'ecclesiastical as well as other observances' is an extraordinarily comprehensive formula.

The last words of the sentence, *regulae vestigiis sunt adaequati seu conformati*, are as problematic (to me) as the opening ones. For *vestigia* simple does not mean 'pathway', it means 'footsteps', 'footprints', 'track' in the sense of a trail left by someone's footprints. And by extension it means the 'soles of the feet' or the feet themselves, and in a derived sense, a 'trace', a 'mark' a 'token', a 'vestige'. But even if we retain 'pathway of the Rule', we are still in for trouble with *sunt adaequati*. Whatever the verb means, it is not 'followed'. Granted that the verbs *sunt adaequati seu conformati* are used figuratively and in a much derived sense, they still necessarily have something to do with 'matching' or 'being equal to' or 'levelling with'. *Vestigiis adaequati*, whatever it means, is not simply 'to follow the pathway'. There is also a problem construing *conformare* with 'pathway'. In basic medieval usage, *conformare* has something to do with 'to take the form of', 'to resemble', 'to be modelled after some other thing'. We may strive to keep on the right path or to follow the path; we make no attempt to take on the form or the shape of the path. Even if we make allowance for the mixing of metaphors and imprecision in the use of terms, the translation seems to fall a bit short of the mark—though the translator has my fullest sympathy, given the problematic nature of the text.

To uncover the meaning of our passage, we need to discover the meaning not only of *ducere rectitudinem*, but of *ducere . . . supra tenorem vitae* we need to get at the sense of the metaphor *vestigiis sunt adaequati* which even the author, who helpfully added the synonym *seu conformati*, must have thought a bit unclear.

We begin with the observation that the vocabulary of the troublesome phrase is based on some idea of movement and walking: *ducere* taken together with *supra* suggests motion: leading, directing, or guiding something over or above something else; and *vestigiis* almost certainly has something to do with foot-prints, tracks, feet. But how does 'rectitude' fit in with this vocabulary of movement? Recourse to a biblical concordance will not help us: the word is non-biblical. We know that Saints Gregory the Great and Anselm and Bernard and a host of others have written wonderful and profound things about *rectitudo* as the condition of man's uprightness (in the literal as well as the metaphorical sense) before the Fall. But the use of 'rectitude' as the direct object of *ducentes* and in conjunction with the preposition *supra* points to a different sort of usage.

A glance at two liturgical texts may throw a bit of light on this enigmatic phrase.

The cistercian repertory of 'monastic canticles', that is to say, the canticles assigned to the third nocturn on Sundays and feastdays, was especially poor. The Cistercians had only six (with three canticles in each formulary), while eight was the minimum elsewhere.[10] The third of the Christmas season canticles concerns us here—the third of the *early* cistercian series, since the order was shifted in the mid-seventeenth century: Is 26:1–12. To set the context, I shall quote the opening lines in the Douai version, with minor adjustments to fit the cistercian latin text.

> Sion, the city of our strength, a savior,
>   a wall and a bulwark shall be set therein.
> Open ye gates, and let the nation enter in,
>   that keepeth the truth.
> The old error is passed away:
> thou wilt keep peace:
>   peace, because we have hoped in thee.
> You have hoped in the Lord for evermore,
>   in the Lord God mighty for ever.
> For he shall bring down them that dwell on high,
>   the high city he shall lay low.
> He shall bring it down even to the ground,
>   he shall pull it down even to the dust.

10. The best recent study on the western tradition of monastic canticles is by Michael Korhammer, *Die monastischen Cantica in Mittelalter.* Münchener Universitäts-Schriften, Texte und Untersuchungen zur englischen Philologie, Band 6 (München, 1976). The author is chiefly concerned with Anglo-Saxon interlinear translations; but his summary of the various branches of western practice in the use of these canticles is extremely helpful.

The foot of the Poor One shall tread it down,
   the steps of the needy.
The way of the just is right,
   the path of the just is right to walk in . . .

The pertinent latin text of the last lines in bold type, as found in
all the oldest cistercian liturgical manuscripts, is:

> *Conculcabit eam pes pauperis,*
>   *gressus egenorum.*
> *Semita iusti recta est,*
>   *rectus callis iusti ad ambulandum.*

A lovely text, but not a word about *rectitudo*. But look at the canticle
text as exegeted by Saint Jerome in his *Commentariorum in Esaiam
Libri XVIII.*

Jerome's latin text is a bit different at *Conculcabit eam pes pauperis,*
where his version rightly reads: *Conculcabit eam pes, pedes pauperis.*
The question: Who is this poor man, whose feet (or foot) will tread
down the high city? Jerome answers: *haud dubium quin Christi;*[11] the
feet 'of Christ, beyond a doubt'. He adds that this exegesis is in
line with his earlier interpretation of Is 25:4—*Factus est fortitudo
pauperi*—where the 'poor man' according to his understanding, is
Christ. What about 'the steps of the needy', the *gressus egenorum?*
This refers to the apostles, who imitated and followed the Lord in
his poverty: *Gressus egenorum, apostolorum scilicet, qui imitantes Domini
paupertatem, etiam virtutis eius privilegium consecuti sunt.*[12] Here any
monk would have thought not only of the apostles, but of all who
have lived the 'apostolic life' in the medieval sense of the term *vita
apostolica.* And who is this 'just man' whose way is just; *Semita iusti
recta est?* Isaiah is still referring to Christ, Jerome tells us: *Adhuc
propheta de Christo loquitur. . . .*[13] This brings us to the critical text:

> *Huius ergo iusti semita recti est, sive, ut verbum novum fingam,*
> **rectitudines**, *quas Graeci vocant* euthutetas, *et nos* aequi-

11. Marcus Adriaen, *S. Hieronymi Presbyteri Commentariorum in Esaiam
Libri I–XI. CCL* 73:332/35–36.
  12. *Ibid.,* 11.38–40.
  13. *Ibid.,* 1.8.

tates *Latinius possumus appellare, dicuntur Hebraice* messarim. *In una igitur Christi semita omnes iustitiae reperiuntur,
et propterea eam suo calcavit et rivit pede, ut quicumque per
eam voluerit ambulare, cursu ambulet inoffenso.*[14]

The path of the just man is right or—to coin a new word—
rectitudines. The greek term is eu'thútētas; the latin
equivalent would more properly be *aequitates*; and the
hebrew term is *messarim*. In this one way of Christ, then,
all 'justices' [*rectitudines, aequitates*] are to be found; and
this is why he trod it down and wore it smooth, so that
whoever should wish to walk along this way, may do so
without obstacle.

Jerome therefore defines *semita recti* (and its parallel in the next line,
rectus callis) as *rectitudines* or (to use a more 'latin' term) *aequitates*.
And this name is fitting, our exegete indicates, because **all** 'justices'
are to be found in or on this one single path carefully cleared for
us by Christ the Poor Man: *in una igitur Christi semita omnes iustitiae
reperiuntur*. In other words, everything we need as disciples of Christ
is to be found on the path which he, the Poor Man *par excellence*,
first trod and smoothed and walked so that we, after him and his
immediate followers the apostles (*pedes egenorum*), might walk this
path without encountering obstacles.

The problematic text from the *Exordium Parvum* begins to have a
bit more inner coherence if we read it in connection with Jerome's
comments on the canticle text. If *semita iusti* is more or less synonymous with *rectitudines aequitates*, but with the nuance that all
perfection is bound up with this path, then *rectitudo regulae* might
well mean something along the lines of the 'right path' or the
'straight path' of the Rule—either the Rule itself as path or the
Rule as pointing out the path—which is curiously in line with the
way the author of the 'Prologue' speaks of the 'strait and narrow
way shown forth by the Rule': *in arta et angusta via quam regula
demonstrat*. Further, it is by no means difficult to construe *rectitudo*
(*semita seu via recta*) with the verb *ducere . . . supra*: 'to direct', 'to

14. *Ibid.*, pp. 332–333, 9–15.

lead', 'to make the path pass over' the entire manner of life, over the whole sum-total of monastic observance: *Sicque rectitudinem regulae supra cunctum vitae suae tenorem ducentes. . . .* This sense of *rectitudo* is also perfectly consonant with the movement-terminology and walking imagery suggested by the words *ducere . . . supra* and *vestigia.* Jerome's contention that *rectitudines* is better expressed in Latin by *aequitates* may also possibly cast a glimmer of light on that rather singular use of the verb *sunt adaequari*, which was unusual enough even to the writer to call for the addition of an explanatory *seu conformari. Aequitas* and *ad-aequare* are cognate terms, and they help us clear up some of the ambiguity of the text. The *regulae vestigia* are the tracks or footprints either left by the Rule or pointed out and shown forth by the Rule. To be *adaequati seu conformati* to these footprints means to match them with our own, to adapt our own course to the tracks left by the One who went before us to lead us on our way. The path of the Rule, or the path shown us by the Rule (it is one and the same thing in the final analysis), is the path of the Poor Man who was the first to walk this way: *conculcabit pes, pedes Pauperis*; the apostles followed their Lord on the same path: *pedes egenorum*; as do we who are disciples of Christ and imitators of the apostles in the *vita apostolica*, understood as the common life lived by the first Christians and paradigmatic for monks of later ages. The Rule shows us the way taken by the Lord. It is a way of obedience, of poverty, of lowliness, of service to the brethren; but all perfection, all 'justices' are to be found in this one single path traced out for us and smoothed down for us by the Lord Jesus. In brief, it is a matter of fitting **our steps in his steps**: *vestigiis . . . adaequati seu conformati.* The first Cistercians loved the Rule, because for them, life according to the Rule meant matching Jesus step for step, stride for stride, as they followed him in his paschal journey from this world to the Father: *regulae vestigiis sunt adaequati seu conformati.*

If Jerome's commentary on the Isaian canticle helps, as I think it does, to explain this problem-text a bit better, one further nuance remains to be noted, and it is not a very irenic one. The canticle text immediately preceding our 'foot of the Poor Man' text describes how the Lord shall bring down them that dwell on high, 'the high city he shall lay low; he shall bring it down . . . he shall pull it down, . . .' Christ, the Poor Man, in Jerome's exegesis, by his poverty tramples down and reduces to dust the proud pretensions of the 'high city' so that those who follow after him can walk on a path that is smooth and level. I suggest that this is a nuance which attaches to *Sicque rectitudinem regulae supra cunctum vitae suae tenorem ducentes.* . . . Exemplary as the Molesme observance was, it did not answer to the absoluteness of the gospel exigencies as understood by the early founders. In the observance of the Rule as practiced at Molesme, there were valleys to be filled up, hills to be toppled down, rough paths to be made plain, and crooked ways to be straightened. The *civitas sublimis* had to be levelled. And this, I suspect, is the nuance which attaches to the somewhat surprising image of leading or directing the *rectitudo*/right path of the Rule straight over (*-supra*) their whole manner of living the monastic life.

Before passing on, let me answer the objection that we ought not to presuppose that Stephen Harding, the alleged author of the *Exordium Parvum* in the traditional view, was familiar with Jerome's commentary on Isaiah. He most certainly was. The Cîteaux manuscript of the commentary is even now one of the glories of the Bibliothèque municipale of Dijon: MS 129 (formerly 96). Charles Oursel, the specialist in cistercian miniatures, dates the manuscript to a period no later than 1115–1125, while allowing for a still earlier date.[15] This is the manuscript which contains the famous Virgin of the Tree of Jesse, styled by Oursel as 'probably the masterpiece of cistercian miniatures'.[16]

In studying the term *rectitudo regulae* with the help of Saint Jerome's remarks on *rectitudines*, the reader may well have been somewhat bemused by the fact that the author wrote *rectitudo regulae* in the singular, rather than the plural *rectitudines*, as in Jerome. Consistency is the sign of a petty soul, of course, and it would be unjust to our author, who uses Scripture, Rule and liturgy freely, to expect him to follow Jerome in a blatantly obvious manner. But I suspect that, in fact, the use of *rectitudinem* in the singular betrays

15. Charles Oursel, *La miniature du XII siècle à l'Abbaye de Cîteaux d'après les manuscrits de la Bibliothèque de Dijon* (Dijon: L. Venot, 1926) pp. 44–45.
16. Paris, Bibl. nationale, MS lat. 2300, f. 40r.

the influence of a collect from the early cistercian liturgy and is not simply an instance of inconsistency.

As their Mass sacramentary the first Cistercians had a version of considerable antiquity. It was substantially the gregorian sacramentary supplemented with material taken from the supplement compiled, as current scholarship now has it, by Benedict of Aniane. There were three formulas in this compilation which made use of the term *rectitudo*. Two of these can be excluded from our consideration right away; both are found in the Mass for the Vigil of Pentecost, where the first collect reads, as transcribed from our earliest extant sacramentary manuscript (from Landais, near Chartres, a bit before 1147):

> *Deus qui in Abrahe famuli tui opere . humano generi obedientie exempla prębuisti . concede nobis . et nostre uoluntatis prauitatem frangere . et tuorum preceptorum* **rectitudinem** *in omnibus adimplere . Per.* [17]

The third collect comes from the formulary in the ancient Gregorian *Sacramentarium Hadrianum* for the Birth of Saint John the Baptist, 24 June. It is a collect *Ad fontes*, that is to say, the collect intended to be said in the baptistery of the Lateran basilica in connection with the procession after Vespers. The collect is not, of course, found here in the cistercian sacramentary, which has little use for evening processions to baptisteries. But it is to be found in the cistercian breviary, where it served as the proper collect for Sext on the feast of the Beheading of Saint John the Baptist, 29 August. The cistercian breviary collects came from the same source as the cistercian Mass collects—a rather ancient form of the gregorian sacramentary supplemented by some very standard formularies so that a number of collects excluded from the cistercian sacramentary nonetheless found a place in the Cistercian Office. As transcribed from our earliest extant breviary-manuscript, written around 1132 and representing the earliest recoverable version of the Cistercian Office, the text reads:

17. *Ibid.*, f. 40r–v. [In the transcription, I've respected the scribe's inconsistency as regards the use of the cedilla-ę.]

140

> *Omnipotens sempiterne deus . da cordibus nostris illam **tuarum***
> ***rectitudinem semitarum** . quam beati iohannis baptiste in*
> *deserto vox clamantis edocuit. Per.*[18]

The formula is extremely ancient, being found already in the *Sacramentarium Veronense*, which contains many formulas dating back to the fifth century. The Latin is beautiful and theologically rich but clumsy when rendered into modern languages, so I refuse to propose an english equivalent. But a literal though gauche rendering of the central part of the collect might run: ' . . . grant to our hearts that "straightness" of your paths which the voice of the blessed John the Baptist, crying out in the desert, proclaimed. . . .' Here we find *rectitudo* in the singular and linked in direct juxtaposition to *semita*, just as in Jerome's remarks about the expression *semita iusti*. And the reader who finds the expression 'to lead the straight path of the Rule (or the straight path shown by the Rule) over the whole manner of life' a bit clumsy should note that the collect is even clumsier: ' . . . give the straightness of your paths to our hearts. . . .'

I believe, too, that the particular meaning of *rectitudo regulae* in Chapter Fifteen of the *Exordium Parvum* is confirmed by the parallel use of *rectitudo* in the final line of the first chapter of the *Charter of Charity* where the author (surely Saint Stephen Harding) states explicitly his intention to retain the *cura animarum* with respect to the houses founded from Cîteaux, for one reason and one only—and here I quote Father Lackner's excellent translation:

> We do wish, however, to retain the care of their souls for the sake of charity so that if they should ever attempt, even if but in a small measure, to stray from their sacred resolve and the observance of the holy Rule—which may God avert—through our solicitude they may be able to return to the **right path** of life.[19]

The Latin text reads:

> *Curam tamen animarum illorum gratia caritatis retinere volumus, ut si quando a sancto proposito et observantia sanctae*

18. Folio 196v of the breviary-MS referred to above, Note 16.
19. *PATC* 91.

*regulae paululum, quod absit, declinare temptaverint, per nos-
tram sollicitudinem ad **rectitudinem** vitae redire possint.*[20]

Here, too, the vocabulary is that of the way, the path: *declinare*, 'to
turn away from', 'to turn aside from', 'to deviate from' with the
etymological force of the word: to get off (*de-*) the path (*via*); and
redire, 'to go back to', 'to return to'. In the Prologue to the Holy
Rule we read (Prologue, 20): *Ecce pietate sua demonstrat nobis Dominus
viam vitae*. But this 'way of life' is synonymous with ***rectitudinem
vitae***, which has the added nuance of being straight and direct.

Finally, I suggest that Saint Stephen's use of the term *rectitudo
regulae* in Chapter Fifteen of the *Exordium Parvum* was prepared for
by the text of Pope Paschal II's *Privilegium Romanum*, transcribed
almost *in extenso* in the preceding Chapter Fourteen. The pertinent
lines are:

*Vos igitur, filii in Christo dilectissimi ac desiderantissimi,
meminisse debetis, quia pars vestri saeculares **latitudines**, pars
ipsas etiam monasterii laxioris minus austeras **angustias**
reliquistis.*[21]

Implicit in this text is a reference to the familiar utterance of Christ:
Quam angusta porta, et arcta via, quae ducit ad vitam: 'how narrow is
the gate, and strait is the way that leads to life' (Mt 7:14); Pope
Paschal is reminding the pioneer reformers that a group of them
(*pars vestri*) have come to New Monastery from the broad, spacious
roads of the world, *saeculares latitudines*, which are quite different
from the *arcta via* of the Gospel; and that another group of them
come from the 'strait' portals of a monastery more 'relaxed' than
their own (*etiam monasterii laxioris*), where, though the portals be
angustiae in conformity with the gospel dictum, they are nonetheless
minus austerae, 'less austere'—either less austere than they should be
or else simply less austere than at the New Monastery.

The text shows that already in 1100 the community at the New
Monastery included not only ex-Molesmites, but brethren who had
entered directly from the world. The pope's references to Molesme

20. *Ibid.*
21. *PATC* 75.

are not particularly derogatory. The 'wide open spaces' he relates to the world; the Molesme observance is designated by the term *angustia*, even though this 'straightness' is *minus austera*, 'less austere'. He does not say *haud austera*, or *minime austera*, but simply *minus austera*, which I take as meaning 'austere, though less austere than at the New Monastery'. Nor does any special opprobrium attach to *monasterii laxioris*, since the phrase refers only to a monastery less strict than the New Monastery.

In spite of the fact that there is not a single word common to the papal text and Mt 7:13–14, it remains nonetheless clear that the diction and the content of these lines from the Roman Privilege depend on the Matthaean text. In brief, the pope is telling the brethren of the New Monastery that they have to remember that they have struck out along the strait and narrow way. The very next chapter, Chapter Fifteen, spells out in summary the way in which the brethren have implemented the pontiff's admonition: they are following right in the path along which the Rule is taking them, and they have made the 'right path' of the Rule pass over absolutely every aspect of their life and observance.

What I am suggesting, then, is that our *rectitudo regulae* in the *Exordium Parvum* is rich with resonances of the Rule, of the liturgy, of the Fathers. For the first Cistercians, fidelity to the Rule meant that they were on the path which was both 'strait' and 'straight', that path which made them companions of the Lord Jesus in his paschal journey. This is the straight way in the desert proclaimed by the Baptist; it is the straight way of the Poor Man of the canticle chanted in Christmastide, when we celebrate the mystery of God's descent into our poverty and lowliness; it is the straight way shown us by the Holy Rule.

On the day of Saint Benedict's death, two of his disciples saw the same vision. In the old seventeenth-century translation which is my favorite, the account reads:

> . . . they saw all the way from the holy man's cell, towards the east even up to heaven, hung and adorned with tapestry, and shining with an infinite number of lamps; at the top whereof a man reverently attired stood,

and demanded if they knew who had passed that way; to whom they answered, saying that they knew not. Then he spake unto them,

> **This is the way** [quoth he], by which the beloved servant of God, Benet, is ascended up to heaven.[22]

All this should make us appreciate the high level of spirituality so evident in monks of the early days of the Order. If Lefevre is right and a liar and a forger such as a pamphleteer of 1151 could lie and forge in terms so rich in meaning and so redolent of Holy Writ, the Rule, and the Fathers, the level of spiritual culture in the Order at large was nothing to be sneezed at. Happy the monastic family in which even fraud and fiction is vibrant with the deep and high things of the Spirit![23]

Have I not, in the preceding pages, sometimes substituted eisegesis for exegesis? When studying and meditating on such texts the mode of communication takes place not only by way of explicit formal statement, but also by way of allusion and theological innuendo; and this calls for a certain degree of 'co-creativity' on the reader's part. But if here or there I have read something into the text which was not meant by the author to be there, I sincerely hope that this 'something' is in basic harmony with the main thrust of the author's meaning and message. Eisegesis is bad, if what we read into the text falsifies or distorts the real meaning. But a writer such as Saint Stephen Harding or Saint Bernard presupposes a readiness on the part of the reader for active collaboration.

If the problem of eisegesis is to be raised, I too can point an accusing finger. The conclusions reached by J.-A. Lefevre and those who follow his lead result in large measure from reading into the texts things which are not there and of failing to notice some of the things that *are* there. There is absolutely no substitute for scientific

---

22. The translator of the Paris edition of 1608 identified himself only as 'P.W.' The text is quoted from the re-edition, *The Little Flowers of Saint Benet* (London: Kegan Paul, Trench Trubner and Co., 1901) p. 121.

23. See below, page 163, note 1.

discipline and methodology. But these must be well used, and not abused; and the point to which they take us is less a point of arrival than a point of departure. An integral historical approach results not only in our knowing a great deal *about* the early Fathers, but—more important—in knowing the Fathers, and loving them. We need, then, scholars whose efforts are directed to helping monks and nuns understand and love our heritage, and to helping so many countless thousands who stand outside this tradition to see a bit more clearly what it is we love and experience.

Robert, Alberic, Stephen, Odo, Letaldus and all the other brethren of early Cîteaux are still speaking to us through those texts. They are inviting us even now to deepen our love for Citeaux, for our own community, and for the cistercian way of life. They are drawing us into a communion of prayer and love that transcends the limitations of time; and from them, we find new courage as we plod along our sometimes weary way to the face to face vision of God.

Biblical Vocabulary as a Reflection of the Spirituality of the Founders of Cîteaux

Denis Farkasfalvy

OUR CISTERCIAN FOUNDERS belonged to a time in which people habitually expressed their theological heritage and conviction through biblical images and vocabulary. By paying close attention to the way the founders used the Bible when speaking of their daily affairs, fundamental goals, and practical organization of life, therefore, historians who, in the face of a lack of reliable original texts, are doubtful even as to the exact sequence of events that led to the foundation, can gain an insight into the concepts of the monastic heritage which motivated their undertaking. Few as the early documents coming from the founders of Cîteaux are, they abound in biblical phrases and allusions which are indicators of the spiritual pedigree of their authors.

Since this method of research yields its best results when one deals with cumulative evidence, rather than in analyzing individual fragments of texts, I intend to assemble some blocks of raw material and to point out the basic concepts appearing in them. Each of these blocks I will attach to a biblical word or expression.[1]

NOVITAS

There is no doubt that the monastery at Cîteaux was first called *Novum Monasterium.* In the medieval mind, the concept of 'novelty'

---

1. I have used J. Marilier, *Chartes et documents concernant l'Abbaye de Cîteaux, 1098–1182*, Bibliotheca Cisterciensis 1 (Rome, 1961) and Jean de la Croix Bouton – Jean Baptiste Van Damme, *Les plus anciens textes de Citeaux*, Citeaux: Commentarii Cistercienses, Studia et Documenta 2 (Achel, 1974).

146

was quite ambiguous. In biblical vocabulary, a *new* man, a *new* life, a *new* spirit meant something of great value; but according to the Pastoral Epistles, also attributed to Paul, the introduction of 'novelties' (*novitates*, cf. 1 Tm 6:20) was not a good thing and so the words *innovare* or *innovatio* had a negative connotation.

There are good signs that the name *Novum Monasterium* was chosen to express the intention of creating a *new kind* of institution. Yet very soon after the foundation the founders appear somewhat defensive about the novelty their monastery represented, both in name and in reality. That the founders of the 'New Monastery' were accused by their contemporaries of innovation is reflected in the letter of Hugh, Archbishop of Lyon to Pope Paschal II. Hugh writes that the brothers of Molesme were displeased by the efforts of their erstwhile brethren now at Cîteaux, 'for they thought that they would be despised by the world if these peculiar and new types of monks were allowed to live among them' (*si isti quasi singulares et novi monachi inter eos habitare videantur*).[2]

Thus, according to the archbishop, the monks of the *Novum Monasterium* need the protection of the Holy See because their being *singulares et novi monachi* provoked hostility among the monks of the region. Interestingly, the word *singularis*, which we might translate in our modern idiom as 'special' or 'exceptional', is also ambiguous. Ancient prayers and sermons use the word about God's special gifts,[3] the best known example being *virgo singularis* in the hymn *Ave Maris Stella*. Yet equally well known is the caricature which Saint Bernard created of the vice called *singularitas* in his earliest treatise, *De gradibus humilitatis*, closely contemporary wit the *Exordium Parvum*. In other words, being *singularis et novus* was a very

2. *Exordium parvum* XII.1. The letter is to be dated to 1100, but its exact wording could have undergone change during the composition of the *Exordium Parvum* See Marlier, 47; Bouton, 72.

3. See H Barré, *Prières anciennes de l'Occident à la Mère du Sauveur, Des origines à saint Anselme* (Paris, 1963), who gives examples—all prior to the twelfth century on pages 45 (*virgo singularis*), 52 (*singulare meritum*), 67 (*singularis sanctitas*), 75 (*singulare meritum*), 136 (*singularis gratia*), 161 (*singulare meritum*), 184 (*singularis virgo*), 220 (*singulare privilegium*), 304 (*o femina mirabiliter singularis et singulariter mirabilis*).

ambiguous compliment for a monk of the early twelfth century, an age marked by reverence for what was ancient and authentic.

The *Exordium Parvum* comes to the defense of the founders' novelty with the help of another Pauline verse: *Exuti ergo veterem hominem, novum se induisse gaudebant* (Having put off the old man, they rejoiced to put on the new), an abbreviated quotation of Ephesians 4:22–24. Further along in the same chapter the founders are called *novi milites Christi.*[4] We may be seeing here a term alluding to the military imagery of the Pauline epistles or hearing an echo of the Rule.[5] We may even think that this is a forerunner of Saint Bernard's title for his treatise on the Templars, *De laude novae militiae.* But here the military aspect remains of little importance; the emphasis in on novelty.

What novelty? The context of the sentence speaks of *the poverty of the founders:* 'the new soldiers of Christ, intent on being poor with the poor Christ, began to discuss among themselves by what ingenuity they could support themselves and their guests, rich and poor alike' (*Coeperunt novi milites Christi, cum paupere Christo pauperes, inter se tractare quo ingenio . . . in have vita se hospitesque divites at pauperes supervenientes . . . sustentarent*). The work *pauper* appears three times in this sentence. The phrase *cum paupere Christo pauperes* appears as a program coined from biblical notions. The underlying verse is 2 Corinthians 8:9, which declares that Christ 'became poor for our sake although he was rich, so that by his poverty you may become rich'. Some may doubt this reference because the Vulgate uses here *egenus* rather than *pauper* and *inopia* rather than *paupertas*. But the reference is correct and closer than might at first be suspected, for in patristic usage, the wording of 2 Corinthians 8:9 in the Vetus Latina retained in this form: pauper *factus est cum esse dives ut eius* paupertate *nos ditaremur.*[6] It was from this variant of

4. *Exordium Parvum* XV; Bouton, 77.
5. RB Prologue 3: *Christo vero regi militaturos;* Prol 40: *oboedientiae militanda;* RB 1.2: *militans sub regula;* RB 58.10: *lex sub qua militare vis;* RB 61.10: *uni regi militatur*
6. See, for example The sermons of Saint Augustine, edited by G. Morin, *Miscellanea Augustiniana* (Rome, 1930) 1:24, 77, 193.

the Pauline verse that the expression *pauper Christi* and the slogan *pauperes cum Christo paupere* entered the founders' vocabulary and became almost a manifesto for their reform of monastic life in the twelfth century, as also later in the reform which climaxed in the Franciscan movement.

The abandonment of the name *Novum Monasterium* in favor of *Sanctae Mariae de Cistercio*[7] and its variants[8] happened in the year 1119 for reasons which must have included the negative repercussions of the founders' claims of novelty and innovation. In the early twelfth century, the ecclesiastic climate measured the authenticity of reforms and customs by the yardstick of antiquity. The name *novum* must have led to continual misunderstanding and misinterpretation. Saint Bernard seems to have succeeded in clarifying this matter: in his vocabulary *novitas* is always positive and joyful; but he rejects and deplores innovations—like those of Abelard—as contrary to authentic tradition.

SERVIRE

The term *servire Deo* appears with some frequency in the ancient documents of Cîteaux. At first I thought this was an overused term with no special significance. A closer look convinced me otherwise. *Servire **Deo*** is a New Testament term. In the Vulgate the

---

7. Marilier 39.IX. This document is supposedly from 1113, but there are signs that the wording of the copy lacks precision. In any case, the other eight documents belonging to the same group of donations (Marilier 39.I-V, pp. 60–61) use the expression *Novi Monasterii* or *sanctae Mariae Novi Monasterii. Sanctae Mariae de Cistercio* also appears in another document, not precisely dated: Marilier 58 (p. 73). The foundation charter of Preuilly in 1118 still has *Novum Monasterium*.

8. The foundation charter of Bonnevaux from 1119 has *fratres a Cistercio* and *Cisterciensi instituto* (Marilier 65, pp. 78–79); a document from 1119 reads *sanctae Mariae de Cistercio* (Marilier 67, p. 80); Pope Callixtus' confirmation of the *Charta caritatis* on 23 December 1119 has *cisterciensis monasterii* (Marilier 69, p. 82); another, slightly later, document has *sanctae Mariae apud Cistercium* (Marilier 79, p. 87); documents from 1130–1140 have *beatae Mariae cisterciensi* (Marilier 81, p. 88) or *sanctae Mariae cistercii* (Marilier 82, p. 88); *cisterciensis ecclesia* (rilier 88, p. 91) or *sanctae Mariae Cistercii* (Marilier 93, p. 95).

Old Testament usually has *servire* **Domino**, where *Domino* stands for YHWH with its usual connotation of the God of Israel. In the New Testament, on the other hand, there are only a few important passages in which the expression *servire Deo* is descriptive of the program of Christian life. The Greek original is not readily identifiable: *servire* in the Vulgate translates either λατρευειν or δουλειν. Even so we have altogether six or seven texts to deal with; only one of them is found in the Gospels: 'you cannot serve both God and Mammon' (Mt 6:24 = Lk 16:13). The rest occur in the Pauline letters: two in Romans (1:9; 6:22), one in Philippians (3:3), one in First Thessalonians (I:9); and one is Hebrews (9:4). The Rule of Saint Benedict uses the concept in the expression *dominici schola servitii*, but does not use the formula *servire Deo* as a description of the program of monastic life.[9]

Some early Cistercian texts focus on this expression. The *Exordium Parvum* spells out the goal of the founders as being *die ac nocte Deo servire*.[10] At first we may think that this refers to Acts 26:27, where Paul is quoted as speaking of the hope of Israel whereby the twelve tribes want to attain *in perseverantia* **nocte ac die deservientes**. A second conjecture, Lk 2:37, concerns the prophetess Anna who stayed in the Temple *serviens die ac nocte*. But the closest biblical parallel—and probably the source—is Revelations 7:15, where the elect are said to have washed their clothes white in the blood of the Lamb and are now therefore before God's throne, serving him day and night (*Ideo sunt ante thronum Dei et serviunt ei die ac nocte in templo eius*).

Not only is this last verse our closest parallel,[11] but it attests to a remarkable consistency in the early spirituality of Cîteaux.

9. The only close parallel is *uni Domino servimus* in RB 65.10, but here, obviously, the emphasis is on *uni*, not on *servire*, and the name of God is *Dominus*.

10. Chapter XVII; Bouton, 81.

11. This can be seen by the context: the sentence of the *Exordium Parvum* speaks of *God's house*, in which the monks want to serve God day and night and so must maintain a special purity of observance Rev 7:15 speaks of *God's temple* in which he is served day and night by those who have washed their robes in the blood of the Lamb.

Most Cistercians know the legend, made famous by the *Exordium Magnum*, about a cleric named Alberic who, in a dream, saw a group of fourteen monks washing their habits in a river. Inquiring about the meaning of this dream, he was advised to go to Cîteaux, where he recognized the same monks whom he had seen in his dream. He entered Cîteaux, later becoming its prior and then possibly abbot of Morimond. This multiple attestation suggests that this legend was based on a true story which had taken place before 1104.[12]

The unintended convergence between the *Exordium Parvum*'s use of Revelation 7:15 and the key role that the same passage plays in Alberic's dream seems to indicate that we are dealing here with fragments of a tradition linking—in the minds of the early witnesses—the ideal of the founders of Cîteaux with this scene of the Book of Revelation.

Put back into its biblical context, the ideal expressed n the phrase *servire Deo* has strong liturgical connotations; it refers to the ideal of *laus perennis*. But there is more to it than merely the wish to participate day and night in the eternal liturgy of the Lamb.

Servire Deo also appears in the *monitum* Stephen Harding attached to his new Bible. Stephen Harding, as we all know, stands out because of his enterprise of correcting the Vulgate and editing a Bible based on the *Hebraica Veritas*. What disturbed him were the interpolations of the Septuagint which had been preserved in certain Latin manuscripts but were missing fro others. To make textual corrections he consulted Jewish rabbis, who helped him in Old French (*lingua Romana*) to bring his Bible closer to the Masoretic text.

The *monitum* Stephen attached to this Bible takes the form of an open letter to all present and future monks of the *Novum Monasterium*. In this document, dated to 1109, Stephen addresses these monks as *praesentibus et futuris* servis Dei. This shows again that the title *servus Dei* was a simple, concise description of the monastic vocation as he conceived it.[13]

12. See Bouton, 80–81, note 2.
13. See Marilier 32, p. 56.

The opening sentences of the *Carta Caritatis Prior* reflect the same idea: 'serving God' is the essence of the monastic vocation. But these sentences insert it into a concise biblical collage:

> Quia unius veri regis et domini et magistri nos omnes *servos* licet inutiles esse cognoscimus, idcirco abbatibus et confratribus nostris monachis quos per diversa loca Dei pietas per nos miserrimos hominum sub regulari disciplina ordinverit, nullam terrenae commoditatis seu rerum temporalium exactionem imponimus.[14]

Many things could be said about this sentence, but I will list only a few of the basic ideas:

As a principle, it is stated that monks and abbots should not engage in exploitation of others by exacting either labor of materials goods.

- As a principle, it is stated that monks and abbots should not engage in exploitation of others by exacting either labor of materials goods.
- This principle is based on the understanding that we 'all are servants',[15] to which is added a quotation from Luke 17:10: are *useless* servants (*servi inutiles*), so that even the title of being God's servants could not become a reason for pride or domination.
- Christ whom we all serve is described as king, lord, and master. The feudal image of king is masterfully balanced by the Johannine image of *dominus et magister*, the title Jesus used at the Last Supper and connected to the washing of the disciples' feet and the commandment of love: 'If I, who am Lord and Master, have washed your feet, you must do the same to each other' (Jn 13:14).
- In this sentences I find a precious compendium of the ancient

14. Prologue; Bouton, 91.
15. This is an implicit quotation of RB 61.10: *quia in omni loco uno Domino servitur, uno regi militatur.*

Cistercian spiritual heritage that speaks about humility, renunciation of riches, greed, and exploitation, as well as the obligation to serve others, not only other monks but all other people. For the text continues by saying: *Prodesse enim* illis omnibusque sanctae ecclesiae filiis *cupientes*[16] *nil quod eos gravet, nil quod eorum substantiam minuat,erga eos agere disponimus.*

- The sentence just quoted ends with a rather strong condemnation of ecclesiastical greed by saying *ne dum nos abundantes de eorum paupertate esse cupimus,* avaritiae malum, quod secundum apostolum idolorum servitus *esse comprobatur, evitare non possimus.* Here Ephesians 5:5 is quoted, but taken out of its context so that it becomes the antithesis of the very first sentence quoted above. By yielding to greed we defeat the purpose of monasticism; we become 'servants of idols' rather than servants of the true God who must be 'our King, our Lord and Master'.

- In this paragraph 'abbots and out brother monks' (*abbatibus et confratribus nostris monachis*) are put on the same footing because all are servants of the same Lord. Furthermore, the text points out that abbots are elected and installed by us 'most wretched men' (*miserrimos homines*). In this way a sharp awareness is expressed that ultimately God's goodness (*Dei pietas*) and not human wisdom or constitutional rights are the source of abbatial authority.)

All this may well reflect the personal attitudes and spirituality of Stephen Harding. In the few authentic documents that have survived from his pen, he twice calls himself the servants, rather than abbot, of his monastery: *frater Stephanus Novi Monasterii minister,*[17] and *cisterciensis ecclesiae servus.*[18]

16. Here *sancta ecclesia* means the universal church, not the particular abbey or the total of all Cistercians.

17. Marilier 31, p. 55.

18. Marilier 88, p. 91. Language of humility is not unique at the time. Abbot Henry of Saint John of the Angels, in a document of donation written before 1131, calls himself *Henricus, servus Angeliacensis indignus* (Marilier 95).

AN INVITATION TO FURTHER RESEARCH

The length of this study does not allow me to go into more detail, yet I would like to list a few matters that deserve similar research

1. *Spiritualis militia* is a theme which has many formulations in our sources,[19] and uses texts and terms taken from Saint Paul. Already in the biblical sources this topic is combined with athletic imagery. The Cistercian sources use a Pauline terminology of a race (*cursus*),[20] of running (*currere*),[21] and of the prize for winners (*bravium*).[22]

2. A very fascinating letter by Stephen Harding was discovered by C. H. Talbot in 1936.[23] Stephen wrote it two or three years before his death to the monks of Sherborne, the English monastery he had left at the beginning of the pilgrimage which brought him eventually to Molesme and finally to Cîteaux. This documents expresses a deep sense of satisfaction about what God's mercy has accomplished through him. It, too, contains many biblical allusions: comparisons with Moses, with Abraham, with Saint Paul as a *vas electum* (in the sense of a container, rather than an instrument), and still others. Stephen writes:

> And now, I who left my homeland alone and
> poor, enter the destiny of all flesh rich and
> accompanied by a crowd of forty. I securely

19. *Exordium Parvum* XVI; Bouton, 80: *Dei misericordia qui hanc militiam spiritualem suis inspiravit.*

20. *Exordim Parvum* XVII; Bouton, 82: *cursum suum consummarent* Cf. 2 Tim 4:17: *cursum consummavi.*

21. *Exordium Parvum* XVII; Bouton, 82; *postea illuc currere; Exordium Cistercii* II; Bouton, 113: [Albericus] *non in vacuum cucurrit.* Cf. Gal 2:2: *ne in vacuum currerem vel cucurrissem,* but more closely Phil 2:16: *non in vacuum cucurri.*

22. *vir Dei Albericus supernae vocationis bravium . . . apprehendit.* Cf Phil 3:14.

23. Marilier 88, p. 91. See above, page $$.

await the one *denarius* promised to the laborers who faithfully worked in the vineyard.

I quote this because of the final allusion to the parable
of the vineyard (Mt 20:1–14). As if preoccupied with
the same image, the prologue of the *Exordium Parvum*
quotes the same parable, but in a rather awkward way.
The founders, speaking in the first person plural (*nos cistercienses, primi huius ecclesiae fundators*), remind the readers
that 'we were the ones who carried the burden and heat
of the day'. In terms of the parable, this accentuates that
the founders were the ones who were hired 'in the first
hour'. The words they cite are, however, ill-suited to
their message, because they quote the complaint raised
by the first laborers when they realized that they would
be paid no more than the later arrivals (Mt 20:12): we
worked longer, we bore the heat and burden of the day,
and now everyone receives the same *denarius*.

Stephen's letter stands in strong—perhaps conscious
—contrast to the use made of this text in the *Exordium*.
He points out that, although he set out on his mission
all alone (*solus . . . egressus sum*), he is now enriched by
a crowd of forty—the forty monasteries issued from
Cîteaux— and, about to die, he looks forward to receiving the *denarius* promised to everyone else as well,
the one and indivisible reward which is God himself.

There are many more biblical echoes in the earliest documents
of Cîteaux which resonated right at the beginning of the Cistercian
experience but which gained increased significance through their
association with other and more biblical documentation in later
time. Of these I will give two examples.

QUIES

The first is a word which represents monastic life style: *quies*—
repose, quietness, leisure. This term appears in various contexts and
is complex. Sometimes *quies* is purely an external term, sometimes
a legal, sometimes a practical or environmental term. Its spiritual

references are often vague. The theme recurs frequently, however, and is found most often in correspondence with episcopal and papal authorities.[24]

But the concept of *quies* is clearly part of a spirituality which, in the works of Saint Bernard—specifically in his *De conversione ad clericos*—takes on unsuspected theological meaning and depth. Bernard must have become acquainted in some way with a very ancient tradition attached to Genesis 4:7 and an Old Latin (*Vetus Latina*) translation based on the Septuagint—probably through reading the works of Saint Ambrose.[25]

Genesis 4:7 is a divine oracle from heaven addressed to Cain after he killed his brother. The Septuagint translated it by two words which the old Latin version renders as '*Peccasti? Quiesce.*' Bernard uses this verse and, even more, the patristic tradition attached to it, to explain that the first step of conversion must be a separation from one's sinful self. *Quiesce*, in this context, means both 'calm down' and 'quit' or 'settle'; which is to say, 'stop sinning, change your way of life'. In Bernard's understanding, therefore, *quies* signifies not just an external condition, but the whole context of conversion. To reach *quies* we ought to make a clean break with our old ways of life. Monastic *quies* means separation from a sinful environment as well as a sinful past; detachment from all the tumult arising from sinful memories, passions, lack of internal peace. *Quies* signifies a

24. *Exordium Parvum* II (Bouton, 58): **quietius** *Domino famulari*; VII (Bouton, 64): *pacem et* **quietem** *molesmensi ecclesiae posse restitui*; X (Bouton, 69): *sub apostolicae protetionis alis* **quieta** *et tuta*; XI (Bouton, 71): *Petunt enim . . . de* **quiete** *et suae religionis stabilitate*; XII (Bouton, 72): *eos in***quiet***are non desinunt; ab hinc infestatione et in***quiet***udine liberando*; XIII (Bouton, 74): *in suae* **quietis** *tutelam a vestra flagitant pietate*; XIV (Bouton, 74): *locum illum quem inhabitandum pro* **quiete** *monastica elegistis*; *Privilegium Papae Callixti* (Bouton, 104): *si qua persona . . . tamquam monasticae religionis et* **quietis** *perturbatrix*.

25. Ambrose, *De paenitentia* ii.11; ed. R. Gryson, *Ambroise de Milan: La Pénitence*, Sources chrétiennes 179 (Paris: Cerf, 1971) 196. Cf. D. Farkasfalvy, 'The First Step in Spiritual Life: Conversion', *La dottrina della vita spirituale nelle opere di San Bernardo,* Atti del Convegno Internazionale, Roma 11–15 settembre, 1990 (Rome: Editiones Cistercienses, 1991) 73–74.

spiritual program to be carried out in the secluded and disciplined environment of the monastery. Bernard, with his genius for interiorization, simply inserted the concept of *quies* into an elaborate teaching on conversion.

EREMUM, DESERTUM

What sense *eremum*—hermitage, wilderness, desert—originally conveyed in reference to the New Monastery is not clear and the arguments on the subject are complicated. There is some evidence that Saint Robert's original monastery had to be moved from its first site to its later, permanent location at Cîteaux, close to an ancient road.[26] But even the original place was not abandoned, for a chapel already existed there. In any case, early Cistercian sources soon forged a connection between Cîteaux and the Judean desert to which John the Baptist and then Jesus himself retired 'among wild animals'. By this allusion to Mark 1:13, the term described Citeaux's isolated location is enriched to invoke the example of Jesus and his lifestyle. In any case, the monks quickly civilized Citeaux, for early documents refer back to the past by saying that only *illo tempore*—in those days—was the place deserted and not fit for human habitation. The language used in this context endows the memory of the founders with an heroic glow, but it also urges new generations of Cistercians to deepen the spiritual meaning of the desert as a place in which to combat Satan, who prowls around as a roaring lion (1 Pet 5:8), a specific wild beast to be confronted.

This development reached its peak, I think, in the *Exordium Cistercii*, joined to the *Summa Chartae Caritatis*.[27] There the *eremum* of Citeaux becomes, in terms taken from Deuteronomy 32:10, a place of horror and vast solitude (*locus horroris et vastae solitudinis*).[28]

26. Marilier, 27, p. 53.
27. The dating of these documents is controversial. Because of its biblical rhetoric, I am inclined to Leopold Grill's thesis that the text may be attributable to Saint Bernard. See his 'Der hl. Bernhard als bisher unerkannter Verfasser des *Exordium Cistercii* und der *Summa Cartae Caritatis*', in *Cistercienser Chronik* 49/50 (1959) 43–57.
28. Bouton, 111.

With this citation the image of the 'desert' is attached to a key text of the Pentateuch and brings to mind not only the Life of Saint Anthony and other Egyptian monks, but the whole saga of Israel's journey in the desert—a great spiritual history connected with many more Old Testament texts used in early Christian typology. In this way, with the help of Saint Paul (1 Cor 10:1–12), we come to realize that the beginnings of Cîteaux are a paradigm for our monastic life journey through the desert. The 'exordium' of Cîteaux becomes an *exitus Israel de Aegypto* (Ps 114:1), a spiritual model of what 'happened for the instruction of us, for whom the end of the ages has arrived' (1 Cor 10:12).

I hope that these examples provide a base on which other may begin to explore the biblical imagery used by the founders of Cîteaux as a research tool for studying their spirituality. Their use of their favorite biblical passages and images must be creatively rediscovered and contextually continued to help establish—in the context of contemporary life—a *Novum Monasterium*—in each of our communities.

Successoríbus nostrís

The Cistercian Inheritance

NOS CISTERCIENSES, *primi huius ecclesiae fundatores, successoribus nostris stilo praesenti notificamus: quam canonice, quanta auctoritate, a quibus etiam personis, quibusque temporibus, coenobium et tenor vitae illorum exordium sumpserit; ut huius rei propalata sincera veritate, tenacius et locum et observantiam sanctae regulae in eo a nobis per Dei gratiam utcumque inchoatam ament, pro nobisque, qui pondus diei et aestus indefesse sustinuimus, orent, in arta et angusta via quam regula demonstrat, usque ad exhalationem spiritus desudent, quatinus deposita carnis sarcina, in requie sempiterna feliciter pausent.*

WE MONKS OF CÎTEAUX, the first founders of this church, make it known to our successors by this present writing how canonically, by what great authority, even by which persons, too, and by which stages, their monastery and manner of life had this beginning, so that, with the sincere truth of this matter clearly spelled out, they may more tenaciously love both the place and the observance of the Holy Rule begun in it—at least in some small way—by us through God's grace; that they may pray for us who have tirelessly borne the burden and the heat of the day; and that they may toil in the strait and narrow way which the Rule marks out until their very last breath; until at last, with the baggage of the flesh set down they may repose happily in rest everlasting.

Exordium parvum, Prologue

Liturgical-Patristic Resonances on The Prologue to the Exordium Parvum

Chrysogonus Waddell, OCSO

RESONANCES is a carefully chosen word. When our Cistercian Fathers wished to do so, they could quote a biblical or patristic text with absolute accuracy; and most readers and editors of the texts—editors especially—are grateful so long as the author points clearly to his source. Often enough, however, our cistercian authors, even the better ones, are less than helpful. Their language and their symbols have usually been consecrated by centuries of tradition. A vague allusion (vague, that is to say, to you and me) or a mere hint at a citation sometimes conveyed more to medieval readers than most of us could express in several paragraphs of a conventional prose. Our Fathers are not, perhaps, unlike some of our more important twentieth-century poets and novelists. We can pick up a copy of, say, T. S. Eliot's *Fours Quartets*, and make our way through it with deep pleasure and personal profit—but many of us read with a sense of partial frustration at the realization that, for every symbol perceived and understood aright, there may be a dozen others we have failed to recognize and appreciate at sufficient depth. For us, there is certainly no substitute for direct contact with the author's text, but we are also grateful for books with titles such as *Four Quartets Rehearsed* or *A Reader's Guide to T. S. Eliot*. Yet there is a major difference between the language of such modern writers as Eliot, Faulkner, or Joyce and that of twelfth-century monks. Modern-day poets and novelists often slip easily into their own private and esoteric jargon in which some images are so personal as to be intelligible only to the writer. The Cistercian Fathers, however, meant to write a common language. If we fail to understand them, it is not just that they could and did write badly at times, but that we ourselves are no longer at home in their world of liturgy, Scripture, and Church Fathers.

What a twelfth-century author writes by way of explicit statement generally conveys perfectly well the substance of what he meant to communicate. Formal citations from familiar sources often flesh out this meaning. But there are also allusions and references to less easily identifiable sources which color the meaning of the text and give off a resonance which affects the real meaning of the text.

By way of illustration I want to look briefly at the Prologue of a work well known to anyone interested in the history of Cistercians, the *Exordium Parvum*. This twelfth-century compilation consists of an historical narrative about the foundation and early history of Cîteaux and about the rise of the Cistercian Order; into this narrative have been inserted various official acts and documents connected with the important events described in the narrative sections.[1]

Here, although we shall be dealing with only the final lines of the Prologue, it will help considerably if we situate those few lines in their proper context. In the notes which follow, the English version—whether translation or paraphrase—is my own, unless otherwise indicated. The Latin is from *Les plus anciens texts de Cîteaux*[2] where Father Bouton adopts as his basic text the one

---

1. I have no intention of passing in review the discussions which began in the early 1950s, when a Louvain candidate for a doctorate in history, J.-A. Lefèvre, bruited abroad in numerous publications his 'discoveries' concerning the true nature of the various historical documents connected with the period of cistercian beginnings. The *Exordium Parvum* proved to be, he assured us, a work pieced together for the first time around 1151 by a fraudulent compiler who, using admittedly authentic documents, linked them together with the help of a narrative and commentary of a purposefully misleading, even mendacious sort. Cîteaux had begun by a splinter-group of monks acting on their private initiative without proper authorization of ecclesiastical superiors and in circumstances gravely compromising to the canonical status of the foundation. The *Exordium Parvum* was designed as a cover-up, 'proving' the canonical nature of the venture to the Order's critics who knew what the true story really was.

2. Jean de La Croix Bouton, *Les plus anciens textes de Cîteaux* [PATC] pp. 54–55.

generally held to be the earliest—written around 1150 and included in the MS Laibach (Ljubljana), University Library, Codex 31, from the monastery of Landstrass or Kostanjevica, on the island of Krka (Gurk), although Father Bouton, following the preferred reading of other MSS, inverts the word-order of the final cadence to read *feliciter pausent* rather than *pausent feliciter*, as in the Laibach MS.

> [1] Incipiunt consuetudines cisterciensium.
> [2] Super Exordium cisterciensis coenobii.
> [3] Nos cistercienses, primi huius ecclesiae fundatores, successoribus nostris stilo praesenti notificamus, quam canonice, quanta auctoritate, a quibus etiam personis, quibusque temporibus, cenobium et tenor vitae illorum exordium sumpserit: [4] ut huius rei propalata sincera veritate, tenacius et locum et observantiam sanctae regulae in eo a nobis per Dei gratiam utcumque inchoatam ament, [5] pro nobisque, qui pondus diei et aestus indefesse sustinuimus, orent; [6] in arta et angusta via quam regula demonstrat, usque ad exhalationem spiritus desudent, [7] quatinus deposita carnis sarcina, in requie sempiterna feliciter pausent. Amen.

1 *Incipiunt consuetudines cisterciensium.* Here begins the Cistercian Customary.

The initial rubric is included for consideration because it situates our document in its context, the Cistercian Customary. In the three distinct redactions recoverable from the twelfth century, the organization of this complex compilation is always the same:

> 1. An account of the foundation of Cîteaux and the rise of the Cistercian Order;
> 2. The Charter of Charity together with a series of General Chapter statutes;
> 3. The *Ecclesiastica officia* or customary proper;
> 4. The usages of the lay brothers.

The pre-1147 redaction is recoverable from only one manuscript, Trent, Biblioteca comunale, MS 1711, dating, in all probability, from a bit before 1140. Characteristic of this redaction is that apart from the customary proper, all the introductory material (historical narrative, Charter of Charity, General Chapter statutes) are presented in 'mini-versions'. There is a *short* historical narrative (*Exordium Cistercii*), a *summary* version of the Charter of Charity, and an *abridged* version of selected General Chapter statutes arranged systematically or thematically rather than according to chronological order. Since the manuscript is lacunose at the end, nothing can be said about the lay brother usages, if there were any in this redaction.

The version of around 1147 as well as the further revision of around 1175/1180 have basically the same texts: the historical narrative is provided by the lengthy *Exordium Parvum*, which includes not only narrative, but a number of official documents reproduced virtually *in extenso*; the complete Charter of Charity appears along with a series of General Chapter statutes (*Instituta*) transcribed integrally and left in (presumably) chronological order; then comes the customary proper, the *Ecclesiastica Officia*; finally the lay brother usages. The difference between these two redactions lies simply in the fact that the texts of each constitutive section have evolved between around 1147 and 1180. There are further somewhat 'accidental' differences in many MSS, due to the laziness of scribes who balked at having to transcribe the lengthy introductory material characteristic of the redactions of around 1147 and 1180. So we find them occasionally cheating by substituting for the full-length *Exordium Parvum* and *Carta caritatis* with *Instituta*, the mini-version of the now out-of-date earlier recension.

Why, around 1147, was it found necessary to substitute a more ample series of documents for the abridged versions such as we find in Trent 1711? The following is a personal working hypothesis. In 1147, if not before, a revision of the usages was absolutely imperative in view of the extensive liturgical reform carried out shortly before under the aegis of Saint Bernard.[3] This would not have necessitated a change, however, in the basic shape of the

3. For a description of this reform and references to related material, see my article, 'The Origin and Early Evolution of the Cistercian Antiphonary: Reflections on Two Cistercian Chant Reforms,' in *The*

introductory material which preceded the customary proper; all these texts would have needed a certain amount of up-dating in order to keep them abreast of the Order's evolution. However, 1147 is also the year in which the Savigny congregation entered the Order along with some thirty houses in its filiation, as did Obazine with its several dependencies. Clearly, each cistercian community had to have a copy of the official customary and the essential legislation of the Order. Surely a practical means of providing newly aggregated communities, as well as other houses of the Order, with the updated essential documentation was to combine it all under one cover: the *Exordium Parvum* with the key official texts given *in extenso*, the current version of the *Carta caritatis* along with the updated *Instituta*, the latest revised version of the *Ecclesiastica officia*, and the new recension of the lay brothers' usages. A suitable account of the Order's early days was already conveniently at hand—an account of the foundation written and compiled by a group of the founders themselves. Though not originally written (as we shall see) to introduce the cistercian customary, it could serve this new purpose admirably well with only minor editorial adjustments.

SUPER EXORDIUM CISTERCIENSIS COENOBII
ABOUT THE BEGINNING OF THE MONASTERY OF CÎTEAUX

Whether this title is primitive or represents a later editorial insertion is an interesting question but need not detain us here.

NOS CISTERCIENSES
WE *CISTERCIANS*

I prefer the clumsier 'We of Cîteaux' or 'we [monks] of Cîteaux'. Father Van Damme writes[4] that the term *cistercienses* situates the composition of this 'Prologue' toward 1119. This seems a reasonable enough inference, based as it is on the brief but important study

---

Cistercian Spirit. Cistercian Studies 3 (Cistercian Publications, 1970) 190–223.

4. *PATC*, p. 54.

by abbé Jean Marilier. 'Le vocable *Novum Monasterium* dans les premiers documents cisterciens'. The author, after surveying all known references to the abbey during the first several decades of its existence, concludes that until just before 1119, the abbey was generally referred to as the New Monastery, *Novum monasterium*; the name *Cistercium* designated as a rule the site on which the monastery was built. Around 1119, when the 'New Monastery' was no longer so 'new', usage changed, and the name of the abbey became almost invariably *Cistercium*, 'Cîteaux'.[5] If *Nos cistercienses* would suggest a date of redaction closer to 1119 than to an earlier year—or so the argument runs. But Father Van Damme's inference doesn't necessarily follow. It was standard usage in the Middle Ages for communities of monks to be referred to, not by the abbey-name, but by the *place-name*—especially if there was only one abbey, or only one really important abbey, at a given location. The monks of St-Benoît-sur-Loire were *Floriacenses*, monks of St-Vaast were the *fratres Atrebatenses*, the brethren of Arras; the monks of S-Bénigne-de-Dijon were the *Divionenses*, the monks of Dijon; the monks of St-Martin at Tours were the *Turonenses*; and the monks of the New Monastery were *Cistercienses*. An excellent example of this usage can be found in the lengthy list of communities united to Cîteaux in an association of prayers and included under the date 2 November in the martyrology MS from Cîteaux now at Dijon, Bibliothèque municipale, MS 633 (formerly 378). the list reads in part: . . . *commemoratio . . . monachorum . . . senonensium* [St-Rémi de Sens, or possibly St-Colombe-lès-Sens], *et atrebaensium* [St-Vaast, Arras], *sagiensium* [St-Martin, Séez], *et ebrensium* [Notre-Dame d'Evron], *et cabilonensium* [St-Pierre, Châlons-sur-Saone], *et divionensium* [St-Bénigne, Dijon], *et cadiacensium* [St-Etienne, Cahors (I think)], and so on.[6] When the brethren of the New Monastery are referred to, then,

5. This is analogous to current american practice. Holy Spirit Abbey is usually referred to as 'Conyers', the name of the neighboring town; Mount Saint Mary Abbey is almost always 'Wrentham', and nearby Saint Joseph's Abbey is 'Spencer'; New Clairvaux is 'Vina'—all instances in which the name-place or site-name replaces the 'official' name.

6. Philippe Guignard (ed.), *Les monuments primitifs de la Règle cistercienne publiès d'après les manuscrits de l'Abbaye de Cîteaux* (Dijon: Darantière, 1878)

common usage would easily have admitted the form based on the place-name, that is, *cistercienses* ; and this designation would have been as appropriate in 1099 as in 1119.

The translation 'We Cistercians' automatically registers as 'We members of the Cistercian Order'; and such a usage would be correct only after the multiplication of foundations and the rise of a Cistercian Order in more or less the modern sense of the term 'Order'. I prefer a translation which, though a bit awkward, will not be anachronistic should the Prologue prove to date from a peirod earlier than the one proposed by J.-A. Lefèvre (around 1150) or even by Father Van Damme (towards 1119). Accordingly, I opt for: 'We of Cîteaux' or 'We [monks] of Cîteaux'.

3 *primi huius ecclesiae fundatores*—the first founders of the this church.

Father Bede Lackner translates this, and translates it correctly as, 'the original founders of this *monastery*'.[7] Though he is right in equating *ecclesia* with 'monastery', in monastic parlance the monastic community was the local church (*ecclesia*). The idea is rooted in the traditional understanding of the monastic community as continuator of the first community of believers at Jerusalem,[8] who by their renunciation of personal property and prayer in common and shared community life provided the paradigm for the authentic monastic community.[9] Instinctively, our Fathers referred to their communities as the 'church of Cîteaux', the 'church of Clairvaux'; and it would respect an extremely important ecclesiological dimension of the monastic community if we nowadays were to think of our communities as the 'church of Tre Fontane' or the 'church of Mount Saint Joseph' or the 'church of Gethsemani'. But what concerns us in the text under scrutiny is less the nuance attached to the term *ecclesiae* than the fact that the text purports to be formulated by the

---

393–394. A similar list is found in a twelfth-century addition to the martyrology described by Father Jean Leclercq, 'Textes et manuscrits à la Bibliothèque Vaticane', in *Analecta SOC* 15 (1959) 80.

7. L. J. Lekai, *The Cistercians. Ideals and Reality* (Kent State Press, 1977).

8. Acts 4:32–41.

9. *PATC*, p. 54.

first founders of the place. That they are speaking with authority is suggested by the fact that theirs is the first name in the opening formula. In medieval usage the order of names was important: the one which came first indicated which was 'superior', the writer or the recipient.[10] There is no doubt that the writers are aware of their privileged position, which is that of founders of the local monastery–church. To whom are they addressing themselves?

3 *successoribus nostris*—to our successors.

Curious! There is no mention here or elsewhere in the 'Prologue' of foundations or of communities founded from Cîteaux and organized as an 'Order'. There is not the slightest hint of any kind of geographical extension of Cîteaux. In the terms of the text, the materials which follow have been compiled for the sake of the 'successors' to the pioneer monks at Cîteaux, not for monks at houses founded from Cîteaux. The formula is quite parallel to Saint Stephen's *Epistola de observatione hymnorum*, addressed by Stephen to his successors: *Frater Stephanus Novi Monasterii minister secundus successoribus suis.*[11] This document has been dated to a period early in Stephen's abbacy, because he is concerned exclusively with the future use of his hymnal in the New Monastery, and there is no thought given to those foundations which were made in rapid succession from 1113 onwards. In much the same way the saint's *monitum* to his recension of the Bible—a text which can be dated with precision to 1109—is addressed simply to *et praesentibus et futuris servis Dei.*[12] On the hypothesis that the *Exordium Parvum* was written and compiled around 1151, one would have expected the forger to have the founding fathers address themselves, not to the future generations of the one 'new monastery', but to all the many houses which, already by 1119, looked to *Cistercium* as to *mater nostra*. How easy and how logical it would have been in 1151 to forge

10. Thus, when Saint Bernard frequently put his own name in second place in formulas of address, this was an act of real humility in those numerous instances when the person to whom he was writing ranked below himself in order of ecclesiastical or social preferment.

11. Edited in Marilier, *Chartes et documents concernant l'abbaye de Cîteaux, 1098–1182* (Rome: Editiones Cistercienses, 1961). See above, pages 78.

12. Edited in Marilier, *Chartes*, 56, with references to other editions.

an address similar to the opening of the Charter of Charity: . . .
*abbatibus et confratribus nostris monachis, quos per diversa loca Dei pietas
per nos miserrimos hominum sub regulari disciplina ordinauerit.*[13]

> 3 *stilo praesenti notificamus, quam canonice, quanta auctoritate, a
> quibus etiam personis, quibusque temporibus, coenobium et tenor
> vitae illorum exordium sumpserit.*

> we make it known, by this present writing, how canonically, by
> what great authority, by which persons, too, and by which stages,
> their monastery and manner of life had their beginning.

The terms are clearly technical, but also in part *liturgical*: *Quam
canonice*: 'how canonically', that is to say, in keeping with proper
canonical procedures, as the following documents will show; *quanta
auctoritate*: 'by what great authority' (not simply 'by what authority')—under the patronage of the Supreme Pontiff himself, as the
following documents will show; *a quibus etiam personis*: 'and even by
whom', that is to say, by those Molesmites who, together with their
abbot Robert, committed themselves to the great enterprise, as
the following documents will show; *quibusque temporibus*: 'at which
times' or 'by which stages', for this undertaking passed through a
number of successive stages from the inception of the plan to its
realization—as the following documents will show.

The noteworthy thing about this itemization of matters which
the following documents will demonstrate is less what *is* on the list
than what is *not* on the list. Not one word about the multiplication
of foundations; not one word about the Charter of Charity and
the organization of the administrative system (General Chapter and
visitations). It would be a puzzling oversight on the part of the
perpetrator of that fraud of 1151, that his Prologue summary of
matters to be treated stops short with the consolidation of the New
Monastery. Separate Chapters One through Fifteen from the rest of
the *Exordium Parvum* and you will have a perfect correspondence
between the matters enumerated for treatment in the 'Prologue'

13. *PATC*, p. 91.

and the contents of Chapter One through Fifteen. Chapter Fifteen treats of the basic principles of reform agreed on after the newly founded community had been assured to papal protection towards the end of 1100; everything beyond Chapter Fifteen falls outside the scope indicated by the 'Prologue'. My own personal working hypothesis is that the *Exordium Parvum* began with Chapter 1–15, written and compiled by Saint Stephen Harding, soon after his abbatial blessing in 1108 as part of his efforts to get a bit of order into the archives; that Abbot Stephen expanded his *opusculum* around 1119, when the New Monastery had given rise to a fast-growing Order—by way of addition, without re-writing the 'Prologue' or earlier chapters of the original version; and that the editorial revisions made when this expanded version was incorporated into the collection of consuetudinary material around 1147 were of a relatively minor sort.

On the *liturgical* resonance of this text, I shall touch only lightly, since it is the later section of the 'Prologue', lines 5–7, which really concerns me. Still, the liturgical cachet of the 'Prologue', 3, can be discerned (though but dimly), in the words: *primi huius ecclesiae fundatores* in combination with the phrase *a quibus etiam personis . . . coenobium et tenor vitae illorum exordium sumpserit*. Consider the classical collect for Saints Peter and Paul (June 29—a formula repeated several times in the ancient *Sacramentarium Veronense*, and probably dating from the fifth century: *. . . da ecclesiae tuae eorum in omnibus sequi praeceptum, per quos religionis sumpsit exordium*.[14] On the one hand, the founders of the church at Rome; on the other, the founders of the church at *Cistercium*; notice the parallel use of the phrase *sumere exordium* at the very end of the period, and the words *coenobium et tenor vitae* in the 'Prologue'. It would not have been far-fetched had the author written *quibusque temporibus religio illorum exordium sumpserit*, since *religio*, in a monastic context

14. No sacramentary of the Gregorian or Gelasian tradition is without this formula. For references to the more important representative MSS, see Father Jean Deshusses, *Le sacramentaire grégorien. Ses principales formes d'après les plus anciens manuscrits*. Coll. Spicilegium Friburgense 16 (Fribourg: Editions Universitaires, 1971) 245, second critical apparatus under n. 594.

almost always means 'monastic observance' and not 'religion' in the classical sense.

The author of a series of monastic statutes written for the Congregation of the Paraclete, and based in part on cistercian sources, for example, begins the paragraph on the sources of income with the frank avowal: *Religionis erat de cultu terrarum et labore vivere si possemus.*[15] 'It would be truly monastic for us to live off farming and our own work—if only we could!' Or again, take the lovely Saint Bernard collect authored by Innocent III, but now no longer in our sacramentary, probably because the meaning of the term *religio* was misunderstood. It reads in part: *Perfice quaesumus Domine pium in nobis sanctae religionis effectum.* Modern editions of our books have turned *effectum* into *affectum*; but as originally composed, the formula asks God to 'bring to perfection' the 'effect' or 'fruit' or 'result' of our 'holy monastic observance'—the exercises and observances which make up our monastic day. The hours of prayer, the work, the practice of silence, the fasting, the life of poverty and simplicity and loving service and humility—all these are meant to bear the kind of fruit so evident in the life and teaching of Saint Bernard. So the collect is not about 'a love of holy religion' or 'a love of holy interior devotion', but rather about our monastic observance coming to full flower as it did in the case of Bernard of Clairvaux, who had not yet arrived at the New Monastery (or so I think) when Abbot Stephen Harding, in the name of himself and his brethren, penned the 'Prologue' to the *Exordium Parvum*. My point here, however, is that *religio* in a monastic context is not much different from the expression *coenobium et tenor vitae* in the 'Prologue'. The Peter-and-Paul text refers to the founders of the church at Rome, through whom that Church received its *religio*; the 'Prologue' text, couched in similar terms, speaks of the founders of the church at Cîteaux, the men to whom future generations there will look as the source of their own monastic *tenor vitae*. In no way do I suggest that the parallel was intentional; but parallel it certainly is. Nor is there anything megalomaniac about the implicit equation between the

15. *Institutiones nostrae*, VII.3; M. Chrysogonus Waddell, ed., *The Paraclete Statutes: Institutiones Nostrae*, CLS 20 (1987) 11.

founders of the Church at Rome and the founders of the church at Cîteaux, between the *religio* of the christian community of Rome and the *coenobium et tenor vitae* of the monastic community of the New Monastery. All this simply indicates the basic understanding of monasticism in an ecclesiological perspective. The founding of the church at Cîteaux inserted us somehow into the archetypal event of the founding of the church of Rome. This is not, of course, *explicit* in the text; but it is, I suggest, a resonance given off by the text. The founding of the New Monastery is both historical event and theological happening.

We shall skim hurriedly over the next lines:

> *ut huius rei propalata sincera veritate, tenacius et locum*
> *et observantiam sanctae regulae in eo a nobis per Dei*
> *gratiam utcumque inchoatam ament*

so that, with the sincere truth of this matter spelled out
clearly, they may the more tenaciously love both the place
and the observance of the Holy Rule begun in it by us
through the grace of God, at least in some small way.

A few comments on this text will be included a bit later in some of the remarks about the final lines of the 'Prologue'.

> 5 *pro nobisque, qui pondus diei et*
> *aestus indefesse sustinuimus, orent;*

that they may pray for us, who have borne
untiredly the burden of the day and the heat.

Everyone will easily recognize the reference to Mt 20:12, where the workers who arrive early in the vineyard complain that the latecomers are receiving the same wages paid themselves, who have 'borne the burden of the day and the heat'. But where Matthew wrote *portavimus*, our author has written *indefesse sustinuimus*. *Sustinere* is a very biblical word, as a glance at any concordance easily verifies; and its use in Pauline writings especially is so characteristic that one might almost surmise it enjoyed something of a technical meaning. It is also a word likely to come spontaneously to any monk who has meditated long and hard on the Instruments of Good Works and the Degrees of Humility in the Rule of Benedict: *Persecutionem pro iustitia* sustinens (RB 4.33); . . . *quibuslibet irrogatis iniuriis tacite conscientia patientia amplectatur et* **sustinens** *non lassescat* . . . (RB 7.38); *et ostendens fidelem pro Domino uniuersa, etiam contraria,* **sustinere** *debere, dicit ex persona sufferentium* . . . (RB 7.38). The substitution of *indefesse sustinuimus* for the biblical *portavimus* could add a special intensity to the image of bearing with 'the burden of the day and the heat'—though it would force the facts to say that this is really the case.

> *in arta et angusta via quam regula demonstrat,*
> *usque ad exhalationem spiritus desudent*

> so that they may toil away in the strait and narrow way
> which the Rule shows, up to their very last breath

. . . *via quam regula demonstrat*: the only passage in the Rule where the verb *demonstrare* is linked with *via* is in the Prologue, 20: *Ecce pietate sua* demonstrat *nobis Dominus* viam *vitae*. But here it is the Lord, rather than the Rule, who points out the way of life. It is symptomatic of our author's frame of reference that he can quite unconsciously interchange 'Rule' for 'Lord'. In other passages of the Rule, the road-image is combined with the strait-and-narrow terminology, as in the Prologue, 48: *via salutis, quae non est nisi angusto initia incipienda*; or in 5.11: *Ideo angustam viam arripiunt, unde Dominus ait: Angusta via est, quae ducit ad vitam*. The biblical reference is, of course, to the 'strait and narrow way' of Mt 7:14. It would be interesting to dwell on the import of the phrase, *Quam angusta porta et arta via est quae ducit ad vitam*. The term *arta* (or *arcta*) was the preferred term used by the early Cistercians in discussing the relative merits of different observances. The *artior via* or *arctio observantia* carried with it a reference to Our Lord's *logion* about the 'strait and narrow way' which leads to life. That way of life was *artior* which was more perfectly conformed to the gospel ideal. There is all the difference in the world between *artior* in the twelfth century and *Etroite Observance* in the seventeenth century and *Strictioris Observantiae* in the twentieth century; it is the difference between what is more perfectly in accord with the Gospel and what is simply 'tougher'.

The real focus of interest for us lies in the phrase: *usque ad exhalationem spiritus desudent*, 'so that they may toil away . . . up to their very last breath'. 'Very last breath' falls short of *usque ad exhalationem spiritus*. *Desudare* suggests a particularly energetic kind of toiling: one can almost see the sweat and hear the labored breathing of the workmen. But the expression *exhalatio spiritus* floods this passage with new light. We might think of Lam 2:12, but this text reads *exhalarent animas*, not *exhalarent spiritus*. Several instances of classical usage can be found by consulting any reasonably large Latin lexicon and provide examples of *exhalare animam*. We would be wrong, too, to look to the *tradidit spiritum* or *emisit spiritum* or *exspiravit* of the passion narratives. More than one scribe has been puzzled by the expression, and has substituted *exaltationem spiritus*. I remember the joy with which Father Louis [Thomas Merton] once pounced on this variant: the early Cistercians were encouraged to toil even unto . . . ***ecstasy! mystical rapture!*** Alas, the authentic reading is about toiling, rather, to the last, the very last gasp.

The Mass readings for Septuagesima Sunday in the classic Vatican I lectionary had been chosen with a view to the approaching beginning of Lent, which was just over the horizon. The newly inscribed catechumens listened on that Sunday to Saint Paul describing the race which they themselves were now about to run: 'Know you not that they that run in a race, all run indeed, but one receiveth the prize? . . .' (1 Cor 9:24–10:51). The gospel appointed for the day was similarly appropriate: the parable of the workers in the vineyard (Mt 20:1–16). Monks heard this pericope not only at Mass, but at the Night Office as well, where the third nocturn featured Pope Saint Gregory's homily on the gospel-parable;[16] and in general practice any section of the patristic homily not finished in church was read later the same day in refectory. Gregory's commentary on this parable was almost as standard Septuagesima fare as the

16. *PATC*, p. 55.

periscope on which it is based. Paul the Deacon had inserted it into his collection of homilies in the late eighth century;[17] and it is to be found not only in the Order's manuscript compiled around 1175/1180 (Dijon 114),[18] but also in cistercian MSS of a much earlier period.[19] The Cistercians divided the homily in such a way that the last words of the last reading were: . . . *spiritum exhalavit vitae*. Here we have it, then: *spiritum* construed with *exhalavit*, and in all but immediate juxtaposition to the 'burden of the day and the heat' of the previous line of the 'Prologue', where the link with the parable of the workers in the vineyard in incontrovertible.

In his homily, Gregory begins by explaining the parable in its ecclesial application as relating to the various stages of salvation history:

> This householder [God] sends workers to his vineyard in the morning, at the third, sixth, ninth and eleventh hours, because from the beginning of the world to the end he has not failed to send teachers to instruct the faithful. The morning of the world was from Adam until Noah: the third hour from Noah to Abraham: the sixth from Abraham to Moses: the ninth from Moses to the coming of Jesus Christ: and the eleventh from the coming of Christ until the end of the world.[20]

After this comes the 'moral' interpretation, the application of the parable to the personal life of the individual believer; and here Gregory states that

17. See Father Réginald Grégoire, *Les homéliaires du Moyen Age. Inventaire et analyse des manuscrits.* Rerum Ecclesiasticarum Documenta. Series Maior, Fontes VI (Rome: Herder, 1966) p. 87, n. 69.

18. Folio 24r-v.

19. Troyes, Bibl. mun., MS 869, pre-1147 Night Office lectionary from Clairvaux; MS 394, winter season Night Office lectionary, perhaps from Igny, also pre-1147; Berlin, Staatsbibliothek of the Prüssischer Kulturbesitz, MS lat. in oct. 402, the oldest extant cistercian breviary-MS, dating from around 1132.

20. Translation from Nora Burke (trans.), *Pope Saint Gregory the Great. Parables of the Gospel* (Chicago-Dublin-London: Scepter, 1960) 24.

> We may also apply these diverse hours to the different
> stages in the life of every man . . . As some are drawn to
> a good life in childhood, others in adolescence, others
> in youth, others in old age and some in decrepitude, it
> is as if the laborers were summoned at differing hours to
> the vineyard.[21]

Though individuals answer the call to work at differing stages of
their lives, all receive the same wage. The scriptural example of the
'eleventh-hour' laborer is the thief 'who professed God upon the
cross, and in the next moment breathed forth his spirit all but in
mid-sentence': *et pene enim voce sententiae* spiritum exhalavit *vitae*.[22]

Clearly, then, the line we are examining from the 'Prologue'
to the *Exordium Parvum* is resonant with echoes of the parable of
the workers in the vineyard as exegeted by Pope Saint Gregory
the Great. The author of the 'Prologue' is suggesting that the early
comers to the New Monastery are the founders of the church,
nos cistercienses, primi huius ecclesiae fundatores; and that, for their
successors who come after them to work in this same vineyard
of the Lord, it will always be the 'eleventh hour', the period after
the definitive beginning and foundation. But eleventh hour though
it is, the latter-day brethren of the New Monastery should be
like the good thief who, though a latecomer to belief in Christ,
nevertheless expended his whole being in his profession of faith
usque ad exhalationem spiritus vitae.

So our author is drawing together ideas from two different sections of Gregory's homily. Note the implicit ecclesiological dimension of this borrowed material. The vineyard, Gregory tells us, is the
'universal Church', *universalis Ecclesia*, which has existed, as he saw
it, from the morning of the world and has passed through various
stages between the first hour and the present eleventh hour. The
New Monastery is also a church, and it too has passed through
similar stages: *a quibus etiam personis, quibusque temporibus*.

In brief, the 'Prologue' to the *Exordium Parvum* is best understood
at depth not so much by reference to the parable of the workers in

21. *Ibid.*, 25.
22. PL 76:1156A.

178

the vineyard as to the parable of the workers *as commented on* by Pope Saint Gregory. The meaning of the text is clear even if we fail to grasp a single one of the images and implicit allusions to Scripture, liturgy, and the Rule; but if we do manage to catch the resonances given off by the text, our understanding of it will be deeper and richer.

Only one more line of the 'Prologue' remains, and a crucially important line it is.

quatinus deposita carnis sarcina
in requie sempiterna feliciter pausent. Amen.

until the time when, having laid down the burden of the flesh,
they may repose happily in everlasting rest. Amen.

To render *quatinus* as another 'so- that' purpose clause misses the nuance proper to this conjunction in this context. The newcomers to the New Monastery are not being exhorted to 'labor . . . so that they may repose', but are being urged to 'keep on toiling away *until the time comes when* they may repose'. We return to *quatinus* in a moment.

Father Van Damme gives an interesting note on the word *sarcina*. It is rare, he says, in the singular, and is not to be found in either Rule or Bible. It is chiefly classical poets (Horace and Ovid) who use it, though Saint Jerome does use the expression *sarcina carnis abiecta* in the *Vita Pauli* 12 and in *Epistula* 41.10.[23] I've come across the word fairly often, and in the singular, in Saint Gregory's *Moralia in Job*; and Saint Augustine uses the word (also in the singular) so constantly with reference to the burden of the episcopal office and the burden of our fleshly condition that Maurice Joujon was able to devote an entire article to '*Sarcina*. Un mot cher à l'évêque d'Hippone';[24] and Frederick Van der Meer thought it so characteristic of Augustine

23. *PATC*, p. 55.
24. In *Recherches de science religieuse* 43 (1955) 258–262.

that he uses *Sarcina Episcopatus* as one of the headings in his great book, *Augustine the Bishop*.[25]

In the context of our 'Prologue', however, it is not Jerome, or Gregory, or Augustine who will help us, but Cassian.

In the homily by Gregory already mentioned briefly, the sentence ending with *spiritum exhalavit vitae* is followed by the remark that the good thief, even before Peter, was brought by the Lord into the repose of Paradise: *ad paradisi requiem . . . latronem . . . perduxit*.[26] The ascetic toil *usque ad exhalationem spiritus* on the strait and narrow way pointed out by the Rule is meant to lead to *requies*; and here the author of the 'Prologue', with *requies* as his point of transition, moves from Gregory to Cassian.

The twenty-fourth and final *Conference* of Cassian is devoted to Abba Abraham's discourse *De mortificatione*—though, as so often happens with the *Conferences*, the content of the discussion goes far beyond what the title suggests. The text which here concerns us occurs towards the end of the conference. In Chapter XXII, Germanus asks how Our Lord can say that his yoke is sweet and his burden light (Mt 11:30) when we know from other passages of Holy Writ that the life of discipleship means hardship and even persecution. We should note here that the saying of Christ which here provides the point of reference for the whole discussion comes at the end of the Lord's invitation to enter into his own rest: 'Come to me, all you that labor and are burdened, and I will refresh you. Take my yoke upon you, and learn from me, because I am meek and humble of heart: and you will find rest (*requiem*) for your souls'.

It is impossible to trace here Abba Abraham's presentation of the monastic program in which fidelity to the toilsome labor of the ascetical life leads ultimately to an experiential tasting of the goodness of the Lord in a state of perfect rest. In Chapter XXV of this Conference, Abba Abraham is talking about the same *arta et angusta via* as our 'Prologue'; this is the *via regia*, the royal way

25. F. Van der Meer, *Augustine the Bishop. The Life and Work of a Father of the Church* (trans. B. Battershaw and G. R. Lamb) (London-New York: Sheed and Ward, 1961) 14.
26. PL 76:1156A.

which admits of not the slightest detour to left or right, but leads
straight to the Kingdom. Of itself, it is *suavis et levis*, even though
we, because of our sinful condition, may perceive it as *dura et aspera*
(and here we recognize the line from the Rule, 58.8: the *dura et
aspera per quae itur ad Deum*). But let the brethren continue on their
weary way along this royal road; for the time will come when,
*iam quodammodo terrenarum passionum sarcinam deponentes non laborem,
sed requiem animabus suis Domino praestante repperient;*[27] 'now, laying
down, so to speak, the burden of earthly passions, they will find, at
the Lord's bestowal, not toil, but rest for their souls'. The essential
combination of the three key words of the Prologue-text: *deponere*
and *sarcina* (in the singular) and *requies* are all here. But there is more.

Any monk reading the lines of Cassian would automatically
think of the great prayer from the formulary for monastic profession which, by the twelfth century, was in general usage in the
monastic worlds of Cluny and Cîteaux: *Domine Iesu Christe, qui es
via....* [28] Central to this prayer is the Lord's *vox invitationis*, his
'voice of invitation', urging us: 'Come to me, all you who labor and
are burdened, and I will give you rest'. The prayer continues with
the request that this *vox invitationis* may grow stronger and stronger
in the heart of the monastic neophyte, until the time comes when,
casting off the burden of sin, he may taste the Lord's goodness and
receive refreshment and nourishment from the Lord. At this point
our *quatinus* of the 'Prologue', is important, for it polishes off the
terminological parallels between Cassian, the profession prayer, and
the 'Prologue':

PRAYER: *quatenus peccatorum onera deponens*
'PROLOGUE': *quatinus deposita carnis sarcina*
CASSIAN: *terrenarum passionum sarcinam deponentes*

27. Text as edited by Father E. Pichéry, though it reproduces the version
established by Petschenig for the *CSEL* edition; in *Jean Cassien. Conférences*,
T. III. Sources chrétiennes 64 (Paris: Cerf, 1959) 198.
28. See my article, 'A Letter to Brother Aidan about the Cistercian
Prayers for the Blessing of a Monk', in *Liturgy O.C.S.O.* 12/2 (1978)
93–130, with special reference to pp. 116–122.

In our context, *onus peccatorum, carnis sarcina,* and *terrenarum passionum sarcina* come to the same difference: our sinful human condition. And could it be that our author, who had taken part in all too many and too frequent burials at the New Monastery, was a bit influenced by the prayer in the ancient monastic ritual, *Deus apud quem mortuorum spiritus vivunt et in quo electorum animae **deposito carnis onere** pleno felicitate laetantur . . . ?*[29]

The final words of the 'Prologue' seem to be the utterance of someone who may have had no intention of referring explicitly to any particular text, but whose phraseology was nonetheless conditioned by familiarity with Mt 11:30, Cassian's *Conference* XXIV, the monastic profession prayer, and (I tentatively suggest) the ritual prayers for the burial of a monk. For the comfort of those of us for whom 'last gasp' is a sorry come-down from 'exaltation of the spirit', we may note that the point of arrival here in the final line includes everything and more than would have been expressed by *exaltatio spiritus.*

A collect for Saints Peter and Paul, a gospel parable exegeted by Saint Gregory the Great, Cassian, and a profession prayer: all seem to have combined to influence to an extent impossible accurately to measure the diction and even content of the 'Prologue' of the *Exordium Parvum.* But the directness of an author's allusions is sometimes toned down in part by an overriding concern for literary elegance. For example, a few lines back I suggested, without attaching to much importance to it, the vague possibility that our author may have had in mind the prayer *Deus apud quem,* which has not only *deposito carnis onere,* but also *felicitate* as the second last word of the phrase, exactly where *feliciter* occurs in the 'Prologue'. The obvious objection is: if the author really had the burial prayer floating around in his subconscious, he would have written: *quatinus deposita carnis sarcina, in requie sempiterna feliciter **laetentur*** to preserve the parallelism with the burial prayer. But I answer: Impossible! This is a Prologue, and the writers of Prologues are particularly finicky

29. The version in the Cistercian *Rituale* of 1689 is faithful to the early MS-version; see the modern re-edition, *Rituale Cisterciense* (Belgium: Westmalle, 1949) Lib. V, Cap. IX. *Quo ordine efferatur ad tumulum,* p. 221.

about literary spit and polish. Here our author is obviously taking pains with his rhyming phrase endings, as Father Van Damme points out in his appended note:[30]

> ut . . . locum et observantiam . . . *ament,*
> pro nobisque . . . *orent;*
> in arta et angusta via . . . *desudent,*
> quatinus . . . in requie . . . *pausent.*

To break the rhyme scheme by ending the 'Prologue' with *laetentur* would be like substituting a b-minor chord for the final chord of Bach's 'Saint Anne' Fugue in E-flat Major. The link with the burial prayer is much too tenuous to be urged; but I think it worth while to make the point that literary allusions of a vague sort, as well as direct citations of an obvious sort, are sometimes modified in points of detail in the interests of good style and literary effect.

In scrutinizing our text for fine points which might otherwise escape us, we run the risk of missing the main message of the text. J.-A. Lefevre, followed by Father Louis Lekai in his classic *The Cistercians. Ideals and Reality,*[31] noted the emphasis in the 'Prologue' attached to the words *quam canonice, quanta auctoritate.* If the *Exordium Parvum* is concerned to demonstrate the canonicity of the foundation of the New Monastery, the implication is, obviously, that there was something 'rotten in the state of Denmark'. Lekai, like his belgian mentor, concludes that, the author of the *Exordium Parvum*

> turned out not to have been Abbot Stephen [Harding], but a member of Saint Bernard's generation who had published it some time after Stephen's death in 1134. It was written as a Cistercian 'white paper' to defend the legitimate nature of Cîteaux's foundation against the

30. *PATC,* p. 55.
31. The documentation is used extensively in the chapter, 'The Fundamentals of Cistercian Reform', pp. 21–32, as well as in the preceding chapter, 'From Molesme to Cîteaux', pp. 11–20. As he remarks in the Bibliographical Notes to Ch. 3, pp. 407–408, 'The views expressed in this chapter on the *Exordium parvum* are based on Lefevre's research'.

charges of the Cluniac 'Black Monks' who had argued that the New Monastery had been established without due canonical formalities. With the intention of proving 'how canonically' the disputed action had been carried out, the author assembled and transcribed a number of documents. . . . [32]

But if we take the 'Prologue' as it stands, the account of the foundation of the New Monastery, with all the details about its canonical basis, sponsorship by highly placed persons, personnel, and the stages in the unfolding of the enterprise, seems intended, not as an answer to hostile critics, but:

> 1– to deepen the love of monks to come for their monastery and the way of life established there by the founders;
>
> 2– to ensure a communion of prayer linking future generations of New Monastery monks with the first-generation founders;
>
> 3– to encourage later generations to toil energetically to their last gasp in this challenging program of monastic life.

The structure of the 'Prologue' is clear:

WHO?	*Nos cistercienses*
WHAT?	*successoribus . . . notificamus*
WHY?	**ut** *. . . ament,*
	orent,
	desudent,
	pausent.

But according to Lefevre and company, the discerning critic should come up with a quite different analysis:

WHO?	We founders [= forger]
WHAT?	provide our critics with documentary evidence

32. Lekai, *The Cistercians*, 22.

WHY?   to prove the legality of our founding of Cîteaux.

Our 'forger' could, of course, be diabolically clever. He could be pretending to be compiling a monastic testament for future generations while really meaning it to be used for self-defense against hostile criticism. My impression, however, is that twelfth-century polemicists were generally a bit less subtle in their strategy. When Saint Bernard wishes to address himself to the problem of White Monk versus Black Monk, he does so directly in the *Apologia* and in his correspondence with Peter the Venerable. Critics of Cîteaux were for their part just as direct, lamentably direct. Had the rebuttal of critics been the real intent of the compiler and author of the *Exordium Parvum*, he would have expressed this in the *ut*-clause which states the purpose of material which follows. No matter who wrote the text, and no matter what the real purpose of it, the 'Prologue' in its present form is a unique witness to the communion the Cistercian Fathers wished to ensure between themselves and future generations of monks. Nine-hundred years later they are still speaking to us in the 'Prologue' and throughout the other sections of the *Exordium Parvum*.

We can, of course, read the *Exordium Parvum* as a political pamphlet directed against hostile critics and written with explicit intent to cover up the embarrassing irregularities attendant on the foundation of the New Monastery. Or we can read it as a narrative addressed by our Fathers to ourselves for the purpose of deepening our love for the rule and our particular monastic tradition, in order to unite us with themselves in a communion of gratitude and prayer, and in order to encourage us as we travel our own sometimes toilsome way to the heavenly kingdom.

If the author of the 'Prologue' was really writing sometime around 1151, his pious fraud bears the stamp of genius. For the style of the 'Prologue' is precisely the style of the letter written by Saint Stephen Harding to his brethren of Sherborne, England, shortly before his death.[33] In both texts we find the same avoidance of direct

---

33. For an edition of the text with references to other versions, see J. Marilier, *Chartes*, p. 91; and above 88-89.

citation; the same technique of combining vague biblical, patristic, and liturgical allusions to give the main affirmations a richer dimension; the same concern for literary agreeableness; the same ability to say more, with the help of allusions, than most twelfth-century stylists were able to say in pages of explicit statement; and the same love of and enthusiasm for the monastic way of life. These are, you may counter, characteristics common to many twelfth-century cistercian and non-cistercian writers. But compare this 'Prologue' or the letter to the brothers at Sherborne to letters by Abelard or Peter of Celle or Bernard of Clairvaux or Peter the Venerable! I certainly write under correction; but my impression is that the 'forger', if forger he is, could write in Stephen Harding's style as well as Stephen himself could.

The First
Foundations

BEFORE THE CISTERCIAN abbeys had begun to flourish, Dom Stephen, the abbot, and his brothers ordained that, in order to avoid any cause of conflict between prelate and monks, no abbeys could ever be founded in the diocese of any bishop until he had recognized and confirmed the decree drawn up and confirmed between the cenobium of Cîteaux and the others which had issued from it. In this decree, therefore, the aforesaid brothers, taking precautions against the future shipwreck of their mutual peace, explained and determined and left to their posterity, by what pledge, or in what manner, indeed with what charity, their monks in abbeys in various parts of the world, though separated in body, could in mind be indissolubly bonded together. They considered that this decree should be called the Charter of Charity because, averting all burdensome levying of any exactions, its legislation pursues only charity and the advantage of souls in all things divine and human.

The Charter of Charity

1113, the week of 18 May.
Monks from Cîteaux establish a new foundation at la Ferté, in the diocese of Chalon-sur-Saône:[1]

There was so great a number of brothers at Cîteaux that the supplies they had were not sufficient for all of them, nor could the place where they lived adequately support them. It pleased the abbot of the place, Stephen by name, and the other brothers to seek another place at which some of them might serve God devotedly and according to the Rule, separated from the others in body, though not in spirit. While the abbot was diligently and doggedly searching for such a place, the undertaking came to the ears of Lord Walter, bishop of Chalons, and of the canons of that same city, and to the ears of the two counts, Savery and William, and of other highborn men. Rejoicing greatly and surveying their lands in the area, by God's will, they discovered the perfect spot for the monks to serve God and live according to the Rule. . . .

1114, 30 or 31 May.
Monks from Cîteaux establish a second foundation at Pontigny, in the diocese of Auxerre:[2]

Since by the mercy and boundless goodness of God the new monastery, that is Cîteaux, built in Burgundy is flourishing in the discipline of the Rule and expanding in the abundant throng of monks, a certain priest named Ansius, more than passably graced by true religion, who lived in the region of Auxerre, petitioned Dom Stephen, abbot of the New Monastery and the monks of his place to establish an abbey in his area, which is called Pontigny, by sending monks and an abbot there. . . . Then Dom abbot Stephen and Ansius

1. Marilier, item 42, pp. 65–66. The full text appears in *Gallia Christiana* 4:1019–1020.
2. Marilier, item 43, p. 66. Full text in T. Hümpfner, *Exordium Cistercii cum Summa Cartae Caritatis et fundatio primarium quattuor filiarum Cistercii* (Kapisztrán Nyomda, Vác., 1932) 19–21.

the priest, coming laid their case for the establishment of an abbey in the aforesaid place before bishop Humbald of blessed memory. . . . And with the assent and on the authority of the lord bishop Humbald and of the entire chapter of his church and of the reverend priest Ansius, the lord abbot Stephen accepted the Church at Pontigny for the establishment of an abbey there. . . .

1115, 25 June.
Monks from Cîteaux make a third foundation at Clairvaux, in the diocese of Langres:[3]

> God put it into the heart of Abbot Stephen to send out his brothers to build a new house at Clairvaux. As they were about to leave, he appointed Dom Bernard as their abbot, much to their amazement. For they were mature, hardy men in monastic life as previously in the world, and they flinched at Bernard's tender, young age, his physical frailty, and his limited experience in external business.
>
> Now Clairvaux was a place in the diocese of Langres, not far from the river Aube. It was a longstanding den of thieves and had formerly been called Wormwood Vale, either with reference to its lush growth of absinth or to the anguish of those who had fallen into the robbers' clutches there. There, in that place of horror and vast loneliness, these men of virtue settled down to make of that robbers' den a temple of God and a house of prayer.

1115.
Monks of Cîteaux make a fourth foundation at Morimond, also in the diocese of Langres:[4]

> First a layman named John, a disciplined man both in dress and in spirit, requested and received the site of Morimond from

3. William of Saint Thierry, *The First Life of Saint Bernard,* 125; PL 185:211.
4. Marilier, item 45, p. 67. *Gallia Christiana* 4:149.

Lord Odolric of Acrimont and Adeline, his most noble wife. Then this same John approached Robert, at the time ordinary of Langres, and having received his blessing and permission, by my intervention, faithfully and to the best of his ability built the place up. . . . After the death of the ordinary, by the leave of Josserand, who succeeded Robert in the bishopric, and on the advice moreover of Lord Odolric, the aforesaid John offered the place he had been given to the abbot and chapter of the New Monastery and granted it to them for the better amendment of life. And abbot Stephen of the New Monastery, coming to visit, accepted the site from Odolric and his wife and from the bishop and chapter of Langres. . . . And he created as abbot in that place a highly respected man named Arnold,[5] admonishing the monks faithfully to observe the Rule of blessed Benedict which they had pledged.

1124.

Abbot Bernard of Clairvaux[6] on the relationship of abbots of daughter houses to their Abbot-Father[7] and monks to their abbots under the Rule:

All else aside, there are two things handed down to us who dwell in monasteries for special observance. One is submission to the abbot, the other is stability within our monastery. And these two are to be observed in such a way that there is no conflict between them. That is to say, we should not be led by our stability to scorn subjection to the abbot, or by our subjection to the abbot to lose stability. Furthermore, if you

5. Arnold later left his post, intent on going on pilgrimage to the Holy Land. By acting without first consulting Stephen—or anyone else apparently—he precipitated a crisis in the Order. See the next extract, Bernard's letter to one of the monks who accompanied him. In the event, Arnold died within a year without ever having left Europe.

6. Bernard of Clairvaux, Letter 7, to Adam, one of the monks who had accompanied Abbot Arnold when he left Morimond.

7. The abbot of the monastery from which the abbot's house was founded. In Latin the term is *pater abbas*; in modern usage, the term is *Father Immediate.*

abominate someone who, although persevering in stability yet ignores the commands of his abbot, can you wonder if I censure the obedience you adduce as the cause or occasion of your losing stability by leaving your monastery? Especially as in our regular profession while stability is explicitly promised there is no mention at all of it being subject to the abbot.

But perhaps you will ask how I reconcile the stability I confirmed at Cîteaux with living elsewhere. I answer that while it is true that I was professed a monk of Cîteaux in that place and was sent by the abbot to live where I do, yet I was sent in peace, without any scandal or discord, according to the customs and common observance of our Order. Therefore so long as I persevere in the same peace and concord wherein I was sent, so long as I stand fast in unity, I am not preferring my private judgement to the common observance. I am remaining quietly and obediently where I was put. I say my conscience is at peace because I have not broken the bond of unity, because I have not left the firm ground of peace. And if under obedience I am absent in body from Cîteaux, yet by a fellow devotion, by a life in all things the same, I am always there in spirit. But the day on which I begin to live by other rules (which God forbid!) and other habits, to keep other observances, to introduce new things and follow different customs, on that day I shall no longer believe I keep my promise of stability. I say, therefore, that the abbot is to be obeyed in all things, but according to the tenor of our profession. You who were professed according to the Rule of Saint Benedict, when you promised obedience, you promised as well stability. So if you should be obedient, but not stable, by offending in one, you offend in all, and if in all, then also in obedience.

Do you now see the force of your vow of obedience? That it cannot, in fact, suffice to excuse the transgression of stability, not even having the force to support itself. We make our professions solemnly and according to Rule in the presence of the abbot, but only in his presence, not at his pleasure.

The abbot witnesses, but does not dictate the profession. He is there to help, not to hinder, its fulfilment. He is there to punish, not to instigate, infringement. What then? Do I leave in his hands what I have confirmed by my mouth and hand before God and his saints, knowing from the Rule that if every I act otherwise I will be condemned by Him whom I mock? If my abbot, or even an angel from heaven, should command what is contrary to this, I shall boldly excuse myself from an obedience that I know would render me a transgressor of my vow and a perjurer before God. I know from Scripture that out of my own mouth I shall be justified and condemned, because 'the mouth that speaks lies kills the soul' and because we chant before God, 'you will destroy all those who speak a lie' and because 'Everyone shall bear his own burden' and 'Everyone of us shall render an account of himself to God. Were it otherwise, how could I dare to sing before God: 'I will render to thee the vows my lips have uttered'? It is the duty of my abbot to consider how he may best follow the explicit direction of the Rule that 'he should maintain the present rule in every particular'. In the same way it is also laid down in the Rule as a general principle from which no one may be excused: 'Let all follow the Rule as their guide, and from it let no one rashly turn aside'. And I have determined to follow my abbot always and everywhere, providing that he never by his teaching departs from the Rule which, in his presence, I have vowed and determined to keep.

1133.

Stephen Harding resigns and a successor is elected

Having entered the monastery of Molesme, the venerable Stephen labored with utmost zeal and endeavored in every way to have the site and the Order of the Cistercians founded. And later—by God's ordaining—he was made its distinguished pastor and teacher. When he reached old age, he resigned his pastoral charge—for his eyes had grown dim and he could not see—to devote himself to the Lord alone. A man undeserving of the honor named Guy succeeded him, however, and like a whitened sepulchre, while not doing badly in external donations he was inwardly befouled with the rottenness of vice. When at the very outset of his promotion to office, he received the brothers' profession in the usual manner, the servant of God Stephen saw an impure spirit come over him and enter his mouth. Hardly a month had passed until—by God's revelation—his impurity was laid bare and the misbegotten transplant, which the heavenly Father had not set in place, was eradicated from God's paradise.[8]

The Cistercian Order at the End of Stephen's Life

When [Alberic] died, Stephen, an Englishman by birth, a man of great monastic fervor and wisdom, succeeded him. And, brilliantly outstanding in his teaching and his holy deeds, he held the office more than twenty-four years and in his day the monastery in the wilderness grew many times over. While he was still alive and at his order, abbot Guy of Trois Fontaines,[9] was elected [as next abbot] and not long afterwards his venerable predecessor died. Guy, however, disgracefully discharged the office taken over from his father and after two years he resigned in disgrace. Then Reginald, the young son of Count Milo of Bar-sur-Seine, was elected and was consecrated abbot by Walter, bishop of Chalons.

It is now almost thirty-seven years since abbot Robert, as was said, settled at Cîteaux[10] and in so short a time such a crowd of men have converged on it that from it sixty five abbeys have sprung up, all of them, with their abbots, subject to the governance of Cîteaux. They all do without trousers

---

8. Herbert of Clairvaux, *De miraculis* 2.24; PL 185:1333–1334.

9. Founded from Cîteaux in 1118 in the diocese of Chalon.

10. Orderic was, therefore, writing about 1135, shortly after Stephen's death in 1133.

and animal skins, abstain from flesh and fat, and by their many good deeds shine like lamps lighted in a dark place. At all times they maintain silence[11] and they use no dyed clothes. They work with their own hands and produce food and clothing for themselves. Every day, except Sunday, from mid-September to Easter, they fast.[12] They bar their gates and keep their quarters absolutely cloistered. They admit no monk of another church within their enclosure nor do they allow anyone to enter the chapel with them for Mass and other services. Many noble athletes and profound thinkers have flocked to them because of the novelty of their unique practices and, willingly embracing the unusual strictness, they chant hymns of joy to Christ. In bleak and wooded places they have built monasteries by their own labor and with skillful foresight have given the such holy names as House of God, Valley of Light, Good Mount, and Almonry[13] and many others of this kind, so that those who hear them are quickly stirred by the nectar of the name along to experience how much blessedness is denoted by so unusual a name.[14]

11. Cf RB 42.1.
12. RB 41.6.
13. Maison Dieu, Clairvaux, Bonmont, and L'Aumône
14. Orderic Vitalis, *The Ecclesiastical History*. This follows immediately the selections given above, pages 19–25, 26–27, and concludes Orderic's description of the Cistercians.

The Earliest Churches of the Cistercian Order

Jean Owens Schaefer

CISTERCIAN ARCHITECTURE has received considerable attention in the past quarter century. Much of this attention has been focused on the existence or non-existence of the 'Bernardine plan'.[1] As important as this debate is, it has led scholars to overlook the fact that there existed a good number of cistercian churches which were built before the purported imposition of this type-plan. A proper study of these pre-bernardine churches throughout Europe should offer significant contributions to the discussions of, on the one hand, the relationship between the early architecture of the Order and the local architectural environment and, on the other hand, the relationship between the early architecture of the Order and the local architectural environment and, on the other, of the spirituality of the movement at its beginnings.

One fragment of the question of pre-bernardine architecture shall be presented here, the issue of the earliest churches of the five founding monasteries in Burgundy: Cîteaux, La Ferté, Pontigny, Clairvaux and Morimond. To separate the architecture of these five houses from the other examples of early architecture is in many ways

---

1. Karl H. Esser, 'Die Ausgrabungen des romanischen Zisterzienserkirche Himmelrod als Beitrag zum Verständnis der frühen Zisterzienserarchitektur', *Das Münster* (1952) 221–223; *Idem*, 'Les Fouilles à Himmelrod et le plan bernardien', *Mélanges saint Bernard, XXIVᵉ Congrès de l'association bourguignonne* (1954) 311–315; François Bucher, *Nôtre-Dame de Bonmont und die ersten Zisterzienserabteien der Schweiz* (Bern, 1957); and Ingrid Swartling, 'Cistercian Abbey Churches in Sweden and the Bernardian Plan', *Nordisk medeltid: Konsthistoriska studier tillängnade Armin Tuulse, Stockholm Studies in the History of Art*, no. 13 (Uppsala, 1967) 193–198.

artificial. The justification for their special treatment rests in their special place within the Order and in the special character given these first foundations by the original leaders of the movement.

One aspect of the history of the founding of the Cistercian Order which has been brought into focus in recent years in the work of such scholars as Jean Leclercq and Louis Lekai[2] is the relation of Cîteaux and its founders to the eremetical movement of the late eleventh-century. The men who left the abbey of Molesme in 1098 to establish the 'New Monastery' and who guided it through its first perilous years had long experimented with the eremetic life. Saint Robert, the Order's founder, had lived with a small group of devout hermits in the forest of Colan and had joined with them in founding Molesme. Along with Alberic and Stephen Harding, he had retreated from Molesme to live a more isolated and ascetic life at a site known only as Vivicus. These three men, Robert, Alberic and Stephen, destined to become the key figures in early cistercian history, were among those signing a document of 1096–1097, encouraging the monks of Aulps in their experiment of combining the rigors of the hermit's life with a strict observance of the Rule of Saint Benedict.[3] It is proper, therefore, to see their 'New Monastery' as the last and most successful of their exercises at creating, in Leclercq's apt if unusual phrase, an 'eremetic community'.[4]

The earliest examples of cistercian ecclesiastic architecture, the first churches at Cîteaux, La Ferté, Pontigny, Clairvaux and Morimond, are given only the briefest mention in the documents and, since they were often of wood, no trace of them remains today. Because the remains are so scanty, it is essential, first, to present

2. Jean Leclercq, 'L'Erémitisme et les cisterciens', *L'Eremitismo in occidente nei secoli XI e XII* (Milan, 1965) 573–580; Idem, 'The Monastic Crisis of the Eleventh and Twelfth Centuries', *Cluniac Monasticism in the Central Middle Ages*, ed. Noreen Hunt (London, 1971) 217–237; Louis Lekai, 'Motives and Ideals of the Eleventh-Century Monastic Renewal', *The Cistercian Spirit*, ed. Basil Pennington (Cistercian Publications, 1970) 27–47; Idem, *The Cistercians: Ideals and Reality* (Kent, Ohio, 1977).

3. J.-A. Lefèvre, 'Que savons-nous du Cîteaux primitif?' *Revue d'histoire écclesiastique* 51 (1956) 19.

4. Leclercq, 'The Monastic Crisis', p. 226.

what documentary evidence we do possess concerning these earliest churches.

When Robert, Alberic, Stephen and their followers set out on their experiment, they retreated to a desolate site near Dijon, which was described in the traditional phrase as *locum horroris et vastae solitudinis, vepribus, et spinetis densum.*[5] In spite of this description, the site may have included among other structures a small oratory dedicated to the Virgin, which could have served as the very first chapel of the Cistercians.[6] In any case, soon after their arrival, the men set about to build a small wooden oratory of their own, in which to carry on the rites of the monastery. Of this building the *Exordium Parvum* says

> After they had cut down and removed the dense woods and thorny thickets, they began to construct a mona-stery . . . and with the aid of Lord Odo, the duke of Burgundy, they completed the wooden monastery.[7]

Manrique, in his *Annales* of 1642, refers to the building as 'a monastery built of sections of roughly squared trees'.[8] That is the extent of our knowledge of the first church built at Cîteaux.

The building which replaced the wooden oratory at Cîteaux (Fig. 1) was still standing in 1708 when it was described by Dom

5. Angelo Manrique, *Cisterciensium seu verius ecclesiasticorum annalium a conditio cistercio* (Lyon, 1642) 1:10, borrowing from Deut 32:10.

6. J. Marilier, 'Les Debuts de l'abbaye de Cîteaux', *Mémoires de la société pour l'histoire du droit et des institutions des anciens pays bourguignons, comtois, et romands*, 15 (1953) 120, n. 6.

7. *Exordium Parvum*, III, quoted in the translation of Lekai, *Cistercians*, p. 452. The Latin text reads: ' . . . nemoris et spinarum densitate precisa ac remota monasterium . . . construere ceperunt . . . . Tunc domnus Odo dux burgundie sancto fervore eorum delectatus. sancteque romane ecclesie prescripti legati litteris rogatus. Monasterium ligneum quod inceperunt de suis totum consummavit. Illosque inibi in omnibus necessariis diu procuravit. Et terris ac pecoribus abunde sublevavit.' Philippe Guignard, *Les Monuments primitifs de la règle cistercienne* (Dijon, 1878) 63.

8. Manrique, p. 10: 'monasterium de sectorum arborum male dolatis lignis fabricarunt'.

198

Martène and Dom Durand in their *Voyage littéraire*. The Benedictines said that

> it is one of the most venerable spots at Cîteaux for it was
> the sanctuary of the first monks and the church in which
> Bernard was received. The church was consecrated in
> 1106 by Gautier, bishop of Chalon. It was quite small,
> I do not believe it could be more than fifteen feet
> wide; the length is proportionate; the choir could be
> thirty feet. It is vaulted and very pretty. There are three
> windows in the sanctuary and two in the nave.[9]

We can draw from this description no conclusions on the precise
appearance of this little chapel;
but we are on relatively safe
grounds to say that it was small
and barrel-vaulted. From the plan
of Prinstet of 1702,[10] it appears
to be angular, and not internally
divided into bays.

From the example at Cîteaux,
the first buildings of each of the
succeeding foundations appear to
have been temporary in character, intended to serve the needs
of the small community and to be
replaced as growth required and
means permitted.

The first daughter-house of
Cîteaux was founded in 1113 and

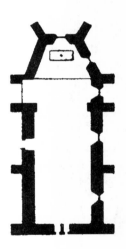

Figure 1. Cîteaux, consecrated
1106 (after Dimier, *Recueil des
plans des églises cisterciennes, II*)

9. My translation. Edmond Martène, *Voyage littéraire de deux religieux
bénédictins de la congrégation de saint-Maur. . . .* (Amsterdam, 1717) pp. 223–
224.

10. In the archives of the Côte-d'Or; published in Marcel Aubert,
L'Architecture cistercien en France (Paris, 1947) 1:109, where it is marked by
the letter 'M'.

called La Ferté. According to Janauschek, the founding party left Cîteaux on 16 May and arrived the following day at the new site; the church was dedicated on 18 May.[11] It has been inferred from this that the buildings were prepared in advance, either by an advance party of Cistercians or perhaps by a combination of monks and lay craftsmen.[12] The advanced preparation of the monastic buildings would be in keeping with a later statute of the General Chapter decreeing that new foundations could not be established until structures were available in which the regular life of the monastery could be maintained.[13] It is unfortunate that we have no information at all on the nature of these first buildings, whether of timber or stone; but they were replaced by larger churches and no accounts of them remain.

After the foundation of La Ferté, the number of monks in the Order continued to grow. Therefore, when Ansius, a hermit priest, asked to offer his oratory to the White Monks, Stephen Harding agreed to accept it. The Cistercians took formal possession of the site on 21 May 1114, and founded the third house, Pontigny.[14] The first chapel was dedicated to the Assumption of the Virgin, but no dedication date has been given for it. Its ruins were visited by Martène and Durand, who describe it only as being behind

11. Leopold Janauschek, *Originum cisterciensum* (1877; reprint Ridgewood, NJ, 1964) 1:3. See also [GCh IV] *Gallia Christiana* 4: col. 1019; Instr. col. 238, 240.

12. Archdale King, *Cîteaux and her Eldest Daughters* (London, 1954) pp. 107–108; and Philippe Erlanger, *Merveilles des châteaux de Bourgogne et de Franche-Comté* (Paris, 1969) pp. 36–37.

13. Guignard, p. 253. In the *Consuetudines*, cap. XII: 'Duodecim monachi cum abbate tertio decimo ad cenobia nova transmittantur: nec tamen illuc destinentur donec locus libris. domibus et necessariis aptetur. libris duntaxat missali. regula. libro usuum. psalterio. hymnario. collectaneo. lectionario. antiphonario. graduali domibusque oratorio. refectorio. dormitorio. cella hospitum et portarii. necessariis etiam temporalibus: ut et vivere et regulam ibidem statim valeant observare.'

14. Georges Fontaine, *Pontigny, abbaye cistercienne* (Paris, 1928) 4–5, citing the cartulary of Pontigny; see also GCh 12: col. 439–441.

the later church and 'small but pretty enough for its time'.[15] Although it was shown on the monastery plan drawn in 1760, there is nonetheless some confusion in later publications as to its shape (Fig. 2). The 1760 plan was reproduced by two authors, Chaillou des Barrès and Henry; both reproduce the plan as rectangular and without an apse.[16] Later authors have, however, discussed the chapel as apsidal.[17] We have no information whether the chapel was vaulted.

The founding of Clairvaux took place the following year.[18] The first task which faced Bernard and his companions was to erect

Figure 2. Pontigny I
(after Chaillou des Barrès)

the temporary buildings for the monastery. Both Vacandard, in his biography of Saint Bernard, and Paul Jeulin, in his architectural study of Clairvaux, refer to these buildings as 'a modest chapel and

15. Martène, p. 58.

16. Abbé Henry, *Histoire de l'abbaye de Pontigny* (Avallon, 1839); Chaillou des Barrès, 'L'Abbaye de Pontigny', *Annuaire historique du département de l'Yonne*, 1844.

17. Aubert, I: 153, n. 2; and Anselme Dimier, *Recueil des plans des églises cisterciennes* (Paris, 1949) 2: pl. 235. See Fontaine, p. 26, fig. 9, for a reproduction of the plan showing the small chapel without an apse; and p. 23 for a discussion of the inexactitudes of the eighteenth-century plan. For the fullest discussion of the earliest church at Pontigny, see Terryl Kinder, 'Some Observations on the Origins of Pontigny and Its First Church', *Cîteaux: Commentarii Cistercienses*, 31 (1980) 9–19.

18. GCh 4: col. 796. the earliest document of confirmation is dated 1121; GCh 4: Instr., col. 156.

fragile huts of wood.'[19] Manrique gives a fuller account of the early buildings.

> After the monks cleared away the thorn bushes by hand, . . . they prepared a dwelling place out of trees. It was of the kind that Molesme had formerly, and like those at the beginning of Cîteaux. Today the humble chapel still exists; [it is] about twenty feet long and fourteen wide, dedicated to the blessed Virgin. It was built in a few days, and it is believed to have served for the divine office for some time.[20]

As with the first church at Cîteaux, we can infer little about the exact nature of these wooden buildings. Since, in each case, they were meant for only thirteen men, it is reasonable that they were small. From Manrique's account, it would appear that they were simple but adequate, and that they were meant to be replaced with more permanent buildings.

The chapel which was built as the first permanent oratory in 1116 stood to the west of the present buildings, although there has been

19. Elphège Vacandard, *Vie de Saint Bernard* (Paris: 1910) 1:66–67; Paul Jeulin, 'Les Transformations topographiques et architecturales de l'abbaye de Clairvaux', *Mélanges saint Bernard* (1954) 325.

20. Manrique, p. 80: 'Tum dumeta fratrum manibus excisa, gratulantibus incolis, et crediderim etiam adiuuantibus, atque ex arbustis habitatio preparata, qualem Molismus olim, qualem Cistercium in suis primordiis habuit. . . . Extat hodieque Oratorium humile, longitudine ad viginti pedes, latitudine ad quatuordecim extensum, beatea Virginis sacrum quod paucis tunc diebus constructum, creditur divinis officiis inseruisse per tempus aliquod'.

There is a nagging concern that the chapel which Manrique describes here, a chapel which he seems to have visited, is in fact the same one discussed below. Since it is widely but falsely assumed that the chapel described on Milley's plan as *vetus monasterium* was of stone, it has been disassociated form the 'modest chapel of wood'. It is remotely possible that it is the same oratory visited by our informants in the sixteenth and seventeenth centuries. The dimensions given by Manrique, however, do not conform to the shape of the building on Milley's plan. See below.

202

some debate about the exact location.[21] The consensus is that the former monastery is represented on the plan of Dom Milley as the *monasterium vetus* and the *capella* (Fig. 3, nos. 12 and 13, and Fig. 4, nos. 16 and 17). Thanks to this plan,[22] we have an idea of the entire layout of a primitive cistercian monastery. The information of the plan can be augmented by two descriptions, one of the sixteenth-century, and one from the seventeenth. In 1517, the queen of Sicily made a visit to Clairvaux; and, in a letter resulting from that visit, the old monastery is described:

> Within the exclosure of Saint Bernard, at the entry gate is the room where Pope Eugene was received. This room is in a small garden; it is of wood, quite small and low, in the old fashion.
>
> After it comes the refectory, the length of which is between eighteen and twenty paces; it is very low and panelled. It is quite old. Above is the dormitory of equal size. At the top of the stairs is the chamber of Saint Bernard, which is very small. His bedstead, which is of wood and the head of stone, is close to the roof, where there is a window. Close to and adjoining this room is the old church, which is a chapel of wood, into which Saint Bernard could see through a window which was in his room. There is a small garden in front, and the entire thing is enclosed by a wall.[23]

The second account is from Dom Joseph Meglinger, a cistercian monk who journeyed to a meeting of the Chapter General in 1667:

> A single roof covers the church and the living quarters of the monks, and a simple ceiling separates the refectory

21. Philippe Guignard, 'Lettre . . . sur les reliques de saint Bernard et de saint Malachie et sur le premier emplacement de Clairvaux', in PL 185:1697–1714; Vacandard, 1:69; and Aubert, 1:13.

22. Published in Vacandard, 1:420. One complete set of the engravings is in Paris, Bibliothèque Nationale Estampes: Topographie de la France, Aube, Arrondissement Bar-sur-Aube, folios 27, 28, 29).

23. Didron, 'Un Grand Monastère au XVIe siècle', *Annales archéologiques* 3 (1845) pp. 236–237.

from the dormitory above; in the former there is only bare earth for the floor. The kitchen abuts the refectory; it is very small but sufficient. From there [i.e., the refectory], one climbs to the dormitory which is the same size as the refectory. Near the stairs is the cell of the mellifluous father, Saint Bernard; [it is] quite small, more like a dungeon than a room.

From there we descend to the oratory which is the very temple of poverty. The altar is as bare as Saint Bernard left it; above is a bad painting on wood of Christ on the cross. Outside of the choir . . . are altars, to the right, of Saint Lawrence, and, to the left, of Saint Benedict.[24]

From these descriptions and from the Milley plan, an image of this oratory begins to emerge. It was small and austere; it was square in plan, with an aisle running along all four sides of the undivided central space. It is usually assumed that these buildings, and the chapel in particular, were of stone.[25] However, the account of 1517 makes it quite clear that the latter was constructed of wood. We shall see that this is entirely consistent with the form of the chapel shown in the eighteenth-century plan and view.

Morimond, like Pontigny, was founded at the site of a hermit's dwelling. The original charter of foundation is lost, but a letter of confirmation, dated 1126, survives. It tells of a hermit Johannes who, in the episcopate of Robert, bishop of Langres, founded his oratory on land granted him by two nobles. Josserand, Robert's successor, asked him to offer his hermitage to the Cistercians and Johannes agreed. Late in 1115, the White Monks were installed.[26]

What, however, is known of 'Old Morimond'? Very little—only that, as Eydoux says: 'it was a place in which a hermit had built an

24. Henri Chabeuf, 'Voyage d'un délégue au chapitre générale de Cîteaux en 1667', *Mémoires de l'académie des sciences, arts et belles-lettres de Dijon* (1883–4) 314–317.

25. Aubert, 1:13–15; Jeulin, p. 326.

26. Aubert, 1:65; Janauschek, p. 5; and *Gallia Christiana* 4: Instrumenta 159.

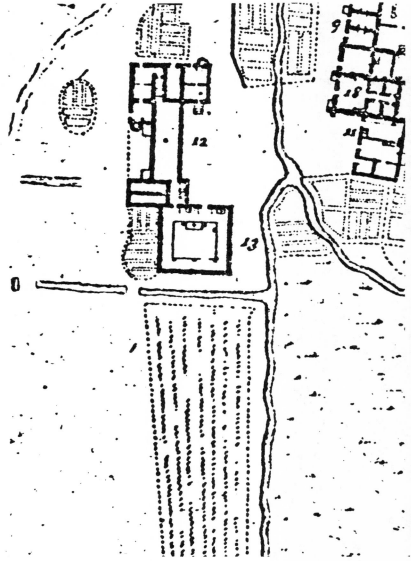

Figure 3. Clairvaux I: plan (after Milley)

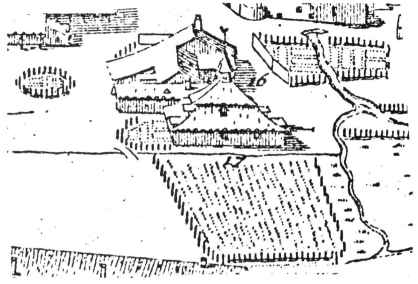

Figure 4. Clairvaux I: plan (after Milley)

oratory which was destined to become the first receptacle of the cistercian establishment.'[27]

An evaluation of these first churches on the basis of these scanty fragments reveals one fact as absolutely certain: the cistercian romanesque plan as seen at Fontenay, the 'bernardine plan', had not yet developed. At this stage the monks were building small, simple oratories. These should be considered in two groups, those of wood and those of stone.

The wooden churches for which we have documentation are those at Cîteaux and Clairvaux. Of these only the church at Clairvaux can be discussed in detail. The descriptions of the sixteenth and seventeenth centuries and the plan and view of the eighteenth century make clear that this was a square, wooden church with a peripheral aisle and a taller central space. Both the plan and

27. Henri Paul Eydoux, 'Morimond, 1954', *Cîteaux in de Nederland* 5 (1953) 131.

206

the view show us a building entirely consistent with timber stave construction.[28] Although most of the surviving stave buildings are in Scandinavia, their use was more widespread throughout the medieval period.[29] The characteristics of stave construction are, first, the staves which are erected at intervals around a rectangular core and create a narrow aisle on all four sides, and, second, the steep pitched roof which rises in stages to a small belfry.[30] These are precisely the characteristics of the church at Clairvaux. Furthermore, close examination of the plan of Milley (Fig. 3) reveals small half-round projections at intervals around the inner square—almost certainly the representation of the staves themselves.

There is no information on the architectural form of the earliest stone churches at La Ferté and Morimond. The church of 1106 at Cîteaux was a small, angular, box-like church without internal divisions. It was vaulted, in all probability with a simple barrel vault (Fig. 1). The church at Pontigny was angular and very simple (Fig. 2).

In connection with what architectural tradition should these simple structures be viewed? Perhaps it will help to answer that question if we remember the close association, even spiritual sympathy, which existed between the leaders of early Cîteaux and religious hermits of

28. I would like to thank Professor Jean Bony for this suggestion. Bony was also kind enough to point out interesting similarities between this plan of Clairvaux and the late anglo-saxon chapel of Saint Benedict within the precincts of Bury Saint Edmunds. This is a stone building, but Bony has suggested it may be a translation into stone of a familiar timber type. See A. B. Whittingham in the *Archeological Journal* 108 (1951) p. 181 and the plan opposite p. 192. I would also like to thank Professor Walter Horn for his frequent advice and encouragement on matters of medieval timber architecture.

29. See Walter Horn, 'On the Origins of the Medieval Bay System', *Journal of the Society of Architectural Historians* 17 (1958) 2–23. There is an early example of stave building in England, at Greenstead in Essex. On this and other stave buildings in England see Thomas Paulsson, *Scandinavian Architecture* (London: 1958) 77; and Gerda Boëthius, *Hallar, Tempel och Stavkyrkor* (Stockholm, 1931) 118–119.

30. Gustav Künstler, *Romanesque Art in Europe* (London, 1973) pp. 311–312, and pl. 244; Paulsson, pp. 31–38, 76–80.

the time; and if we remember as well that Pontigny and Morimond were established at existing hermitages.

Is there any reason why men who are in such spiritual accord with the hermits that they replaced the humble buildings already erected to serve God? Surely a tiny oratory could suffice for thirteen. At Pontigny and at Morimond just as at Fontenay, Hautecombe, Les Dunes, Aulps and at other sites,[31] the Cistercians took the hermit's structures for their own. In these examples, the earliest cistercian architecture is a direct continuation of the hermit architecture of the eleventh century. What of the other early churches, especially the first wooden and stone buildings at Cîteaux and Clairvaux? It may be rash to compare vanished structures to a tradition of architecture which has left almost no trace,[32] but it is reasonable to argue that these buildings had more in common with the simple oratories of hermits than with the distinctive style of church architecture which architectural historians call 'cistercian'.

31. Janauschek, p. 8; and Watkin Williams, *Saint Bernard of Clairvaux* (Manchester, 1935) 55, 63–64.

32. Hermit architecture is not an area attracting much art historical attention; see Jean Humber, 'L'Erémitisme et l'archéologie, *L'Eremitismo in occidente nei secoli XI e XII* (Milan, 1965) 462–487.

The First Cistercian Nuns

1120–1125 The Abbey of Tart is Established

Wherefore we make known to those present and those to come that in the time of Bishop Guilence of Langres, while Hugh was governing the duchy of Burgundy, nuns were gathered in a place called Tart; and by the permission and confirmation of the chapter of Langres, there was put in charge of them an abbess named Elizabeth, under whom a certain Mary acted as prioress. At the request of, indeed by the purchase by, said duke and Mathilda his wife, a certain knight, Arnulf Cornu, with his wife named Amelina— who was later buried there—gave this place to the nuns through the hand of Dom Stephen, the abbot of Cîteaux, in accordance with the disposition of woods and waters, springs, arable and non-arable lands first made by Lord Christopher or Lord Josserand, then bishop of Langres. . . . This gift is given into the hand of Abbess Elizabeth and of Prioress Mary in the presence of Bishop Josserand, Duke Hugh and his son Odo, and Robert de Cristol, Maurice de Genle and his son Hugh, and Simon de Vergy.[1]

c. 1200 The Abbot of Cîteaux Affirms the Account of the Foundation

I Guy, styled abbot of Cîteaux,[2] make known to those present and those to come that Arnulf Cornu and his wife Amelina, with the consent of and through the purchase by Hugh, Duke of Burgundy, have through the hand of dom Stephen, abbot of Cîteaux, given to certain nuns, who had attached themselves[3] to the house at Cîteaux, the place called Tart for the purpose of building an abbey there. At this place, the same Abbot

1. This document, dated to 1132, records the donation retrospectively PL 185:410A Cf. B. Hene, 'Einiges über die Cistercienserinnen', *Cistercienser Chronik* 9 (1897) p. 88, n. 6.
2. Guy was abbot from 1194 until his resignation in 1200.
3. *reddiderant*

Stephen of Cîteaux set up an abbey for nuns living according to
the constitutions of the Cistercian Order, and he established the
abbess there according to the practice[4] of the Cistercian Order.
Let everyone therefore take note that the aforesaid abbey of Tart is
a proper daughter of the house of Cîteaux and that the abbot of
Cîteaux shall have full authority to correct and direct whatever is
in need of correction or direction there, as regards the superior as
well as the members, and in the election and removal of the abbess
there, according to the practice of the Order . . . .[5]

4. *formam*, translated in the following article as 'manner'
5. PL 185:1413–1414.

The Abbey of Tart

Elizabeth Connor, OCSO

JULLY, A PRIORY of Molesme, had close cistercian ties. Its first prioress, Elisabeth, was a sister-in-law of Bernard of Clairvaux, and its second prioress was his own sister Humbeline. Sometime between 1118 and 1132, the abbot of Molesme, Guy of Châtel-Censoir, aided by the advice of four cistercian abbots, Hugh of Pontigny, Bernard of Clairvaux, Godfrey of Fontenay, and Gaucher of Morimond, drew up new rules or usages for the Jully nuns.[1] These bore a greater resemblance to cistercian customs than did the usages which the nuns had previously been observing, even though the general organization of the rapidly growing convent remained modeled on cluniac structures. At about the same time, c. 1120, Josserand, bishop of Langres, commissioned a nun of Jully to found an abbey which would follow cistercian observances.[2] This abbey would be Tart. The nun given this assignment was another Elisabeth, daughter of Elisabeth of Vergy, a great benefactress of Cîteaux.

We are not well informed about the establishment of the new monastery for cistercian nuns, but a document dating from 1132 lists five distinct donations to the abbey and permits an attempt at reconstruction of how the foundation came about.[3] It would appear that the idea for the monastery emerged from discussion among three persons: Elisabeth of Vergy, Abbot Stephen Harding, and Bishop Josserand. But in order for it to be brought to realization, it was necessary to involve a whole network of persons. Apparently

---

1. J. Bouton, B. Chauvin, E. Grosjean, '*Tart et ses filiales*', in B. Chauvin, ed., *Mélanges à la mémoire du Père Anselme Dimier* II. *Histoire cistercienne. 3. Ordre, Moines* (Pupillin, 1984) p. 21.

2. *Ibid.*

3. *Ibid.*, pp. 21–23.

Josserand and someone named Christopher—who cannot be identified with precision—suggested to Duke Hugh of Burgundy and
his wife Mathilda that a certain piece of property which included
forests, springs and streams, and land both cultivated and unculti-
vated, would be suitable for the nuns. The duke and his wife, in
turn, asked the owner, Arnulf Cornu, Lord of Tart-le-Haut and
a vassal of the lords of Vergy, to donate the land to the abbot of
Cîteaux for the purpose proposed by Josserand. The duke seems to
have borne the expense.[4] The donation was made by Arnulf and his
wife Amelina, and confirmed by his vassals. Amelina urged Arnulf
to make other donations, too: tithes, fishponds, and fishing rights.
These were made directly into the hands of the new abbess and her
prioress, Mary, in the presence of the duke of Burgundy, his son,
and several other persons. Josserand was also present.

On 10 October 1125, Josserand resigned as bishop and was
succeeded by Vilain d'Aigremont. With his approval the parish
priest of Tart-la-Ville ceded the tithes of that place to the nuns.
The duke of Burgundy confirmed all these donations and offered
the nuns still another: the *locus* of Marmot at Fauverney. The new
abbess had been married to the Lord of Fauverney, Thierry III of
Mailly, and had had several children. One of them, Harvey, became
a Cistercian and abbot of La Ferté. The foundation, begun in the
time of Josserand, and completed in the time of Vilain, took time.

The Charter of Abbot Guy

A number of the details given in the document of donation are
corroborated by a charter of the abbot of Citeaux, Guy de Paray,
dated between 1196 and 1200 by various historians. This same
Guy—who later became archbishop of Rheims and also cardinal—
had only shortly before visited the spanish women's monastery of
Las Huelgas and had personally received the donation of the royal
abbey from Alphonsus VIII. The circumstances which occasioned
the letter are unknown, but it gives an account of the foundation

---

4. The *Charta* of Abbot Guy has: *de assensu et emptione Hugonis ducis
Burgundiae. . . .*

of the monastery of Tart and other information which is of interest to us.[5] We will examine it section by section.

> A charter of Abbot Guy of Cîteaux about the foundation of the abbey of Tart and about the monasteries subject to it.
>
> I, Guy, abbot of Cîteaux, make known to persons present and future that Arnulf Cornu and his wife Amelina, with the assent of Hugh, Duke of Burgundy, and his wife Mathilda, and by a purchase made by him,[6] founded, by the hands of Lord Stephen, Abbot of Cîteaux, an abbey of nuns living according to the *instituta* of the Cistercian order, and established the abbess in this same place according to the prescribed manner (*formam*) of the Cistercian Order. Therefore, let all people know that the aforementioned abbey of Tart is Cîteaux's own (*propria*) daughter-house, so that the abbot has full power of correction and setting in order (*ordinandi*) those things which he finds should be corrected or set in order, both as concerns the head and members, and that he has power of appointing (*eligendi*) the abbess and deposing her according to the prescribed manner of the Order.

From this first paragraph of Abbot Guy's charter we can see how dependent the abbey of Tart was on the abbot of Cîteaux. He was responsible for the quality of cistercian life in the monastery. At the time this charter was drawn up, the abbess was still appointed, not elected. The direct relationship of the community to the Abbot of Cîteaux probably continued during most of the twelfth century. It is not known at what date Tart became incorporated into the Order. The first mention of incorporation in the Statutes of the Order comes in 1213, and then more or less as an aside in a statute having

5. *Gallia Christiana*, 4, Instrumenta, col. 157. This charter is reproduced by Mme M. de Fontette in *Les religieuses à l'âge classique du droit canon* (Paris: J. Vrin, 1967) pp. 35–36, note 51. See also PL 185:1413–1414.

6. By her generosity Mathilda may be considered the outstanding benefactress of the nuns. See 'Tart et ses filiales', p. 29.

to do principally with enclosure.[7] What is particularly significant for us in this charter is that the abbey of Tart was following the *instituta* of Cîteaux.[8] But this does not imply that the General Chapter had anything to do with either the organization of the monastery or its administration.

Abbot Guy continues with a list of monasteries dependent upon—or rather 'belonging to' (*pertinent*) Tart: 'And if any others will belong to it in the future, they will belong by right and in perpetuity to the care (*cura*) and governance (*ordinationem*) of the house of Cîteaux'.

Had the filiation existed for some time already or had Guy brought the idea for it back from Spain after his visit to the royal abbey of Las Huelgas, founded there in 1187? What was the reason for the filiation? Did Cîteaux wish to promote a congregation of nuns within the Order? This seems unlikely, for the charter of Guy is very explicit that all the houses of the filiation are to be dependent on Cîteaux. The questions raised by this filiation that we meet full-grown, so to speak, cannot be answered. Documents do not exist.

Eighteen houses are mentioned. Six were in Burgundy, relatively close to Tart. Five were in Champagne, and of those, three were close to Langres. The other seven houses were in various parts of France, the two most distant being Lum-Dieu (or Fabas) in Haut-Comminges, in the approaches of the Pyrenees, and Rieunette, near Carcassonne. Several houses were founded very early, that is, about the same time as Tart: Belmont (1127) and Belfays (1128), founded by the abbot of Morimond. Others were founded in the middle of the twelfth century, and still others quite late: Valboyon (about 1181), Lieu-Dieu (about 1180). Lum-Dieu founded three other monasteries in France and became the mother-house of the first monastery of cistercian nuns in Spain: Tulebras, from which nuns went out to found Las Huelgas. The eighteen houses do not

---

7. J.-M. Canivez, *Statuta Capitulorum generalium Ordinis cisterciensis ab anno 1116 ad annum 1786* (Louvain, 1933–1941). I, p. 405, cap. 3. See Sally Thompson, 'The Problem of the Cistercian Nuns', in Derek Baker, ed. *Medieval Women, Studies in Church History*, 1 (Oxford, 1978) 236.

8. 'Tart et ses filiales', p. 24.

in any way represent the totality of cistercian monasteries of nuns at the time. Far from it. We would like to know how these particular eighteen came to form the filiation of Tart. It has been suggested that when new communities were being formed, Tart sent several nuns to join other women aspiring to the cistercian life.[9] Existing communities also no doubt asked to be affiliated with Tart. Collonges, in the diocese of Besançon, was founded (before or in 1139), through the mediation of Godfrey de la Roche-Vanneau, bishop of Langres, former monk of Clairvaux and cousin of Saint Bernard. The large community of Esclache (1159), near Clermont-Ferrand, founded Bussières (about 1159), another house of the filiation, near Montluçon. Poulangy was attached to the Order in 1149 by Saint Bernard. His niece, Adeline, was abbess. This monastery, however, returned to its former benedictine observance in 1254.[10] Several of the monasteries made transfers in later centuries; none of them survived the Revolution.

The rest of Guy's charter concerns the Chapters of nuns which were to meet at Tart under the supervision of Cîteaux :

> Besides, let it be known that the abbesses of the abbeys mentioned above are to meet at the aforesaid abbey of Tart each year on the feast of Saint Michael at the General Chapter at which the abbot of Cîteaux presides, either himself or someone he has delegated, except those [abbesses] who stay away by favor of the Abbot of Cîteaux himself.
>
> At this General Chapter of abbesses proclamations should be made before the abbot of Cîteaux or his delegate according to the prescribed manner (*formam*) of the Order, and those things which should be corrected and set in order (*ordinanda*) are to be corrected and set in order without any objection to his judgment and decisions.

9. The community would not have been large enough to permit many regular foundations (i.e. twelve nuns and a superior).

10. A. Dimier, 'Chapitres généraux d'abbesses cisterciennes', in *Cîteaux* 11 (1960) p. 267.

The date of the Chapter is perhaps significant, coming so shortly after the General Chapter of abbots at Cîteaux. Although the abbot of Cîteaux was to preside, at three of the Chapters for which we have the Acts he was replaced by delegates: the abbot of La Bussière and the prior of Cîteaux. This may have been common practice. From the Acts of the Chapter[11] which we will examine it may be surmised that the abbesses discussed at their Chapters how they could implement in their monasteries the decisions made by the abbots at their Chapters. The proclamations spoken of refer to faults against the Rule of Saint Benedict or the usages (*consuetudines*) of the Order. Was it really necessary to say that the president's judgement and decisions should be accepted without any objection (*sine omne contradictione*)? Did he foresee, or had he already experienced, difficulty in correcting faults at the Chapters? We will never know.

To call the assemblies General Chapters was something of an exaggeration. Besides the fact that only a small number of houses was represented, the Acts reveal that the abbess of Tart had very limited authority. A document from 1233, concerning a disagreement between Tart and Poulangy, states certain rights of the abbess of Tart: she can make visitations in abbeys which are under her 'jurisdiction', establish rules, and preside at the election of superiors.[12] This is the only time that the word 'jurisdiction' is encountered in reference to the abbess of Tart, and one may wonder if it is meant to be taken in its technical sense.[13] In her study on canon law, Madame de Fontette states firmly that the abbess of Tart had no jurisdictional power.[14]

11. The Acts of 1268, 1272, 1290, and 1302 are examined in the original paper, published in *Hidden Springs* (see Acknowledgements) Because they all occurred in the thirteenth century, this section has been omitted here.

12. 'Tart et ses filiales', p. 26, with reference to Bouton, 'L'établissement des moniales cisterciennes' in *Mémoires de la Société pour l'Histoire du Droit et des institutions des anciens pays bourguignons, comtois et romands*', 15th fasc. (1953) pp. 100–101.

13. In documents dealing with questions about the abbess visitor's attributes, the expression *statuant quae viderint statuenda* (they should make whatever rulings they see should be made) never occurs although it is always found in references to an abbot visitor's authority.

14. de Fontette, p. 37.

That the Chapters of Tart were not to be considered as parallel to
those of Cîteaux is clear from a text in the *Instituta* of the General
Chapter of 1258, which expressly states that the abbesses do not have
a Chapter. The text concerns the regular visitation, asking pardon
for faults, proclamations and corrections.[15] Promulgation of the
Instituta did not prevent the Tart Chapters from going on, however,
since the extant Acts are all of later date than the *Instituta*. . . .

THE MONASTIC DOMAIN

Although the archives of the abbey of Tart have been, for the
most part, lost, several inventories—one very long, of six-hundred
pages—and some pontifical or seignorial documents have been
preserved. The patrimony of the monastery was established during
the first sixty years of its history.[16] The most important donations,
made at the time of the foundation, have already been mentioned.
The noble families of Fauverney, Licéy, Mailly, Marigny, Pouilly,
and Saux were among the nuns' benefactors.

Whereas common people and churchmen, as well as noblemen,
contributed generously to monks' monasteries, during the first
century of Tart's existence donations came only from nobles. The
nuns had the help of laybrothers for work on their property, but
they also needed some hired workmen.

It was during the thirteenth century that priests and common
people began to make donations to the abbey. From 1240 on,[17] the
nuns purchased land, usually property bordering what they already
owned, in order to consolidate their domain. They reached a total of

15. *Instituta capitulorum generalium* Dist XV, *De monialibus, cap.vi: De
habitu monialium.* J. Paris et H. Séjalon, *Nomasticon cisterciense seu antiquiores
Ordinis cisterciencis constitutiones* (Solesme, 1892) p. 362: *Et quia abbatissae
capitulum generale non habent, venias de suis excessibus tam in visitatione quam
alias quotiens fuerit necesse, coram visitatore petant, et ab ipso visitatore vel de eius
visitatoris praecepto proclamentur et corrigantur.*

15. For this section on the Domain I have followed 'Tart et ses filiales',
pp. 28–35.

16. *Ibid.*, p. 29.

17. *Ibid.*, p. 31.

eight granges which, although normal for monks, was considerably more than the usual two or three which other monasteries of nuns possessed. The abbey prospered. In the spirit of the Rule the nuns had on their domain just about everything they needed for their life. The grange of Beauvoir furnished cereals. Those of Lamblin, Spoy, and Saint-Usage had pastures and fields for growing crops. Hauteserve, near a vast forest, was for the herds. Battault provided cereals and grapes. There were two winecellars and a winepress, four or five mills, and there was salt on the property. Although the nuns administered their monasteries and domains in a purposeful way and with reflection, they seem not to have been intent on profit or the development of their domains. Their land simply permitted them to live their monastic life.[18]

As time passed and the number of laybrothers in the Order diminished, the nuns came to lack hands. Stricter enclosure after *Periculoso* prevented them from going out themselves to work the fields. They began to count more on rents for income. And, toward the end of the thirteenth century, hard times were coming for everyone.

18. *Ibid.*, p. 34.

Ideals and Reality in Early Cistercian Life and Legislation

Louis J. Lekai, O.Cist.

OTH SCHOLARS and amateur historians have stated innumerable times, that the Cistercian Order flourished only as long as it held fast to its original ideals and principles, clearly formulated in the earliest documents of Cîteaux as well as in the first statutes passed by the General Chapter. On the duration of the 'golden age' and the beginning of decline, however, the same authorities disagree, some stating flatly that the downward slide is noticeable as early as the death of Saint Bernard. The principles and legislation, supposedly so soon broken, concern meticulous observance of the Rule of Saint Benedict, strict seclusion from the world, and poverty and simplicity; more specifically they refer to the refusal to accept customary feudal and ecclesiastical revenues coupled with the demand that the monks live by the fruits of their own labor.

That the first Cistercians indeed cherished such ideals is so evident that it needs no further proof. Hosts of other problems, however, must be examined before a balanced judgment can be formed on the validity of the above mentioned and widely accepted opinion on the relationship between broken laws and decline. Were those principles indeed unbroken before 1153? Could occasional defaults be justified? Were what are seen in retrospect as 'laws' really passed and accepted as universally binding regulations? Did the General Chapter 'legislate' as modern legislative bodies do? Was cistercian lawmaking sufficiently orderly and efficient to demand prompt obedience? Even if someone were willing to answer most such questions with a resounding 'yes' there remains the curious fact that nearly four hundred abbeys were founded in rapid succession after 1153, the period of supposed decline. Moreover, some of the greatest and most successful communities of cistercian history were founded only in the second half of the thirteenth century (among them Rauden, Pelplin, Chorin, Goldenkron, Neuzelle, Königssaal, Grüssau).

I do not pretend that I am about to solve all these problems definitively, but I would like to turn attention to certain facts and circumstances which may point to more realistic conclusions than those of our predecessors when grappling with the same elusive issues.

I have shown on a previous occasion that the founders of Cîteaux assumed a peculiarly ambivalent attitude toward the Rule of Saint Benedict.[1] They declared their utter devotion to it, but in fact they used that venerable document with remarkable liberality. They invoked and applied it when it suited their purpose, but ignored or even contradicted it when they thought that they had better ideas. In the latter category we find the exclusion of children and the introduction of lay brothers, liturgical uniformity, restrictions on the power of abbots combined with an emphasis on central authority and control by visitors, along with many other features of the *Charter of Charity* totally beyond the scope of the Rule. If the founders of Cîteaux were indeed as devoted to the Rule as they proclaimed themselves to be, their adherence was certainly more to its spirit than to its letter.

Another supposedly firmly-established principle demanded that abbeys of the Order be established far from populated areas. Cistercian authors habitually described their monastic sites by borrowing the colorful words of *Deuteronomy* (32:10): *locus horroris* **et vastae solitudinis**. Here again we may ask: was this indeed a 'principle', and if so, how firm a principle.

The ambiguity begins with Cîteaux. In spite of the *Exordium Parvum's* best efforts to assure us that Cîteaux was an impenetrable wilderness inhabited only by wild beasts, the site included an ancient chapel and some peasant dwellings; and after the first years of

1. L. J. Lekai, 'The Rule and the Early Cistercians', *Cistercian Studies Quarterly* 5 (1970) 243–251.

expansion the granges of the abbey became immediate neighbors of well-settled villages.[2] Clear indications survive that solitude was not the condition uppermost in the minds of those responsible for the earliest foundations. If the original site of a new abbey closely resembled the cherished landscape of a 'place of horror and vast solitude', but offered no adequate means of safe survival, the monks did not hesitate to move to a location geographically less secluded, but economically more rewarding. According to Donkin, in England alone there were at least twenty-nine such moves away from an uninviting wilderness and closer to more fertile lands, even though the new location lay near populated areas.[3]

The rejection of all feudal and ecclesiastical revenues remains one of the most characteristic features of early Cîteaux. It is firmly established in the first *Capitula* emanating from the annual sessions of the General Chapter. If ever there was a basic law in Cîteaux, the repudiation of 'churches, *altaria*, oblations and burials, tithes of other people, ovens or mills, vills and serfs,' surely formed a cornerstone of cistercian legislation. Nevertheless, the examination of a random selection of cartularies left behind by the earliest foundations must convince anybody that infractions of even these rules were no rare exceptions even before the death of Saint Bernard.

Between 1116 and 1119 Cîteaux herself acquired in Moisey tithes which originally belonged to two priests who transferred their claims to the abbey.[4] The foundation document of Bonnefont (1136–1137) included the donation of tithes, although, as also true in the case of Cîteaux, there is no clear proof that the monks actually collected such revenues.[5] The same was true at the foundation of Otterberg in 1144.[6] Elsewhere in Germany similar cases must

2. J. Marilier, *Chartes et documents concernant l'abbaye de Cîteaux, 1098–1182* (Rome, 1961) 50.

3. R. A. Donkin, 'The Site Changes of Medieval Cistercian Monasteries', *Geography* 44 (1959) 251–258.

4. Marilier, *Chartes*, pp. 76–77.

5. Charles Samaran and Charles Higounet, *Recueil des actes de l'abbaye cistercienne de Bonnefont en Comminges* (Paris, 1970) 50.

6. G. Kaller, *Wirtschafts- und Besitzgeschichte des Zisterzienserklosters Otterberg* (Heidelberg, 1961) 82.

have been wide-spread: Camp received tithes in 1130 from the archdeacon of Cologne;[7] Walkenried accepted at its foundation (1129) three villages; Volkerode, founded in 1131, was soon relieved of grave hardships by the welcome revenues from a mill. A son of the foundress of the same house was buried in the abbey church in 1149. At about the same time, life at Sittichenbach was so hard that Count Friedrich von Beichlingen donated to the monks the village of Ober-Heilingen with an income of thirty-six marks in tithes. The Polish abbey of Łekno, founded about 1147, received at its inception the town of the same name along with the revenues of the local market. Andreow, another Polish house, possessed from 1149 on the town in which the abbey was founded along with seven villages.[8] According to an undated document (surely written before 1139) Preuilly, the sixth 'daughter' of Cîteaux, received a mill on the condition that the monks furnish the donor with half a bushel of rye and the same quantity of wheat each year on the feast of Saint Luke.[9]

What was the reaction of the General Chapter to such manifest infractions of supposedly fundamental rules? I know the answer in only one case, involving the Roman abbey of Tre Fontane, an ancient house incorporated in 1140, with the blessing of Saint Bernard, in spite of the fact that it possessed a village, churches and all kinds of other customary ecclesiastical revenues. There is no indication of subsequent efforts by the abbey to unload the 'illegal' possessions. In fact, to make sure that all was in fact in order, Pope Eugene III turned to the General Chapter of 1152 with the request that the abbey be permitted to retain these sources of income, arguing: *licet enim id ordinis rigor inhibeat, loci tamen necessitas retineri compellit* (though the rigor of the Order forbids it, the necessity of the situation requires they be retained). The pope

7. Giles Constable, *Monastic Tithes from their Origins to the Twelfth Century* (Cambridge, 1964) 191.

8. Franz Winter, *Die Zisterzienser des nordöstlichen Deutschlands* (Gotha, 1867–1871) 1:32–81.

9. Albert Catel and Maurice Lecomte, *Chartes et documents de l'abbaye cistercienne de Preuilly* (Paris, 1927) 14.

assured the Chapter that although he would try to work out some other solution, for the time being the monks could not forego their usual sources of livelihood or they would be forced to go about begging for their food. The General Chapter of 1153 found the exception justifiable and readily consented.[10]

This concession was by no means an isolated incident of an exception granted only under the pressure of papal authority. A veritable floodgate to all such illegalities was opened in 1147 by the incorporation—advocated by Saint Bernard himself—of the Congregation of Savigny (twenty-nine abbeys and three monasteries of nuns). In the same year the small congregations of Cadouin and Obazine followed Savigny's example. All of them were admitted with their previously acquired churches, tithes, and serfs, without the obligation to conform immediately to cistercian restrictions. One can hardly suppose that a man with Saint Bernard's intelligence could overlook the discrepancies between the economic basis of the newly admitted abbeys and that of the original cistercian foundations; neither could he fail to realize the potential effects such wholesale concessions would have on the rest of the Order. Why then did he promote the consolidation? As I see it, the only logical answer is that, in the judgment of Saint Bernard, the spiritual benefits of the union outweighed the drawbacks of the compromise.[11] But it would be unfair to blame Saint Bernard for what followed; the General Chapter took the same lenient attitude even after his death. In 1157, for example, the Chapter permitted the newly incorporated abbeys to hold on to their mills until they received other

10. J. Canivez, *Statuta Capitulorum Generalium Ordinis Cisterciensis* (Louvain, 1933–1941) 1:43–45, 51–52. Henceforth: *Statuta*.

11. 'Cum Savigniacenses in nostri Ordinis societatem transire decreverunt, dispensatione in hac parte habita ecclesias et earum beneficia permissi sunt habere. Durum numque visum est loci cognita infecunditate ab huiusmodi eos prohibere beneficiis. Si quis ergo de perceptione talium beneficiorum adversus eos obloquitur, noverit sinceritas vestra huius Ordinis patres misericorditer hoc eis indulsisse.' Letter of William, abbot of Clairvaux, to Achard, bishop of Avranches (after 1161), quoted by B. Griesser, 'Registrum Epistolarum Stephani de Lexington,' ASOC 8 (1952) 189.

instructions. Meanwhile, as one could easily anticipate, these well-publicized concessions encouraged other communities to reach out for hitherto forbidden possessions. By 1169 the abuse had become so widespread that Pope Alexander III addressed a strongly worded bull to the Order, calling attention to the alarming deviations from the 'holy institutions' of the founding fathers.[12]

Uniformity in daily life and discipline did not fare much better. Irish communities posed the greatest problems, despite the great care and direct supervision lavished on the foundation of Mellifont in 1142 by Saint Malachy and Saint Bernard. The Clairvaux-trained monks found so much resistance to cistercian customs among the Irish that they were forced to return; among them was Robert, the architect of Clairvaux. Saint Bernard refused to be discouraged, although he must have realized that no foundation could take root on the island without compromise with the ancient forms of irish monasticism. After renewed efforts, some abbeys were constructed according to cistercian requirements, but the native monks continued to live in small huts around the cloister, in the immediate vicinity of nuns. By 1190 the situation had become critical, but instead of taking radical measures, the General Chapter merely ordered ineffectual visitations. In 1228, abbot Stephen Lexington of Stanley, after visiting the delinquent houses at peril of his life, could no longer find even the vestiges of cistercian observances among the rebellious Irish. Yet all that the General Chapter did was to effect a temporary break-up of local lines of affiliation.[13]

The phenomenon of peremptory legislation and indulgent execution can be better understood if it is considered within the context of contemporary legal developments. The Gregorian Reform witnessed the rebirth of Roman Law, and the first systematic collections of canon law, together with papal claims to universal authority supported by the ever expanding Curia as the organ of centralized, bureaucratic administration. These revolutionary novelties ran

12. J. Leclercq, 'Passage supprimé dans une epître d'Alexandre III', *Revue Bénédictine* 62 (1952) 151.

13. J. A. Watt, *The Church and the Two Nations in Medieval Ireland* (Cambridge, 1970) 85–107.

into the resolute opposition of those who kept faith with the old traditional concepts of feudal relations based on immemorial customs, local autonomy, and extensive privileges. In the ensuing controversy the papacy fought under the banner of divine truth and freedom from secular entanglements, while the emperor defended his position by invoking the power of unbroken traditions and feudal contracts. The outcome could only be a compromise, but from a papal point of view the Concordat of Worms was certainly a far cry from the categorical claims of the *Dictatus papae*.

The reform program of Cîteaux can be conceived of as the application of gregorian ideals to monastic renewal, in contrast to traditional ways symbolized by Cluny. In the early cistercian documents, fidelity to the Gospel was replaced by strict adherence to the Rule, but cistercian rejection of long-standing customs and their demand for complete freedom from feudal ties reflected the same issues as those involved in the investiture conflict. The parallel goes even further: just as the papacy was forced to recognize that a rigid application of gregorian principles was impossible, the rapid territorial expansion of the Order forced the General Chapter to admit that the tenets of cistercian reform were not always and everywhere applicable. Cîteaux did not sign a formal concordat with local opposition, but in the career of Saint Bernard one discovers at least a disposition towards a tacit compromise.

The great abbot of Clairvaux cannot be unqualifiedly characterized as a protagonist in the Gregorian Reform. When he came to prominence the long strife had already been terminated and he had no ambition to renew it. He was, obviously, an intrepid champion of moral reform, but he had no taste for power politics and the intricacies of canon law. In his well-known *De consideratione* he wrote about the papacy, not in juridical terms but as a moral power, and he described the Church, not as a legal entity, but as the mystical bride of Christ. In a much quoted passage he berated the Curia where 'daily the laws resound in the palace, but they are laws of Justinian, not of the Lord'. In his mind, papal jurisdiction ought to be motivated by spiritual and pastoral considerations rather than by the provocative display of force. When Saint Bernard interfered in the disputed papal election of 1130, he preferred Innocent over

Anacletus, not because of canonical formalities, but because he was convinced that by character the former was better suited to be the Vicar of Christ.[14] When Saint Bernard spoke up in the General Chapter, then, it was entirely logical that he spoke not in behalf of the rigid enforcement of laws and regulations, but in favor of the spiritual welfare of monastic communities. When the two came into conflict, as certainly happened in 1147, he was willing to bend the law to accommodate the large number of worthy monks for their own good and for the glory and spiritual benefit of his beloved Order.

That this was indeed Bernard's frame of mind can also be inferred from his attitude towards the Rule of Saint Benedict. To use the words of Jean Leclercq, Bernard 'considered it not as a code of observances but as the expression of an idea; not as a collection of usages to be followed but as a work of doctrine conveying a spirit and establishing certain fundamental structures; he did not, in fact, attribute to it legislative value'.[15]

Saint Bernard's position was a source of inspiration to many, among them the famed author of the most important canonical work of the twelfth century, Gratian. His *Concordia discordantium canonum*, published about 1140, attempted, as its title indicates, to reconcile the old with the new, to synthesize traditional feudal concepts with gregorian theories of law, and he incorporated much of Saint Bernard's teaching on the Church and papal jurisdiction. This work dominated legal thinking at the time of the most vigorous

14. See this interpretation of the role of Saint Bernard in Hayden V. White, 'The Gregorian Ideal and Saint Bernard of Clairvaux', *Journal of the History of Ideas* 21 (1960) 321–348. See the problem of 'Saint Bernard and the Law' discussed in Stanley Chodorow in *Christian Political Theory and Church Politics in the Mid-Twelfth Century* (Berkeley, Los Angeles, 1972) 260–265. See an attempt to reconcile the legal and purely moral considerations in Saint Bernard's approach by John R. Sommerfeldt, 'Charismatic and Gregorian Leadership in the Thought of Bernard of Clairvaux', in *Bernard of Clairvaux: Studies Presented to Dom Jean Leclercq*, CS 23 (Washington, D.C., 1973) 73–90.

15. J. Leclercq, 'S. Bernard et la Règle de S. Benoît', *Collectanea* 25 (1973) 183.

cistercian expansion and certainly exercised a decisive influence on the attitude of the more erudite members of General Chapter. From our point of view the most important feature of this great work is the introductory part, the *Tractatus de legibus* on the nature and origin of laws, including the relationship between customs and other forms of human laws. After making the distinction between divine and human laws, Gratian defined the latter as *mores jure conscripti et traditi*. Since 'human laws consist of customs, for the same reason they are different according to the likes and dislikes of nations'. Gratian recognized written and statutory laws as well, but he insisted, by listing the attributes of all valid laws, that they must be 'honest, just, possible, corresponding to nature, in harmony with the customs of the country, adapted to place and time, necessary, useful and manifest'. Furthermore, 'laws are instituted when they are promulgated; they are confirmed when they are approved by the customs of the users. Namely, just as in our days many laws have been abrogated by the contrary customs of the users, [other valid] laws have been confirmed by the users' customs.'[16] In a subsequent discourse Gratian carefully delineated the necessary attributes of customs having such force, but in conclusion he still maintained that 'customs should not be resisted as long as they are not contrary to canonical authority; . . . traditions instituted by the fathers should not be broken' and 'daily practices should be taken as laws'.[17]

From these quotations it is obvious that Gratian shared his contemporaries' deep-seated suspicion of novelties and held that law-making was conceivable only if and when laws were related to long-established and living social realities. Medieval rulers, of course, passed new laws long before the emergence of statutory legislation, but, at least during the course of the twelfth century, they were anxious to disguise patent novelties as forgotten and rediscovered customs.[18] That the fathers of Cîteaux were very sensitive to charges of introducing undue novelties and vigorously

16. PL 187:35.
17. PL 187:63.
18. See on the prevailing legal conservatism, M.-D. Chenu, *Nature, Man and Society in the Twelfth Century* (Chicago, 1968) 310–330.

2

8

disclaimed any such intentions is one of the striking features of virtually all sources dealing with cistercian beginnings.

We may go one step further however, and state that the formulation of the basic norms of life at Cîteaux and the nucleus of the Charter of Charity—which fall under the rubic 'legislation'—preceded the existence of the General Chapter, and moreover that this annual convention of abbots did not claim legislative authority and in fact, until about 1180, passed no new laws. The Chapter sessions described in the Charter of Charity were merely conventions at which 'the abbots should consult upon matters that pertain to the salvation of souls and see to the observance of the Holy Rule and the [usages] of the Order. . . .'[19] In 1151 Pope Eugene III in his letter to the General Chapter echoed the same idea when he referred to the assembly as 'dealing presently in unison about the rekindling of the Holy Spirit and the progress of souls', adding that 'whenever you, dearly beloved sons, come together, you must be concerned with corrections of things to be corrected and ordinations that need to be ordained for the salvation of souls and the advancement of the Order . . . therefore you should carefully consider what can be done to prevent deviations from the virtues you have planted, [virtues] that you must bring to fruition.'[20]

As these quotations seem to indicate, the primary goal of the General Chapter was not legislation but spiritual guidance; the Chapter fathers watched over the observance of the Rule, the Charter of Charity and other initial usages of the Order. This may explain the curious fact that, with the exception of a few undated and disjointed fragments, no documentary evidence for the annual legislative activity of the General Chapter exists until about 1180. The collection of rules and regulations published under the auspices of the Chapter in or somewhat before 1152 and featuring the *Ecclesiastica officia*, the *Usus conversorum* and particularly the *Instituta Generalis Capituli* can be described more properly as adaptations,

19. J.-B. Van Damme, *Documenta pro Cisterciensis Ordinis historiae ac juris studio collecta* (Westmalle, 1959) 17.
20. *Statuta*, 1:40–41.

amplifications, and explanations of already established usages and customs than as new legislation.

If, by exception, something undeniably new appeared among these early statutes, it was proposed on a tentative basis, to be approved by the membership or rejected and quietly discarded. A striking example of this attitude is the first statute of 1152, prohibiting new foundations or incorporations.[21] To us this measure sounds perfectly reasonable and sometimes we may wish it had been heeded. But to contemporaries it was so blatantly new and in such manifest contradiction to existing trends that none of them would have taken it seriously. In the face of adverse reaction, this 'law' was never repeated and no effort was made to enforce it.

A further proof of both the tentative nature of new regulations and the broad-minded, compromising disposition of the Chapter fathers can be seen in the wording of virtually countless statutes passed before as well as after 1180. A firm command or rigid prohibition always begins the statutes, but the end lists the exceptions, often enfeebling the text to the extent that it hardly qualifies as more than fatherly advice. The Chapter of 1152, for example, prohibited the use of silk copes, but authorized them at abbatial blessings; it forbade abbots to employ secular servants in the guests' quarters, 'unless there should be many guests'; it excluded meat courses on Saturdays in the infirmary, 'unless there should be someone so sick that he can take nothing else'.[22] Even far more significant statutes contain built-in loopholes, placing local considerations above general rules. Thus, when the Chapter of 1182 was informed of the heavy indebtedness of many houses, it ruled that an abbey owing more than fifty marks was not to buy new land or construct any buildings, 'unless there should be a real necessity for such things, ascertained by the father abbots'.[23] Records of the Chapter of 1184 contains an explicit admission that local customs might override previously passed statutes, such as the prohibition against serving

21. *Ibid.*, 45.
22. *Ibid.*, 1152:16, 17, 19.
23. *Ibid.*, 1182:9.

wine in the granges.[24] Similar examples could be multiplied, as could instances when deviations were encouraged by the soothing connective *nisi*. The busy scriptorium of Pontigny paid no attention to the prohibition of multi-colored illuminations and produced ornate manuscripts with impunity throughout the twelfth century.[25] The experimental nature of all statutes was confirmed as late as 1265 in the bull *Parvus fons* of Clement IV, which restated the well-established rule of thumb that no law passed by the General Chapter was to be considered binding until confirmed by the subsequent session of the Chapter.[26]

One thing seems certain: after 1180 the annual sessions of the General Chapter were better recorded, capitular statutes became ever more numerous, less concerned with spiritual guidance, and more emphatic on purely administrative and financial matters. In this they reflect the new posture of self-conscious legislators. The date of this conspicuous change supports the oft-debated thesis of Rudolph Sohm, who argued that with the triumph of Pope Alexander III at the Third Lateran Council (1179) a break took place in the traditionally 'sacramental' interpretation of canon law, an interpretation which had been firmly upheld by Gratian. Thereafter a new juridical mind set took hold professional lawyers, chiefly concerned with the powers of ecclesiastical office-holders, constitutional structures, and the intricacies of papal administration. Indeed, it is not unlikely that when the Cistercian General Chapter of 1188 ordered that all works on canon law be kept under lock and key and not allowed to circulate among monks, the abbots were instinctively reacting to sensing the changing legal climate as it moved away from the theologically oriented patristic traditions and drifted toward a utilitarian exploitation of canons as legal weaponry in jurisdictional disputes.[27]

24. *Ibid.*, 1184:15.
25. C. H. Talbot, 'Notes on the Library of Pontigny', ASOC 10 (1954) 107.
26. *Statuta*, 3:27.
27. The Sohm thesis is discussed in Chodorow, *Christian Political Theory*, (note 14) 7–11.

The final point of our investigation should be the actual or potential efficiency of the General Chapter from a purely technical point of view, quite apart from the question of the nature of its activity.

The annual Chapter was supposed to bring together all abbots of the Order. The early regulations accepted only one excuse for absence: illness. The speedy geographical expansion of the Order, however, made regular attendance difficult to those in far-off lands. For reasons of great distance, expense, and danger of travel, exceptions were soon granted. Abbots of houses in Syria were required to attend the Chapter only every seventh year and others received similar concessions in proportion to their distance from Cîteaux. On the number of abbots participating in the deliberations of the Chapter during the twelfth and thirteenth centuries no figures have survived. Constant complaints about unauthorized absences, however, lead one to conclude that the ordeals of travel were powerful deterrents. At any rate, the physical facilities for the accommodation of the members of the Chapter at Cîteaux were very modest. Even after the completion of the final gothic cloister in 1193 ('Cîteaux III') the regular meeting place, the chapter hall, was a room of 17 x 18 meters, with a double or perhaps triple row of benches around the walls. It has been estimated that it held about three hundred persons,[28] but whether the hall was ever filled remains highly doubtful. A session with about a third of the abbots in attendance (250) was probably the norm.

How were the absent two-thirds notified of the resolutions of the Chapter? On record-keeping and the promulgation of statutes, twelfth-century documents are silent. The fact that until about 1180 the extant manuscripts give no information whatever about the proceedings of single sessions seems to indicate that the consultations remained unrecorded and the resolutions of the Chapter, if there were any, were passed on orally. The matter was further complicated by the assembly's continually changing membership from year to year; a considerable portion of the abbots at any given occasion

28. G. Müller, 'Studien über das Generalkapitel', *Cistercienzer Chronik* 12 (1900) 248.

was un-acquainted with the discussions held in previous years. The frequent result was the passage of incongruous or contradictory regulations. This led to confusion and a skeptical attitude toward the validity of individual statutes. Important decisions were repeated year after year and were noted in the periodic collection and publication of statutes, such as the earliest *Capitula* about 1119, the *Instituta* of 1152, and the *Libellus definitionum* edited by Arnaud Amaury about 1202. This last collection led the General Chapter of 1204 to issue for the first time an order obliging every abbot to obtain a copy of it, 'so that no abbot could excuse himself in the future under the pretext of ignorance'.[29] Promulgation continued nevertheless, to be a vexing issue. The Chapter of 1212 scolded certain 'less solicitous abbots' who neglected to take home the texts of definitions to be read in their chapter. To make sure that each abbey had been provided with the latest edition of definitions, visitors were enjoined to check on the matter. Abbots who for any reason failed to attend Chapters were obliged to collect from their neighbors, from father abbots, or from visitors the records of the session they had missed.[30]

All these measures fell short of the target. If General Chapter was unable to make up its collective mind on a crucial issue, a flow of conflicting regulations resulted year after year. Leasing or renting monastic land to lay tenants was strictly prohibited by the *Instituta* of 1152, but became inevitable as lay-brother vocations began to decline. Thus, the Chapter of 1208 permitted the leasing of 'less useful land', but the session of 1214 revoked the concession. In 1215 the Chapter not only permitted but ordered the leasing of newly acquired land. In 1220 the fathers returned to the permission of 1208, and in 1224 the Chapter no longer objected to the leasing of any land if such a move seemed desirable.[31]

In other cases the careful reader of records may get the impression that the wording of important statutes was made deliberately so vague or so complicated that it left open a number of possible

29. *Statuta*, I:1204.8.
30. *Ibid.*, 1212.6, 7.
31. *Ibid.*, 1208.5; 1214.58; 1215.65; 1220.5; 2:224.10.

interpretations. Once obvious 'hot potato' was the much criticized cistercian tendency to acquire ever more and more land, a matter discussed at length at the Chapter of 1190. The result was a long paragraph, composed 'in order to curb cupidity' which in fact prohibited 'forever' the acquisition of any real estate. But the new law was to take effect only upon its confirmation by the capitular session the following year and the text exempted pastures and lands held for usufruct, donations *in puram eleenosynam*, and lands from which pensions or tithes were due and, finally, it dispensed all abbeys whose existing estates were insufficient to support thirty monks, a proportionate number of lay-brothers, and the usual number of guests.[32] The repetition of this ruling in 1191 bears eloquent testimony to the fathers' concern about this important matter, but also betrays that it was conveniently innocuous and without practical consequences.

To attribute to the General Chapter a high degree of efficiency at least in disciplinary matters would be another mistake. Here we refer only to one incident which dragged on from 1190 to 1222 without conclusive result. In 1190 the abbey of Bonlieu in the diocese of Bordeaux experienced grave hardships. The Chapter ordered an investigation by the abbot of Bonlieu's 'mother', Jouy. In the event that the visitation failed to ensure the secure support of at least 'twelve regularly-living monks' at Bonlieu, the abbey was to be suppressed. But by 1192 no visitation had taken place, and the abbot of Jouy was informed that if he failed to act, the maternity over Bonlieu would be transferred to Pontigny. As late as 1207 still nothing had been done; the order of 1190 was merely repeated. In 1208 the Chapter added a new threat: if the abbot of Jouy remained negligent in the matter, Bonlieu would be reduced to a grange. In 1212 the exasperated Chapter entrusted the visitation of Bonlieu to two other abbots, who turned out to be equally reluctant. In 1213 the Chapter again rebuked the stubborn abbot of Jouy and renewed the threat of changing Bonlieu's filiation. Finally, in 1222, the abbot of Pontigny was charged to assume the role of father abbot

32. *Ibid.*, I:1190.1; 1191.42, 43.

over Bonlieu; even so there is no evidence of further action in the matter.[33]

In conclusion what observations can we make? Those who see a link between the non-observance of certain original statutes and the decline of the Order identify, at least implicitly, the cistercian reform with a set or regulations; by this logic, broken rules broke the Order itself. Both the presupposition and the conclusion, however, seem to be unjustifiable. The cistercian reform was a movement of spiritual renewal; the initial regulations were merely instrumental in moving toward a new height of monastic perfection. Cistercian ideals certainly included a greater degree of poverty, simplicity, and detachment from the world than was practiced elsewhere; but preconceived principles and rigid adherence to a dogmatic position that admitted of no exception were far from cistercian mentality. Rhetorical flourishes employed by the defenders of Cîteaux in their debates with the Cluniacs should not mislead us. Cistercian regulations sounded peremptory, but in their application individual abbots as well as the General Chapter were always circumspect and wanting to compromise whenever the welfare of a community demanded concessions. In the minds of the founders of Cîteaux, just laws were closely associated with customs and with the living realities of a specific environment, and in cases of conflicts local needs prevailed. Without such a flexible and tolerant mentality the Order could never have grown beyond the confines of Burgundy, and conversely, the very fact of the speed and extent of growth attest to the universal appeal, not of rules, but of spiritual values. During most of the twelfth-century, the General Chapter neither claimed nor exercised legislative powers in a modern sense of the term. The annual assemblies of abbots served as occasions for a collective examination of conscience. The chapter abbots were watching primarily over the spiritual welfare of communities. New regulations, if indeed there were any, were passed on a tentative basis and gained validity only upon the approval of a broad segment of the membership. Even when the Chapter did eventually assume

33. *Ibid.*, I:1190.22; 1192.25; 1207.13; 1208.24; 1212.33; 1213.39; II:1222.28.

legislative functions, its efficiency was seriously hampered by in-soluble problems of attendance, record-keeping, promulgation and enforcement. A tolerant and flexible attitude, then, far from being a sign of decay, was in fact a necessity, and its judicious practice should be taken as evidence of health and vitality and not of decline.

This is why I cannot find indications of a universal cistercian decline until at least the fourteenth century. The growing number of disciplinary cases dealt with in General Chapter is not a reliable gauge of declining standards of morality. By the end of the thirteenth century the Order easily had ten thousand members, and with growth came an increase in the number of delinquents. Nor was the much castigated greed and land-grabbing an unfailing symp-tom of spreading materialism at the expense of spiritual values. A largely agrarian economy was always full of hazards. Failing crops or pestilence among farm animals often brought otherwise prosperous communities to starvation, forcing the temporary dispersal of the monks. If, after such a disaster, the abbot attempted to broaden the economic basis of his house by new land acquisitions, it was proof of his foresight and solicitude for the welfare of his subjects. The abandonment of direct cultivation and the leasing of large tracts of monastic land to lay tenants was simply imposed on the Order by drastically changing social conditions and economic factors and cannot be construed as a deliberate breach with early Cistercian practices. Similarly, the progressive commercialization of monastic economy was simply part of a universal trend that monks could not ignore if they wished to provide for themselves.

What then should be taken as the first signs of decay? The sudden arrest of cistercian expansion after 1300 (the number of new foundations between 1250 and 1300 was 50; between 1300 and 1350: 10; between 1350 and 1400: 5. A precipitate drop in membership and an inability to recover from a physical or financial disaster all point to the period between 1300 and 1350. For the fragmentation, all point to the period between 1300 and 1350. For the sake of convenience I suggest as the dividing line the year 1348, the terrible year of the great plague, a fatal calamity that struck even contemporaries as a portent of impending doom. Among other external causes one may point to the fall of both the Empire and Papacy, political chaos in Germany and Italy, the disappearance of the Crusader States, the menace of turkish expansion and the outbreak of the Hundred Years' War. All these were of course, merely symptoms of a fast changing civilization that had lost faith in its old institutions, but had not yet been able to find acceptable alternatives. Western monasticism, and within it the Cistercian Order, shared the fate of other medieval organizations. It grew and flourished so long as it enjoyed the enthusiastic support of society, but it was forced to contract when appreciation changed to suspicion and resentment. No religious order can possibly thrive in uncongenial surroundings.

Abbreviations

CCL   Corpus Christianorum, Series Latina. Turnholt: Brepols.

CCP   *Carta Caritatis Prior*

EC   *Exordium Cistercii*

EM   *Exordium Magnum Cisterciense*

EP   *Exordium Parvum*

PL   Patrologia Latina, edited J. P. Migne.

PTAC   *Les plus anciens textes de Cîteaux.*, edited Jean de la Croix Bouton, OCSO and Jean Baptiste Van Damme, OCSO. Achel 1985.

SBOp   *Sancti Bernardi Opera*, edited Jean Leclercq, H. M. Rochais, C. H. Talbot

SCC   *Summa cartae caritatis*

SCh   Sources chrétiennes

Stat.   *Statuta* of '1134'

FuRther Reading

If you have enjoyed this introduction to the New Monastery and the Cistercian Order, you may want to explore the history of its foundation and development in more detail. Among the available literature, we recommend:

> *Legislative and Narrative Texts from Early Cîteaux: An Edition, Translation, and Commentary* by Chrysogonus Waddell ocso. Cîteaux: Commentarii Cistercienses: Studia et Documenta 7. 1998.

> Louis J. Lekai, O.Cist., *The Cistercians: Ideals and Reality.* Kent, Ohio: Kent State University Press, 1977.

> James France. *The Cistercians in Medieval Art.* Cistercian Publications (USA) and Sutton Publishing (UK) 1998.

> André Louf, ocso. *The Cistercian Way.* Cistercian Publications 1983.

Acknowledgements

PRIMARY SOURCES

Bernard of Clairvaux, Letter 7. 15–17. Latin text in *Sancti Bernardi Opera* 7. Rome: Editiones Cistercienses, 1974: 43–44. English translation, adapted, from Bruno Scott James, *The Letters of St Bernard* London: Burns & Oates, 1953; rpt. Stroud: Sutton - Kalamazoo: Cistercian Publications, 1998.

Exordium parvum. Latin edition in *Cîteaux. Documents primitifs.* Cîteaux: Commenarii cistercienses, 1988. Translations by E. Rozanne Elder and M. Chrysogonus Waddell, OCSO. A new critical edition of the early cistercian documents, with English translation by Father Waddell, will be available in 1998 from *Cîteaux: Commentarii Cistercienses, Studia et Documenta.*

Foundation charter of Cîteaux translated by E. R. Elder from J. Marilier, *Chartes et documents concernant l'Abbaye de Cîteaux, 1098–1182*, Bibliotheca Cisterciensis 1. Rome, 1961: item 23, pp. 49–51.

The Life of Robert of Molesme. Latin edition by Kolumban Spahr SOCist., *Das Leben des hl. Robert von Molesme.* Freiburg/Schwiz: Paulusbruckerei, 1944. Translated by Brian Kerns, OCSO and Jeremiah F. O'Sullivan. A translation of the full *Life of Saint Robert* will appear in a volume of Early Cistercian Lives.

Orderic Vitalis: *The Ecclesiastical History*. Latin edition with English translation by Marjorie Chibnall, *The Ecclesiastical History of Orderic Vitalis*. Oxford: Clarendon Press, 1969–1980. Translation by Jane Patricia Freeland.

Stephen Harding. Eulogy for Abbot Alberic, attributed to, but almost certainly not by, Stephen Harding. Translated by E. R. Elder from Marilier, *Chartes et documents,* item 30, pp. 54–55.

240

―――. Letter to the Monks of Sherborne. Latin edition and translation by M. Chrysogonus Waddell, OCSO, from *Noble Piety and Reformed Monasticism*, Studies in Medieval Cistercian History 7. Kalamazoo, 1981.

―――. On the Cistercian Hymnal. Translated by E. R. Elder from M. Chrysogonus Waddell, ed., *The Twelfth-Century Cistercian Hymnal*, Volume 2: Edition (Gethsemani Abbey, 1984) 11–12.

William of Malmesbury, *The Deeds of the Kings of England*. Translated E. R. Elder from *Patrologia Latina* 179: 1288–1290.

SECONDARY WORKS

Elizabeth Connor, OCSO, 'The Abbey of Tart' is abridged and revised from 'The Abbeys of Las Huelgas and Tart and their Filiations', in John A. Nichols and Lillian Thomas Shank, OCSO. *Hidden Springs: Cistercian Monastic Women*. Kalamazoo: Cistercian Publications, 1995.

H. E. J. Cowdrey, '*Quidem frater Stephanus nomine, Anglicus natione:* The English Background of Stephen Harding' is reprinted from *Revue Bénédictine* 101:3/4 (1991) 322–340, with the kind permission of *Revue Bénédictine* and the author.

Denis Farkasfalvy, O.Cist., 'Biblical Vocabulary as a Reflection of the Spirituality of the Founders of Citeaux' was presented at the 1997 Cistercian Studies Conference of the 32nd International Medieval Studies Congress, Kalamazoo.

Louis J. Lekai, O.Cist. 'Ideals and Reality in Early Cistercian Life and Legislation', revised and reprinted from *Cistercian Ideals and Reality*. John R. Sommerfeldt, ed. Cistercian Studies Series, Number 60. Kalamazoo: Cistercian Publications, 1978.

Jean Owens Schaefer, 'The Earliest Churches of the Cistercian Order', revised and reprinted from *Studies in Cistercian Art and Architecture* 1. Cistercian Studies Series, Number 66. Meredith Parsons Lillich, ed. Kalamazoo: Cistercian Publications, 1982.

Chrysogonus Waddell, 'An Exegesis of the Letter of Saint Stephen Harding', from *Noble Piety and Reformed Monasticism*, Studies in Medieval Cistercian History 7. Kalamazoo, 1981.

———. 'Liturgical–Patristic Resonances on "The Straight Path" ' and 'Liturgical–Patristic Resonances of the Prologue' appeared together as 'Notes on the Liturgical-patristic Resonances of Two Fragments from the *Exordium Parvum*' in *Liturgy OCSO* 15:2 (1981) 61–107. Revised and reprinted with the permission of the author and editor.

———. 'The Molesme Cistercian Hymnal'. Reprinted from 'The Introduction' to *The Twelfth Century Cistercian Hymnal*, Volume 1: *Introduction and Commentary,* Cistercian Liturgy Series, volume 1. Gethsemani, 1984: 7–22.

———. 'Viduata suo pastore: A Brief Note'. Reprinted from *Liturgy OCSO* 22:1 (1988) 7–16.

CISTERCIAN PUBLICATIONS, INC.
TITLES LISTING

—CISTERCIAN TEXTS—

BERNARD OF CLAIRVAUX

Apologia to Abbot William
Bernard of Clairvaux, Letters of
Five Books on Consideration: Advice to a
    Pope
Homilies in Praise of the Blessed Virgin Mary
Life and Death of Saint Malachy the Irishman
Love without Measure: Extracts from the
    Writings of St Bernard (Paul Dimier)
On Grace and Free Choice
On Loving God (Analysis by Emero
    Stiegman)
Parables and Sentences (Michael Casey)
Sermons for the Summer Season
Sermons on Conversion
Sermons on the Song of Songs I–IV
The Steps of Humility and Pride

WILLIAM OF SAINT THIERRY

The Enigma of Faith
Exposition on the Epistle to the Romans
Exposition on the Song of Songs
The Golden Epistle
The Mirror of Faith
The Nature and Dignity of Love
On Contemplating God: Prayer &
    Meditations

AELRED OF RIEVAULX

Dialogue on the Soul
Liturgical Sermons, I
Mirror of Charity
Spiritual Friendship
Treatises I: On Jesus at the Age of Twelve,
    Rule for a Recluse, The Pastoral Prayer
Walter Daniel: The Life of Aelred of Rievaulx

JOHN OF FORD

Sermons on the Final Verses of the
    Songs of Songs I–VII

GILBERT OF HOYLAND

Sermons on the Songs of Songs I–III
Treatises, Sermons and Epistles

OTHER EARLY
CISTERCIAN WRITERS

Adam of Perseigne, Letters of
Alan of Lille: The Art of Preaching
Amadeus of Lausanne: Homilies in Praise of
    Blessed Mary
Baldwin of Ford: Spiritual Tractates I–II
Gertrud the Greata: Spiritual Exercises

Gertrud the Great: The Herald of God's
    Loving-Kindness
Guerric of Igny: Liturgical Sermons I–[II]
Helinand of Froidmont: Verses on Death
Idung of Prüfening: Cistercians and Cluniacs:
    The Case of Cîteaux
Isaac of Stella: Sermons on the Christian
    Year,
    I–[II]
The Life of Beatrice of Nazareth
Serlo of Wilton & Serlo of Savigny: Seven
    Unpublished Works
Stephen of Lexington: Letters from Ireland
Stephen of Sawley: Treatises

—MONASTIC TEXTS—

EASTERN CHRISTIAN TRADITION

Besa: The Life of Shenoute
Cyril of Scythopolis: Lives of the Monks of
    Palestine
Dorotheos of Gaza: Discourses and Sayings
Evagrius Ponticus: Praktikos and Chapters on
    Prayer
Handmaids of the Lord: Lives of Holy
    Women in Late Antiquity & Early
    Middle Ages (Joan Petersen)
Harlots of the Desert (Benedicta Ward)
John Moschos: The Spiritual Meadow
Lives of the Desert Fathers
Lives of Simeon Stylites (Robert Doran)
Luminous Eye (Sebastian Brock)
Mena of Nikiou: Isaac of Alexandra & St
    Macrobius
Pachomian Koinonia I–III (Armand Vielleux)
Paphnutius: Histories/Monks of Upper
    Egypt
Sayings of the Desert Fathers
    (Benedicta Ward)
Spiritual Direction in the Early Christian
    East
    (Irénée Hausherr)
Spiritually Beneficial Tales of Paul, Bishop of
    Monembasia (John Wortley)
Symeon the New Theologian: The
    Theological and Practical Treatises &
    The Three Theological Discourses (Paul
    McGuckin)
Theodoret of Cyrrhus: A History of the
    Monks of Syria
The Syriac Fathers on Prayer and the
    Spiritual Life (Sebastian Brock)

WESTERN CHRISTIAN
TRADITION

Anselm of Canterbury: Letters I–III
    (Walter Fröhlich)

CISTERCIAN PUBLICATIONS, INC.

TITLES LISTING

Bede: Commentary...Acts of the Apostles
Bede: Commentary...Seven Catholic Epistles
Bede: Homilies on the Gospels III
The Celtic Monk (U. O Maidín)
Gregory the Great: Forty Gospel Homilies
Life of the Jura Fathers
Maxims of Stephen of Muret
Meditations of Guigo I, Prior of the
    Charterhouse (A. Gordon Mursell)
Peter of Celle: Selected Works
Letters of Rancé I–II
Rule of the Master
Rule of Saint Augustine
Wound of Love: A Carthusian Miscellany

CHRISTIAN SPIRITUALITY

Cloud of Witnesses: The Development of
    Christian Doctrine (David N. Bell)
Call of Wild Geese (Matthew Kelty)
Cistercian Way (André Louf)
The Contemplative Path
Drinking From the Hidden Fountain
    (Thomas Špidlík)
Eros and Allegory: Medieval Exegesis of the
    Song of Songs (Denys Turner)
Fathers Talking (Aelred Squire)
Friendship and Community (Brian McGuire)
From Cloister to Classroom
Life of St Mary Magdalene and of Her Sister
    St Martha (David Mycoff)
Many Mansions (David N. Bell)
Mercy in Weakness (André Louf)
Name of Jesus (Irénée Hausherr)
No Moment Too Small (Norvene Vest)
Penthos: The Doctrine of Compunction in
    the Christian East (Irénée Hausherr)
Rancé and the Trappist Legacy
    (A.J. Krailsheimer)
Russian Mystics (Sergius Bolshakoff)
Sermons in a Monastery (Matthew Kelty)
Silent Herald of Unity: The Life of
    Maria Gabrielle Sagheddu (Martha
    Driscoll)
Spirituality of the Christian East
    (Thomas Špidlík)
Spirituality of the Medieval West
    (André Vauchez)
Tuning In To Grace (André Louf)
Wholly Animals: A Book of Beastly Tales
    (David N. Bell)

—MONASTIC STUDIES—

Community and Abbot in the Rule of
    St Benedict I–II (Adalbert De Vogüé)
Finances of the Cistercian Order in the
    Fourteenth Century (Peter King)
Fountains Abbey and Its Benefactors
    (Joan Wardrop)

The Hermit Monks of Grandmont
    (Carole A. Hutchison)
In the Unity of the Holy Spirit
    (Sighard Kleiner)
Joy of Learning & the Love of God:
    Essays in Honor of Jean Leclercq
Monastic Odyssey (Marie Kervingant)
Monastic Practices (Charles Cummings)
Occupation of Celtic Sites in Ireland
    (Geraldine Carville)
Reading St Benedict (Adalbert de Vogüé)
Rule of St Benedict: A Doctrinal and Spiritual
    Commentary (Adalbert de Vogüé)
Rule of St Benedict (Br. Pinocchio)
St Hugh of Lincoln (David H. Farmer)
Stones Laid Before the Lord (Anselme
    Dimier)
Venerable Bede (Benedicta Ward)
What Nuns Read (David N. Bell)
With Greater Liberty: A Short History of
    Christian Monasticism & Religious
    Orders (Karl Frank)

—CISTERCIAN STUDIES—

Aelred of Rievaulx: A Study (Aelred Squire)
Athirst for God: Spiritual Desire in Bernard
    of Clairvaux's Sermons on the Song of
    Songs (Michael Casey)
Beatrice of Nazareth in Her Context
    (Roger De Ganck)
Bernard of Clairvaux: Man, Monk, Mystic
    (Michael Casey) [tapes and readings]
Bernardus Magister (Nonacentenary)
Catalogue of Manuscripts in the Obrecht
    Collection of the Institute of Cistercian
    Studies (Anna Kirkwood)
Christ the Way: The Christology of Guerric
    of Igny (John Morson)
Cistercians in Denmark (Brian McGuire)
Cistercians in Medieval Art (James France)
Cistercians in Scandinavia (James France)
A Difficult Saint (Brian McGuire)
Dore Abbey (Shoesmith & Richardson)
A Gathering of Friends: Learning &
    Spirituality in John of Forde (Costello
    and Holdsworth)
Image and Likeness: The Augustinian
    Spirituality of William of St Thierry
    (David Bell)
Index of Authors & Works in Cistercian
    Libraries in Great Britain I (David Bell)
Index of Cistercian Authors and Works in
    Medieval Library Catalogues in Great
    Britian (David Bell)
Mystical Theology of St Bernard
    (Étienne Gilson)
The New Monastery: Texts & Studies on the
    Earliest Cistercians

CISTERCIAN PUBLICATIONS, INC.
TITLES LISTING

Nicolas Cotheret's Annals of Cîteaux
(Louis J. Lekai)
Pater Bernhardus (Franz Posset)
A Second Look at Saint Bernard
(Jean Leclercq)
The Spiritual Teachings of St Bernard of
Clairvaux (John R. Sommerfeldt)
Studies in Medieval Cistercian History
(various)
Studiosorum Speculum (Louis J. Lekai)
Three Founders of Cîteaux
(Jean-Baptiste Van Damme)
Towards Unification with God (Beatrice of
Nazareth in Her Context, 2)
William, Abbot of St Thierry
Women and St Bernard of Clairvaux
(Jean Leclercq)

MEDIEVAL RELIGIOUS
—WOMEN—

Lillian Thomas Shank and John A. Nichols, editors
Distant Echoes
Hidden Springs: Cistercian Monastic Women
(2 volumes)
Peace Weavers

—CARTHUSIAN—
TRADITION

Call of Silent Love (A Carthusian)
Freedom of Obedience (A Carthusian)
Guigo II: The Ladder of Monks & Twelve
Meditations (Colledge & Walsh)
Interior Prayer (A Carthusian)
Meditations of Guigo II (A. Gorden Mursell)
Prayer of Love and Silence (A Carthusian)
Way of Silent Love (A Carthusian Miscellany)
Wound of Love (A Carthusian Miscellany)
They Speak by Silences (A Carthusian)
Where Silence is Praise (A Carthusian)

—STUDIES IN CISTERCIAN—
ART & ARCHITECTURE

Meredith Parsons Lillich, editor
Volumes II–V are now available

—THOMAS MERTON—

The Climate of Monastic Prayer (T. Merton)
The Legacy of Thomas Merton (P. Hart)
The Message of Thomas Merton (P. Hart)
The Monastic Journey of Thomas Merton
(P. Hart)
Thomas Merton/Monk (P. Hart)
Thomas Merton on St Bernard
Toward an Integrated Humanity
(M. Basil Pennington, ed.)

CISTERCIAN LITURGICAL
—DOCUMENTS SERIES—

Chrysogonus Waddell, ocso, editor
Hymn Collection of the...Paraclete
Institutiones nostrae: The Paraclete Statutes
Molesme Summer-Season Breviary (4 vols.)
Old French Ordinary & Breviary of the
Abbey of the Paraclete (2 volumes)
Twelfth-century Cistercian Hymnal (2 vols.)
The Twelfth-century Cistercian Psalter
Two Early Cistercian *Libelli Missarum*

—STUDIA PATRISTICA XVIII—
Volumes 1, 2 and 3

*Editorial queries & advance book information
should be directed to the Editorial Offices:*

Cistercian Publications
1201 Oliver Street
Western Michigan University
Kalamazoo, Michigan 49008
Tel: (616) 387-8920 • Fax: (616) 387-8921

*Cistercian Publications is a non-profit
corporation. Its publishing program is restricted
to monastic texts in translation and books on
the monastic tradition.*

• • •

*North American customers may order these
books through booksellers or directly by
contacting the warehouse at the address below:*

Cistercian Publications
Saint Joseph's Abbey
167 North Spencer Road
Spencer, Massachusetts 01562-1233
Tel: (508) 885-8730 • Fax: (508) 885-4687
email: cistpub@spencerabbey.org

• • •

British & European Orders:

Cistercian Publications
Mount Saint Bernard Abbey
Coalville, Leicester LE67 5UL
Fax: [44] (1530) 81.46.08

• • •

*A complete catalogue of texts in translation and
studies on early, medieval, and modern
monasticism is available, free of charge, by
contacting any of the addresses above.*